Minette Walters and
the Meaning of Justice

Livonia Public Library
CIVIC CENTER #32
32777 Five Mile Road
Livonia, Michigan 48154
734.466.2491

Minette Walters and the Meaning of Justice

Essays on the Crime Novels

Edited by
MARY HADLEY *AND*
SARAH D. FOGLE

McFarland & Company, Inc., Publishers
Jefferson, North Carolina, and London

ALSO OF INTEREST

British Women Mystery Writers:
Authors of Detective Fiction with Female Sleuths
by Mary Hadley (McFarland, 2002)

LIBRARY OF CONGRESS CATALOGUING-IN-PUBLICATION DATA

Minette Walters and the meaning of justice : essays on the
  crime novels / edited by Mary Hadley and Sarah D. Fogle.
    p.   cm.
  Includes bibliographical references and index.

  ISBN 978-0-7864-3842-6
  softcover : 50# alkaline paper ∞

  1. Walters, Minette — Criticism and interpretation.
  2. Walters, Minette — Interviews.   I. Hadley, Mary,
  1949–   II. Fogle, Sarah D.
  PR6073.A444Z78   2008
  823'.914 — dc22   2008016994

British Library cataloguing data are available

©2008 Mary Hadley and Sarah D. Fogle. All rights reserved

No part of this book may be reproduced or transmitted in any form
or by any means, electronic or mechanical, including photocopying
or recording, or by any information storage and retrieval system,
without permission in writing from the publisher.

Cover photograph ©2008 Shutterstock

Manufactured in the United States of America

McFarland & Company, Inc., Publishers
  Box 611, Jefferson, North Carolina 28640
    www.mcfarlandpub.com

Acknowledgments

We would like to thank our wonderful contributors, without whose scholarship and hard work this book would not exist. We would also like to thank our families, friends and colleagues, especially Donna Barbie, Mary McLemore, and Libbie Searcy, for their insightful suggestions.

Table of Contents

Acknowledgments	v
Introduction *Mary Hadley and Sarah D. Fogle*	1
Truth and Justice *Mary Hadley*	5
Soul Murder: Children in Minette Walters' Novels *Sarah D. Fogle*	23
Body of Evidence/Body *as* Evidence in *The Sculptress* *Caren J. Town*	49
Shakespeare, Scolds, and Self-Fashioning: The Making of Mathilda Gillespie in *The Scold's Bridle* *Rhonda Knight*	66
A Wounded World: Victim/Victimizers in *The Scold's Bridle*, *The Dark Room,* and *The Breaker* *Lois A. Marchino and Deane Mansfield-Kelley*	88
British Social Issues *Donna Waller Harper*	103
The Impenetrable M and the Mysteries of Narration: Narrative in *The Shape of Snakes* *Tilda Maria Forselius*	118

Table of Contents

Society, Evil, and Other
   Nancy Eliot Parker   137

The Tangled Web of Justice and Revenge: Narrative Devices and Subtexts in *The Devil's Feather*
   Gerri Reaves   157

Everyday Heroes: Women of Valor
   Rachel Schaffer   185

Online Interview with Minette Walters
   Minette Walters and Contributors   205

Notes on Contributors   211

Index   215

Introduction

Mary Hadley *and* Sarah D. Fogle

Continuing in the tradition established by Dorothy Sayers, Agatha Christie, and others in the Golden Age of detective fiction in the 1920s and 1930s, Minette Walters has revitalized the tradition of the stand-alone psychological thriller. Standing shoulder to shoulder with writers like P. D. James and Ruth Rendell, she has achieved worldwide recognition and success.

Walters was born in Bishop's Stortford, Hertfordshire, England, in 1949. At age twelve, after the death of her father from injuries suffered in World War II, she was sent to Godolphin boarding school in Salisbury, Hampshire, England. When discussing her education, Walters says the teachers made her very independent and pushed her academically. Having finished school, she spent seven months on a kibbutz in Israel, before going to Durham University where she majored in French. It was at university that she met her future husband, Alec.

After graduation, Walters worked for IPC magazines (the UK's leading consumer magazine publisher) as a subeditor on a romantic fiction magazine where she wrote articles, short stories, and novelettes. In 1978, she married Alec and had two sons, Roland and Philip. For seven years she stopped writing and kept busy with the boys and another of her loves, renovating old houses. When Roland and Philip went off to school, she began her first book, *The Ice House*, which was published in 1992 to great acclaim. It won the Crime Writers Association John Creasey award in the

UK for best first novel and within six months was published in several languages. Since then Walters has published twelve more novels in over thirty-five countries and has won numerous awards, including the Edgar Allan Poe Award and the CWA Gold Dagger Award. The BBC televised versions of the first five novels have brought her even more fans.

Having lived in Hampshire, Wiltshire, and now Dorset, Walters sets her novels in these three counties of England; but rather than continuing in the cozy tradition of Christie, her novels are often very harsh and bleak. They include a great deal of commentary and focus on the societal ills that beset the United Kingdom today. When her mother once asked her why she did not write "nice little murders," Walters replied that they "would be too easy." She prefers to have contemporary events, which in her recent novels include global problems, to inspire her stories, so that she can "root the story firmly for [her] readers and they know what [she's] talking about" (Rao).

Along with the importance of current events and setting, another influence in her life and writing was her grandfather Joshua Jebb, who was Surveyor General of British prisons in the nineteenth century and brought about numerous reforms. Following in his footsteps, Walters has been a prison visitor for much of her life and is shocked that many of these institutions have changed so little in the last century. Although she has said she does not use the prisoners' own crimes as a focus in her work, her interviews with them have certainly helped shape her narratives. She has noted in many interviews that 50 to 75 percent of prisoners are illiterate and their illiteracy often exacerbates their criminal tendenciescrimes. In Walters' opinion, "If you can't read and you can't admit to people you can't read, you do lash out" (Sibree). She maintains that she can really understand why criminals, especially males, become angry and violent. As youngsters, they often skip school, and then when they cannot keep up with their peers, they become frustrated and may start bullying. Walters says, "I think it's so important to keep children in school long enough for them to have the tools to enable them to get out into society" (Sibree). Many of Walters' characters reflect the limitations brought about by the lack of a strong nuclear family and proper education.

While many crime writers have invested in a single series main character, Walters has confounded both her publishers and her critics by successfully writing only stand-alone novels. She feels that series crime fiction can be formulaic when authors use the same characters and setting with just a different death each time. Stand-alone novels allow her to create a completely different world and shift her focus with each new narrative. "I do not want to get into a pattern," she says. "It would bore me to always use the same people" (Spelman).

Although she always focuses on contemporary issues in her novels, Walters is very aware of the long female tradition of British crime writers. While Ngaio Marsh, Margery Allingham, and Dorothy Sayers were "more concerned with the upper-class eccentricities of their protagonists than they were with the bulk of society, Christie tore apart middle-class attempts at being genteel, revealing everything about their lives" (Patrick). This tearing away is one of the aspects of Christie's writing that Walters most admires, as This, too, is what Walte wants to do as she also she depicts characters drawn from all classes of society and shows how even her "heroes" can have flaws that make them more capable of understanding what other people have suffered. As Walters has said, "It's the psychology of crime that interests me.... What set of circumstances conspire to make a person commit an evil act" (Jacobson). In Walters' work, her major themes emerge from these impelling circumstances: inadequate social and justice systems, dysfunctional families, abuse and neglect of children, homelessness, racism and the treatment of "other," and body politics.

Beyond her determination to write only stand-alone novels, Walters' narrative techniques are unique. Throughout her work, she uses "extrafictional" sources of information such as newspaper articles, doctors' reports, police documents, and e-mails to augment her narratives. While these bring real-world elements into the novels, they also reveal the multiple ways in which a story may be presented and interpreted by her characters. The deliberate use of multiple perspective on events, in fact, is a salient feature of Walters' writing. At times, she purposefully creates ambiguity about the truth of what happens and who commits what actions in her novels by creating a variety of texts and subtexts to advance the action of the plot.

Considering the popularity and acclaim that Minette Walters enjoys, as well as frequent comparisons of her to P. D. James, it is surprising that no major critical study of her work has yet been done. Although some are writing dissertations and others have done independent articles about her crime fiction, we felt it was time for a book of critical analyses of her entire body of work. This collection of essays provides in-depth studies of *The Sculptress, The Shape of Snakes, The Scold's Bridle,* and *The Devil's Feather,* and broader examinations of Walters' major themes throughout *The Ice House, The Echo, The Breaker, The Dark Room, The Shape of Snakes, Acid Row, The Tinder Box, Fox Evil,* and *Disordered Minds.* We are also honored to be able to include an interview with Minette Walters, which she was kind enough to do electronically.

Works Cited

Jacobson, Michael. "The Sinister Small Mind." *Gold Coast Bulletin* 28–29 Nov. 1998. 21 Nov. 2006. http://www.minettewalters.co.uk/about_minette/articles/inst_aus.htm.

Patrick, Bethanne Kelly. "Acid Reign." 21 Nov. 2006. http://www.minettewalters.co.uk/about_minette/articles/acid_rn.htm.

Rao, Kavitha. "Killer Queen." *Sunday Morning Post* 27 Nov. 2006. 10 Mar. 2007. http://www.kavitharao.net/journalism/minettepdf.pdf.

Sibree, Bron. "Mind of Minette." *The Saturday Mercury* 19 Nov. 2000. 5 Nov. 2006. http://www.minettewalters.co.uk/about_minette/articles/mind1.htm.

Spelman, Judith. "Minette Walters: An Intelligent Approach to Crime." *Writers News* June 1994. 5 Nov. 2006. http://www.minettewalters.co/uk/about_minette/articles/winternw1.htm.

Truth and Justice

Mary Hadley

Minette Walters doesn't believe in evil (Berlins); however, she is very interested in the issues of truth and justice. As early as 1994, she said in an interview that she was fascinated with the nature of truth, and she believes one of the major problems of contemporary society is that people are "at sea" because of the abandonment of values and they have to manage the "new sets of values" (Spelman); as her prison visiting has taught her, even old-fashioned justice, in the form of the police, the courts, and the rehabilitation of prisoners, is affected by new sets of values. Because of this interest in the psychology of the criminal, it is not surprising that Walters has not followed in the footsteps of the Golden Age mystery writers. For writers like Agatha Christie and Dorothy Sayers, for example, the criminal is seen as aberrant, and once he or she is apprehended, the status quo returns and everyone is satisfied. This is not the case with Walters.

Her works have more in common with the early American hard-boiled detective story, which grew out of a specific desire on the part of certain male writers to write differently than the traditional British writers of the 1930s and 1940s. Because he is going to expose and judge societal problems as well as one particular criminal, the hard-boiled detective is often under pressure by the police and is frequently threatened verbally and even physically by them. "The detective is ... a marginal figure who for readers explores in fantasy the border between the law and unlawfulness" (Walton and Jones 191). In the hard-boiled traditions too, the police are often seen as corrupt or corruptible and the truth as ugly. Dashiell Hammett and Raymond Chandler, for example, are important to an analysis of Walters because they were enormously influential to the first female hard-boiled writers of the 1980s — among them, Marcia Muller, Sue Grafton, and especially Sara Paretsky — and these authors, in turn, affected Walters.

When we look at the female hard-boiled authors who are contemporaries of Minette Walters, we see that justice can sometimes be better served by letting a criminal go free, as Val McDermid does in her novel *Union Jack* (1993). A prison visitor for much of her life, Walters know prison is not the answer in all cases. She believes strongly in penal reform and even wrote to former president Bill Clinton protesting capital punishment. "Seventy-five percent of prisoners are wasting taxpayers' money by being there," she said (Berlins). In addition, Walters believes that "justice and revenge are two sides of the same coin.... It's something society needs to look at ... [because] it's dangerous to have very angry people who feel they have not got justice and that justice then becomes a desire for revenge" (Sibree). As critic Maureen Reddy states, not only is justice for the feminist authors of the 1980s and 1990s problematic, but also "there is no single universal truth ... rather truth is always relative, dependent on the perspective and on circumstances" (176). This feminist viewpoint is clearly seen in Minette Walters' first novel *The Ice House*, published in 1992, which gives a complex picture of justice in the form of the bad behavior of the British police.

In *The Ice House*, the plot concerns the discovery of a rotted, severely mutilated corpse in the ice house of Streech Grange, a beautiful village mansion owned by Phoebe Maybury. Ten years ago Phoebe's husband David disappeared and was presumed to have been murdered by her. Because they were unable to convict her then because of lack of evidence, the local police now jump at the idea that the body in the ice house is David's and believe this time justice will be served and Phoebe will go to prison. The investigation reveals the true nature of Chief Inspector Walsh and Detective Sergeant Andy McLoughlin and gives the reader a portrait of the British police that is both very realistic and extremely disturbing.

The unflattering depiction of the police in *The Ice House* follows the example set by several female mystery authors who began writing in the 1980s. British writers Liza Cody, Val McDermid, and Lynda La Plante all showed how the sexist behavior of the police not only affected personal relationships within the force, but sometimes the outcome of a case, when the police refused to believe evidence if it challenged their narrow opinions. La Plante's television series, *Prime Suspect,* which was popular on PBS, clearly demonstrated these problematic behaviors and was in marked contrast to other police shows such as *Dixon of Dock Green* and *Z Cars,* which aired in Britain in the 1960s and 1970s. While the early programs depicted the police as avuncular or helpful, the police in *Prime Suspect* are jealous, mean spirited, and above all misogynist. These traits could all be attributed to the two policemen in Walter's *The Ice House.*

At the start of the novel, Chief Inspector Walsh and Detective Sergeant McLouglin appear to have many similarities, and indeed they work well together. Walsh thinks of McLoughlin as a "conscientious type, honest, intelligent, dependable" (*The Ice House* 16), but this description is at variance with how McLoughlin behaves toward Phoebe and her friends Anne Cattrell and Diana Goode, with whom she now lives. We first see him described in strong contrast to Walsh's view: "he had brought with him the irritability of the Police Station, concentrated, malignant" (10). Phoebe believes McLoughlin's dislike must be based on what happened ten years ago; but since Anne and Diana were not present when David disappeared, these women feel they have not merited such animosity, and Anne is determined to discover why McLoughlin is so angry.

As the novel progresses, readers learn that Walsh and McLoughlin are both moody and have bad marriages. McLoughlin's wife has just left him for a fellow officer, while Walsh's regularly rejects him in bed and is cold and uncaring. It would be easy to claim that the reason why both men have difficulties dealing with the strong personalities of all three women at Streech Grange is that they are unhappy with their home lives. However, there is much more to their characters.

In both Walsh and McLoughlin, there are tendencies toward violence and abuse of power which are key to their personalities. When Walsh tells Phoebe that he wants to interview her children as to the identity of the corpse in the ice house, Phoebe is furious and doesn't want them upset again. She tells him that he was very stupid when she first had dealings with him and he won't have changed (36). Her remark inflames Walsh, who would never admit that women are smarter than he is. Later, when McLoughlin asks Diana why the three women are trying to protect Phoebe's daughter Jane, Diana tells him that she is a recovering anorexic and still very fragile and if he does interview Jane, she will be traumatized to no avail since she knows nothing (48). In another situation, when challenged by Anne Cattrell as to his views of women and his drinking problem, McLoughlin responds by savagely kissing her. Although he tells her he is sorry, he also feels revenged by his action, and his behavior points once again to the violence and abuse of power often common in the police.

The question of the equality of women is also discussed at length when McLoughlin talks to Anne about all the renovations that Phoebe has made in the house. He is shocked that she is capable of doing major repairs and reminisces about his mother and his wife. His mother thought all jobs outside the kitchen were the domain of the man of the house, while his wife maintained she was an enlightened career woman but according to him was a lazy complainer. The narrator comments, "He had come away from both relationships with a sense, not of his own inadequacy, but of theirs. He had looked for equality and found only irritating dependency" (80). When he does find a woman in Anne with whom he could have an equal relationship, however, he is, at first, deeply worried and wary.

Throughout the novel, there is little in the two policemen to admire. They are not thoughtful, intelligent men who are painstaking in their investigation of the crime, determined to seek out the truth. Rather, they are prejudiced and easily swayed by rumors. As they try to discover the identity of the body in the ice house, the true facts of the disappearance of David Maybury unfold. A man who was violent toward his wife, David had also been raping his daughter Jane since she was seven. It was pure chance that Phoebe returned home early from her evening job to discover David actually molesting Jane. She maintained at the time and ever after that her husband left the house that same night and never returned. Walsh didn't believe her, but as Anne tells McLoughlin, Walsh agreed not to pursue the investigation as long as Phoebe agreed to have weekly sexual relationships with him (256). When Phoebe refused to play Walsh's game, he spread the rumors about her and her friends being lesbians and witches, which led to their being ostracized by the villagers. Here, Walters follows other feminist crime writers by depicting the long-term ramifications of the first crime, and implying that truth has no place in Walsh's pursuit of justice.

As the plot unfolds, and readers discover the facts about the past and the identity of the body in the ice house, Walters shows a more humane, conscientious, and intelligent policeman in the changed character of McLoughlin. At the end of the novel, Anne is able to confide the facts of David's death to McLoughlin as she trusts he will not reveal the truth to Walsh because he is in love with her and has grown sufficiently in self-knowledge to recognize that he and Anne are similar. Once McLoughlin claims that he can now respect strong independent women, Anne believes he sees the merit of female solidarity and the power of female friendship, and McLoughlin realizes that justice would not be served by incarcerating the murderer because David deserved to die.

Having enjoyed enormous success with her first novel, Walters has gone on to write several more stand-alone books, always focusing on contemporary societal issues that particularly disturb her. Her seventh novel, *The Shape of Snakes*, published in 2001, was inspired by the horrific death of Stephen Lawrence in April 1993 and the subsequent investigation into the police action. According to an article entitled "A Fight for Justice: The Stephen Lawrence Story," Stephen was an eighteen-year-old black man who was returning home with a friend on the evening of April 22, 1993, when he was set upon and severely beaten by a group of five white youths in Eltham, an area of southeast London that has had a great deal of racial tension. Stephen urged his friend to run away and he did, but he later returned along with an off-duty policeman to find Stephen dead in a pool of blood. Charges against two of the white boys were dropped in July of the same year, and in April 1996 all charges were dropped. In 1997 a government inquiry was initiated because the first examination of the police behavior stated that there had been "no evidence of racist conduct" ("A Fight for Justice").

In a personal interview, Walters said that she was horrified by the death of Lawrence and thought the handling of it was a "ridiculous situation." Because the boys who committed the crime had been named in the newspapers, the judiciary thought they would not have a fair trial, and so they were never tried or even charged. Although essentially everybody knew they had done the crime, there was no justice or resolution for the

Lawrence family. In addition, when the Kent Police were engaged to look into the accusation by Stephen's parents that the Metropolitan Police's initial investigation was flawed, they "found no evidence to support the allegation of racist conduct by any Metropolitan Police Officer" ("Racism" 1). While they may not have found specific officers guilty of racist comments, the report does state the following:

> The failure of the first investigating team to recognize and accept racism and race relations as a central feature of their investigation of the murder of Stephen Lawrence played a part in the deficiencies in policing.... For example, a substantial number of officers of junior rank would not accept that the murder of Stephen Lawrence was simply and solely "racially motivated" ["Racism" 5].

The case of Stephen Lawrence and the actions of the police and the justice system toward the whole family forced Londoners, and indeed everyone in England, to face the fact that institutional racism was rampant within the police force. It was a topic ripe for Minette Walters.

The Shape of Snakes, which takes place in 1999, is a first-person narrative by a Mrs. Ranelagh, "M," who in 1978 found her black neighbor "Mad Annie" dying outside her house in Graham Road. In their initial interview, the police question Mrs. Ranelagh's insistence that Annie was murdered, and the coroner supports them when he rules the death an accident. Although the coroner does lay some blame at the door of social services, he also says there was no real evidence to uphold an "alleged racist campaign" (5). Desperately upset because of Annie's death, Mrs. Ranelagh becomes ill and suffers a slight case of agoraphobia. She loses her job as a teacher, and her husband, angry with her continued concern with what happened to Annie, walks out on her. Finally, her mother comes to see her, saying she cannot jeopardize her marriage for someone who was not even born in the country and is a drain on society (7). For the next twenty years M and her husband Sam, reunited, live overseas, only to return to England in 1999.

Early on in the novel, readers learn that M and her father had kept in touch with numerous people from Graham Road, and had in fact collected newspaper clippings on people like the vicar, Peter Stanhope, and the doctor, Dr. Sheila Arnold. It is because of her knowledge of the doctor's whereabouts that M persuades her husband to rent a house in

Dorset on their return, soon manages to make contact with Sheila, and begins, once again, to examine the events of the crime.

As Dr. Arnold tells M, Annie was not mad at all but a victim of Tourette's syndrome, which made her shout out inappropriate remarks and caused her to twitch. Her white adult neighbors hate her because she has more money than they had, as well as beautiful souvenirs of her Caribbean homeland. In many ways Annie is superior to them because her behavior is neither vicious nor slatternly, and her love of cats shows a gentle side to her character which is not present in many of the other women. While the adults are angered by the abusive words Annie shouts at them, at first they take no action against her. However, soon they want to force her to leave and encourage their children to victimize Annie by brutalizing several stray cats and pushing them through her cat flap. When Annie dies, twenty cats are found in horrible conditions. Although the authorities believe she harmed them in her demented drunken state, this is revealed as untrue.

The portrayal of the authorities in the form of Sergeant Drury, Dr. Benjamin Hanley, the pathologist who performed the postmortem on Annie, and the Royal Society of Prevention of Cruelty to Animals inspector, John Howlett, clearly shows Walters following in the footsteps of earlier feminist crime writers. As critic Maureen Reddy states,

> Traditionally, authority — the power to judge, the right to command, the power to persuade based on knowledge or experience — inheres in the masculine role, with that role part of a social structure based on male superiority. From a feminist standpoint, authority based on such a structure is necessarily illegitimate. Feminist crime writers lay bare this illegitimacy and offer different bases of authority, most often an understanding rooted in relatedness, empathy and care [177].

In *The Shape of Snakes* the figures who empathize and care, Dr. Arnold and the narrator M, learn the truth about Annie's murder. Dr. Arnold cared enough in her lifetime to be a frequent visitor in Annie's house, and M is determined to gain justice for Annie by revealing that her house was burgled and she was the victim of a vicious racist-based harassment campaign by her neighbors.

Far from being superior, the authority figures of Sergeant Drury and

Dr. Benjamin Hanley are shown as deeply flawed. While Drury inspired confidence in M in 1978, in 1999 M says he was utterly dishonest (156). Dr. Benjamin is also shown to be untrustworthy because he wrote false postmortem reports which were directed by the police (178). While not being negligent in his duties, John Howlett was an authority figure who, in his uniform, frightened Annie. His inaccurate report on the cats allowed the police to lay all the blame for the chaos in her house and her own poor condition on Annie herself, and to claim she'd been hit by a passing truck. The truth, of course, is very different.

The year 1978, when the fictional murder took place, was a time of unrest in England when people were deeply disturbed by the actions of the government, and finally brought about the downfall of the labor government (369). At this time, similarly to the time of the Stephen Lawrence murder, people did not expect that the death of a black woman would be given the same amount of attention as that of a white one. One of the reasons that the coroner returned a verdict of accidental death on Annie was that the police presumed that she was a drunk, since numerous empty bottles of spirits were found in her house after she died. They never took into account that these bottles were vodka, the drink of choice of her neighbor Maureen Slater, and not rum, which Annie liked. In addition, Sergeant Drury made no attempt to contact Annie's doctor to learn the true facts about her "madness"; rather, he refused to investigate the possible theft of valuable property from her house. Although Dr. Arnold remembered several articles of value in the house and had been given a bracelet by Annie worth two hundred pounds, the police claimed that since she was mad, Annie could very easily have spent all her money on drink during the last weeks of her life (48). This belief about Annie immediately after her death never changed in the five years afterward, despite several letters over the years from Dr. Arnold pleading with the police to re-open the case. The excuse of the Police Superintendent in 1983 was that since Annie was dead and there was no accurate inventory of her possessions, there would be no purpose in re-investigating the death. However, M believes the police superintendent was negligent because Annie was black.

Walters makes clear her views on the institutional racism of British police forces when she has M's father read an article about Stephen Lawrence's death, describing the inquiry following the murder in some depth. In this way Walters weaves the facts of the Lawrence case into her description of the ugly truths about the events that led to Annie's death and the subsequent terrorizing of M. In both the real murder of Stephen and the fictional one of Annie, people of color do not receive justice because the police do not care as much about their fate as they would have had they been white.

The issues revealed in *The Shape of Snakes* are familiar Walters' concerns: poverty, child and domestic abuse, marital infidelity, victimization of women, and a new addition, cruelty to animals. This last is depicted in utterly horrific graphic detail. Knowing Annie's love of cats and determined to upset her so much that she will move house and allow Graham Road inhabitants not to have to suffer having a black woman living there, the children put glue in the mouths of several emaciated stray tomcats, tape their muzzles shut, and push them through her cat flap. Desperate to rescue them, she mistakenly puts a piece of furniture across the cat flap exit, but most of them are too far gone to save. Indeed, later the RSPCA inspector has to put most of them to sleep.

After Annie's death, some of these same neighbors begin to terrorize M to stop her from vilifying them to the police, and she hears scratching beneath her own floorboards. At the time she does not know what it is and fears rats, but on her return to England in 1999 when she learns the truth about the cats in Annie's house, she realizes that she too had dying animals under her house.

The lives of less-than-quiet desperation of the inhabitants of Graham Road reveal the truth of how poverty, racism, and lack of education can turn entire families into evil monsters. The behavior of two of the children is the result of failing in school, a social problem that Walters addressed in an interview:

> There are a lot of knock-on effects when a child begins to have behavioural problems. In Britain we're excluding so many children from school when their behaviour is bad because the schools can't cope with them, but there doesn't seem to be anything in place to help them address this problem [Sibree].

The illiterate Derek Slater is violent and his brutalizing of his wife Maureen leads her to be extraordinarily violent toward her son Alan and to

Annie's favorite marmalade cat to stop Annie from shouting obscenities at her. The article by Bron Sibree also mentions that this book is, "Walters strongest statement yet on women and their influential role in families, and, by implication, in criminal behavior." We see in Maureen and other women that, as Walters states, "The mother is absolutely the linchpin around which families operate" (Sibree). From Derek to Maureen to Alan there is a clear knock on effect.

At the end of the novel Annie's cursing of most of her neighbors brings about her fatal beating and reiterates the message that, as Walters has pointed out in other novels, children of abuse will abuse in their turn. Although the narrator M does get her revenge on her former neighbors and the truth Annie's death is revealed, the final justice of seeing Annie's murderer prosecuted does not occur. Since feminist writers don't see the value of the return to the status quo, and "order [can be seen as] the *source* of crimes against women and therefore as the antithesis of real justice" (Reddy 176), Walters shows clearly in the epilogue of the book that "there may often be higher values than abstract truth or justice, such as preserving lives and relationships" (Reddy 176). M and Sam, along with their friend Jock Garth, are working on restoring the old Dorset farmhouse and continuing their lives companionably. M is slowly making her peace with her mother, and her marriage with Sam is strong and happy.

Abstract truth and justice are very much at the forefront of Walters' eighth book, *Acid Row,* published in 2002. This novel continues the themes of the far-reaching consequences of poverty and lack of education and shows how the police find it almost impossible to be effective in the type of council estate described in the novel.

While the behavior of the teenage boys in *The Shape of Snakes* is to some extent controlled because everyone meddles in their neighbors' business, and Graham Road is a very different setting from Bassindale, the crime of the Bassindale Estate flourishes unchecked by the police because of the layout of the streets and the palpable fear of the inhabitants. As Walters has said, "My heart *bleeds* [her italics]for those condemned to live behind barred doors.... In my view alienated people get very, very angry.... " (Thomson), and she shows this anger in the riots caused by the troubled Wesley Barber and his friends after a pedophile is relocated to Acid Row.

At the start of the book, WPC Hanson arrives at the ugly sink hole estate to interview the angelic-looking Wesley Barber. According to the headmaster of the school, fifteen-year-old Wesley enjoys snatching the pension money from the purses of elderly women. WPC Hanson thinks that Wesley may not be home and is considering her options when she sees a gang of youths approaching her. They run off after seeing the police car, but one yells threateningly at her and Hanson's reaction is one of horror. She has been afraid of the inhabitants of the estate for some time, but she receives no understanding from her superiors, who think she's being a typically emotional scared female. Their behavior towards her is reminiscent of scenes from *Prime Suspect* where not only was Jane Tennison put down by her team, but other female officers were also not taken seriously.

Hanson, however, has reason to be afraid of the estate since its architecture is such that the only two thoroughfares provide only four points of access, which effectively turn the entire area into a fortress nearly impossible to penetrate. When a riot begins, the angry youths blockade all four exits. Two policemen, who have been interviewing someone earlier about the disappearance of a child, Amy Biddulph, are lucky to be on the outside, looking at the Molatov cocktails being created. WPC Hanson is less lucky and is trapped inside the home of a senior citizen who has reported being robbed. Quickly she realizes that he is senile, and the money might not be missing at all; but her pity for him, as she examines his squalid living conditions, turns to self pity when he becomes angry with her because he obviously wanted to see a big, burly male policeman responding to his phone call and not the "namby-pamby" (68) Hanson. The old man might just be voicing his own dislike of female police officers, but Hanson's fears do make her an ineffective police officer.

Hanson, however, is not the only frightened person on the estate. The female residents become ever more disturbed as they see the youths gathering. They frantically call for police help, only to receive the message that the emergency lines are all busy (69). The dismissive message is the extent of the assistance the police can give the inhabitants; they not only cannot get into the estate but also do not really want to help. As an officer says of the problems, the planners caused them because the layout of the estate makes it a "concrete jungle" (71). Bassindale is a typical 1960s housing estate of high rise apartment blocks filled with the poor, elderly and very young. While many of these estates started off well, they very quickly became major sources of crime. When elevators ceased working, mothers with very young children and the senior citizens were trapped in their apartments. Stairwells became places to conduct drug and other criminal activity, and adolescents skipped school and formed gangs to while away their boredom. The portrait Walters paints compares well with Dashiell Hammett's and Raymond Chandler's "mean streets." And as Chandler wrote in "The Simple Art of Murder," "It is not a very fragrant world ... but it is the world you live in" (218). The not-very-fragrant world of Bassindale is an excellent background for Walters to discuss her concerns about alienated youth.

The action of *Acid Row* begins when Fay Baldwin, a health visitor, learns of the re-housing of a pedophile onto the estate. She informs one of her patients, Melanie Patterson, of the fact, and Melanie decides to stage a peaceful protest. Unfortunately, the youth of the estate display their ignorance and deep-rooted prejudice, and while throwing bricks at the pedophile's house, begin a riot of mammoth proportions. When Dr. Sophie Morrison enters the Hollis house to help the father who is having an asthma attack, the out-of-control rioting teenagers break the downstairs windows, and Franek Hollis and his son Nicholas take Sophie hostage. Only then does she realize that what the boys had been chanting was "pervert" (86), and that she is now at the mercy of the pedophile.

While Fay Baldwin and the mothers of the estate are deeply worried to have a pedophile housed on their estate, other members of the Nightingale Health Center do not seem to want to take any action since they believe that even if it was unwise to move a pedophile to an area full of children, the decision was made by the police, and they could do nothing about it (3). Minette Walters addressed the whole topic of pedophiles in an interview with Liz Thomson, in which she recalled a "name and shame" campaign which took place in Britain some years before she wrote *Acid Row*. She is concerned that the public does not differentiate between pedophiles who are psychopaths and those who are just "pathetic people who are *desperately* [her italics] lonely." She also mentions that men who expose themselves are not necessarily really dangerous and sending these individuals to prison where they may learn to be killers is not the answer. Her possible solution is more research into the whole topic of serious personality disorders. As she says, "Being attracted to children isn't a phase — it's been around for a hell of a long time and it was perfectly acceptable in the Victorian era. So we have to sit down and understand where it's coming from" (Thomson).

The problems with the riot and the pedophile cause a lot of tension in the plot of *Acid Row* which is cleverly developed by Walters. As in all her novels, she uses police reports and memos to sustain the realism, and she moves the action from the different street scenes to the pedophile's house, to the health center, and to the police command center. There the police are able to view what is happening around Bassindale via police helicopter footage but do not have the men to take action. Later, the town council would blame the police for not having acted, while the police would tell the council that they never should have built a development with so few access roads. However, everyone agrees with one of the officers, who says that the press will really take them to task (159).

In this novel, some of the police are depicted as ineffective. As the doctor in charge of the Nightingale Health Center and Sophie Morrison's boss tells her fiancé, the police were caught unawares when the troubles erupted, claiming they couldn't have stopped the riot because they didn't have the men to react effectively since several of them were busy dealing with Amy Biddulph, the missing child from Bassindale (141). However, Detective Chief Inspector Tyler is very different from the police in the previous novels and shows a progression in the way Walters is depicting them. He is shown as concerned, thoughtful, sympathetic, and intelligent as he heads the search for Amy. When Amy's look-alike, Franny Gough, telephones from Majorca, abandoned there by Edward Townsend, Tyler immediately realizes that Townsend might be involved in child pornography and might have been using Amy as a subject while he was living with her and her mother, Laura.

Trying to learn more about the whereabouts of Amy, DCI Tyler tells Franny's mother to send the money to Majorca to bring her daughter home as Franny isn't ready for the responsibility of looking after herself. She may have made poor choices and been wasteful with money, but she needs guidance, Tyler says, not abandonment. For many girls, lack of money prompts them to turn to prostitution as a solution. Tyler tells Franny's mother that after he arrests young prostitutes, most return to their former ways since selling themselves provides them with an easier source of money to spend on drugs than working a minimum wage job (138).

Tyler may not have children himself, but his caring nature is apparent in his behavior toward Laura Biddulph. While it may have been hard for readers to believe in McLoughlin's transformation in *The Ice House*, Walter's depiction of Chief Inspector Tyler shows that there are admirable police officers in positions of authority, and perhaps reflects how the investigation into irregular practices by the London Metropolitan police in the 1990s led to a more effective and less corrupt force.

Throughout his actions to find Amy and learn the truth about Townsend and his friend Rogerson, C.I. Tyler is shown as clever and considerate. When Laura criticizes his colleagues, he defends them, and we're told: "His kindness destroyed her" (179). Later in the investigation, we see him taking chances and finally discovering how Townsend was making videos of several young girls, along with their mothers, although he claimed to the end that he was not involved in Internet pornography. Well-deserving of his position, Tyler is a very different policeman from Walsh in *The Ice House*.

While some of the police in *Acid Row* are shown as effective, most have a real problem curbing the violence of the boys of the estate. The high-rise apartment blocks and lack of green space of sink-hole estates give rise to fear and violence and only within close-knit communities can the effects of angry, uneducated youths be contained. In the novel relationships, not police intervention, are shown to be the saving grace of difficult situations. While the uncaring relationship Martin Rogerson has with his daughter Amy has far-reaching negative consequences, the loving one Gaynor Patterson has with her son Colin and daughter Melanie overcomes numerous difficulties. While seen as a truant and hothead at the start of the riot, Colin, along with his sister, tries desperately to prevent the crazed Wesley Barber from setting the pedophile's house on fire. Colin understands the huge dangers of starting a fire, and it is his love for his pregnant sister and his attempt to protect her from Wesley that lead to his own fate.

Dr. Sophie Morrison also understands the importance of relationships, and seeing the frightening loneliness experienced by so many of her patients on the estate leads her to create Friendship Calling, a group of residents who telephone each other to check on the health and welfare of housebound individuals. Although before the riot the network has a limited role, during the troubles the police are able to use the group to help organize the escape of hundreds of women and children trapped in the streets once the riot begins. And Walters leads us to believe that the network's existence shows a sense of community which promises a better future (258).

At the end of the novel, there is no justice in the form of prison sentences for the rioters because no one would give evidence at trial, except against Wesley Barber, since they were afraid of gang reprisals (252). Showing the harsh truth about youth violence, Walters reiterates two favorite themes: a lack of education as the main cause of the youth of today turning to crime and the problems within the prison system.

In an interview with Bethanne Kelly Patrick, Walters stated that 75 percent of men incarcerated in Britain's prisons are illiterate, and 98 percent of them come from dysfunctional families like those in *Acid Row*. The only way the young men can gain power both inside and outside prison is by being more aggressive and stronger than the next person (Patrick). Sadly, there will never be redemption for young criminals like Wesley Barber because if they do not die while committing the crime and are sent to prison, they are not rehabilitated. Rather, they become hardened by the older criminals with whom they are housed. Over and over again in interviews, Walters, a long-time prison visitor, mentions that far too many of those incarcerated should not be there and are learning nothing positive by being inside.

Minette Walters' 2005 novel *Disordered Minds* continues the theme of the problems with the British justice system. She told interviewer Charles Silet in 1994, "I don't know how much you know about the British judicial system but in our system nobody is interested in finding out the truth; they are only interested in pitting one story against another.... And the jury decides who has told the best story" (185). *Disordered Minds* blends the story of a rape and a murder that occurred in 1970 with the present-day story of Dr. Jonathan Hughes, a university professor who is writing a book about injustice. Having examined numerous cases of illiterate or semi-literate young men who were convicted after a confession was extracted from them by the police when they did not have a solicitor present, Hughes is now looking into the case of Howard Stamp, who was found guilty of the brutal murder of his grandmother. Stamp claimed that Grace Jefferies was already dead when he entered her house, and he ran away because the sight of her mutilated body so upset him. A firm time of death, which would have exonerated Howard, was not given by the pathologist, who changed his original statement from the death having occurred four days prior to two days. Howard committed suicide three years after his conviction.

As Hughes learns the truth behind the murder, he also learns about the events that led to the rape of thirteen-year-old Priscilla Trevelyan by three boys, Roy Trent, Mickey Hopkinson, and Nicholas Hurst. At the time of the rape, Priscilla "Cill" Trevelyan and her friend Louise Burton were encouraging the boys with their flirtatious behavior. Scantily and sexily dressed, they talked to each other and took no notice of the boys (3). Although they thought they were in control of the boys, they were not; and Louise's taunts to one of the boys of "Virgin, virgin, virgin" (5) ended in Priscilla's being gang raped by the boys. Skinny Louise froze, and as she held no attraction for them, the boys let her go and turned to Priscilla for sport.

There is no justice for Priscilla, since she refuses to tell the police what happened out of fear of the beating she will receive from her father. He is already angry with her about her truancy and the provocative clothes she insists on wearing. When Louise admits to the attack, but refuses to identify the boys, Priscilla runs to take refuge in the home of Grace Jefferies. When she never returns home, the police presume that she has run away to London, and the murder of Grace soon takes precedence over the investigation of a runaway teenager.

Like *The Shape of Snakes* and other Walters' novels, *Disordered Minds* reveals the truth behind the earlier crimes one detail at a time. But even when Dr. Hughes and Councillor Georgina (George) Gardener discover the facts, they quickly realize that there will be no clean, comforting justice. While layer upon layer of the convoluted plot unfolds, the reader learns the truth of the nasty secrets being hidden by the father of Louise Burton and two of the three men who as boys committed the rape. Louise, at first portrayed as the victim of her father, is described by her former headmistress as a horrid child who told on her peers in order to gain attention (265). Later it is revealed that she married all three of the rapists. Her first husband, Mickey Hopkinson, introduced her to heroin and then forced her into prostitution to support both of their habits. When he died, Louise, now calling herself Priscilla or Cill, married Roy Trent, who used to be a major drug dealer and needed to keep Louise stoned so that no one would believe her story of the disappearance of the real Priscilla Trevelyan. Finally she married Nicholas (Colley) Hurst.

As readers learn the truth of the old disappearance and where Priscilla's body is buried, they realize that no one would have discovered the body at the later date had Louise behaved differently. The irony of her actions is that because she draws attention to herself, Dr. Hughes and Councillor Gardener discover who murdered Grace Jefferies. The truths that are revealed by Hughes and Gardener lead to a resolution, if not justice. The murderer shows no remorse and may or may not be convicted. Nothing is definite, and the police continue to believe the lies they are told. Louise has not grown into a sympathetic character with the passage of time and still blames her father for abusing her. Priscilla's rapists, Roy and Colley, will never be punished for the crime since too much time has passed.

Although many mystery readers enjoy crime fiction in which the criminal gets his or her just desserts, this outcome is not usually the case in real life. Justice, as we learn from Walters' novels, is not a simple case of locking criminals in prison, and often there is no healing justice for the victims of crimes. Walters has said that "It's the psychology of crime that interests [her]. What set of circumstances conspire to make a person commit an evil act?" (Jacobson). It is clear from all her novels, especially those examined in this chapter, that why people become criminals and how their personal circumstances lead to those crimes fascinate both Walters and her fans.

As Walters describes the sad lives of the dysfunctional families, truth in her novels is often shown as ugly. Many of her characters are, in effect, serving life sentences as victims of poverty or violence. Were they to be punished for their crimes by a prison term, it would not help either their situation or that of their victims. As Walters writes the truth about British society today, she shows how there can be no cleansing justice. The only resolution people may hope for is to be able to continue "actively challenging and directing the course of their lives and not merely waiting to be swept along by others" (Dilley 40).

Works Cited

Berlins, Marcel. "Crime Pays." *Hot Air* Jan/Mar. 1998. 5 Nov. 2006. http://www.minettewalters.co.uk/about_minette/articles/hotair2.htm.

Chandler, Raymond. "The Simple Art of Murder." *The Longman Anthology of Detective Fiction.* Eds. Deane Mansfield-Kelley and Lois A. Marchino. New York: Pearson Longman, 2005. pp. 208–218.

Dilley, Kimberly. J. *Busybodies, Meddlers, and Snoops: The Female Hero in Contemporary Women's Mysteries.* Westport: Greenwood Press, 1998.

"A Fight for Justice: The Stephen Lawrence Story." 6 Nov. 2006. http://news.bbc.co.uk/1/hi/special_report/1990/02/99/stephen_lawrence/281742.stm.

Jacobson, Michael. "The Sinister Small Mind." *Gold Coast Bulletin* 28–29 Nov. 1998. 21 Nov. 2006. http://www.minettewalters.co.uk/about_minette/articles/inst_aus.htm.

Patrick, Bethanne Kelly. "Acid Reign." 21 Nov. 2006. acid_rn.htm.

"Racism." Chapter 6. *The Stephen Lawrence Inquiry* 13 Nov. 2006. http://www.archive.official-documents.co.uk/document/cm42/4262/sli-02.htm.

Reddy, Maureen. "The Feminist Counter-Tradition in Crime: Cross, Grafton, Paretsky and Wilson." *The Cunning Craft: Original Essays on Detective Fiction and Contemporary Literary Theory.* Eds. Ronald G. Walker and June M. Frazer. Macomb: Western Illinois University Press, 1990. pp. 174–187.

Sibree, Bron. "Mind of Minette." *The Saturday Mercury* 19 Nov. 2000. 5 Nov. 2006. http://www.minettewalters.co.uk/about_minette/articles/mind1.htm.

Silet, Charles L. P. "An Interview with Minette Walters." *The Armchair Detective.* 27 (1994): pp. 182–185.

Spelman, Judith. "Minette Walters: An Intelligent Approach to Crime." *Writers News* June 1994. 5 Nov. 2007. http://www.minettewalters.co/uk/about_minette/articles/winternw1.htm.

Thomson, Liz. "Crime and Compassion." *Publishing News* 12 Oct. 2001. 13 Nov. 2006. http://www.minettewalters.co/uk/about_minette/articles/pubnews.htm.

Walters, Minette. *Acid Row.* New York: Berkley Books, 2003.

_____. *Disordered Minds.* New York: Berkley Books, 2005.

_____. *The Ice House.* New York: St. Martin's Press, 1992.

_____. Personal Interview. July 23, 2004.

_____. *The Shape of Snakes.* New York: Putnam & Sons, 2001.

Walton, Priscilla L. and Manina Jones. *Detective Agency: Women Rewriting the Hard-Boiled Tradition.* Berkeley: University of California Press, 1999.

Soul Murder: Children in Minette Walters' Novels

Sarah D. Fogle

The tradition of excellence begun by Agatha Christie, Dorothy L. Sayers, Margery Allingham, and Ngaio Marsh in the "Golden Age" of British crime and detective fiction during the early twentieth century, and continued by Ruth Rendell and P. D. James, has since 1992 been even further enriched by the novels of Minette Walters. In her work on feminism and crime writing, Sally Munt observes that British women writers are "implicated together by the literary world view they share; the explorations into the effects and motivations for murder are expressed as psychological investigations into the darkness of the human psyche for which there is no effective guiding moral principle" (25). Through her very successful and often honored writing career, Walters has developed a reputation for writing dark novels on psychological and social themes that extend well beyond the particulars of the murders and perpetrators that populate her work. While she is not particularly comfortable "being seen as the successor of a purely women's thread of writing" (Morrell 2), Walters acknowledges the strengths of British women's detective writing, especially its qualities of analysis and sophistication that in her opinion set it apart from American women's detective fiction (Morrell 3). What Walters has done to separate herself somewhat from the tradition of which she is a part is to write stand-alone psychological novels instead of a series with a single detective and other reappearing characters, and thereby assert her independence within that tradition — in her words, her "'right to be different'" (Patrick 1).

In the absence of typical series elements, Walters does, however, establish a common thread among her books through her consistent themes of poverty, racism, homelessness, and other forms of social injustice; mob mentality and isolation of individuals; and most, centrally, family relationships, domestic violence, and cruelty to children through neglect, sexual molestation, and outright torture. Without fail, Walters mirrors family dysfunction with societal dysfunction, each reflecting what is off-kilter in each sphere. Walters' fictional themes stem from her outspoken concerns about contemporary society: "The two themes I am pursuing, and probably always will, are firstly the damage that families can do to themselves, and secondly the nature of truth.... I do think we have two fundamental problems: the collapse of the family structure and the abandonment of absolute values" (Spelman 1). When reading her novels occasionally as they are published, even reading all of them over time, one may not be cognizant of the role of children in her work. But when reading them as a body of work over a short period of time, one is immediately struck not just by the presence of children but by the focus on children as some of the most significant characters in her novels. In nearly every case, children are at the epicenter of fractured families and are negatively affected by the absence of values in family and in society. Although children are seldom the victims of murder, children — survivors though they may be — are the real victims in Walters' bleak world.

While Walters may have asserted her right to be different from other British women detective writers, her work belongs in a tradition that extends back to the "foremothers" of modern crime writing (Reddy 8) who wrote gothic and sensation novels in the early nineteenth century. These early writers and then their successors wrote novels "reflective of the societies in which these authors themselves were raised. These societies were convention-bound, and the roles of women in them were restricted" (Swanson 13). Detective novels tended to depict crimes that occurred in the home, in the family, or in some other form of community; such crimes stemmed from the human relationships therein (Swanson 14). And while the early nineteenth century and the Victorian era are long past, Walters' writing depicts a world that has not fully shed the cultural and social values of those times. Further, her novels began to be published shortly after the period during which Margaret Thatcher held office, a time of return to earlier conservative values in England. With economic problems and a scarcity of employment, there was a renewed emphasis on family and the woman's place in the home, while at the same time the government reduced programs and services that women and children needed and thus relegated women even more to the domestic realm (Gardiner 197–98). In "The Heat in the Kitchen," Lynne Segal notes the effects of "Thatcherism" on women as she cites Thatcher's expressed desire to safeguard and enhance the "stability and quality of family life" and to maintain an emphasis on the critical role women play in the home. Further, Thatcher believed that "bringing up a family is the most important thing of all"; she also asserted that families must be "secure and respected" (quoted in Segal 208). According to Segal, Thatcher saw family values as essentially women's values: "Women know that society is founded on dignity, reticence and discipline" (quoted in Segal 208). Such social and cultural attitudes during Thatcher's tenure in office would at least in some ways reinforce earlier Victorian views of the importance of the middle- and upper-class home as the private domain headed by a woman, in contrast to the public domain of men.

Indeed, home and hearth have long been archetypal symbols of security and peace: "Throughout Western civilization, the hearth universally symbolizes safety, warmth, and comfort ... a quiet refuge where a loving family gathers in the evening for happy, contented community. If a home has a heart, surely it must beat within the hearth" (Deats and Lenker 1). In the nineteenth century, the home was considered a "sanctuary, a firelit circle enclosed against the hostile and dangerous external world" (Trodd 1) and the woman of the house was viewed as a "guardian of the inner sanctuary, the 'angel in the house'" (Trodd 6). But popular fiction of the time began to "represent the home not as a place of refuge but as a place of threat" (Sturrock 83), a place where secrets may be kept, where crimes may be committed, usually by women or servants, out of the public eye. Crime within the home created an intersection between the private, female domain and the public, male domain, as the usually male detective investigated the locus of the crime. Although Walters' novels center on the home and the family, especially relationships between mothers and children, she neither embraces conservative attitudes about the role of women in society nor views the home as a sanctuary. To the contrary, she illuminates the detrimental influences that such values have on women and children and depicts the home as an often dangerous place, especially for children. Her adult characters' ancestral pasts, rooted in an earlier, more conservative time, carry into the present of the narrative and affect their children in subsequent generations.

Perturbed by depictions of ineffectual women in crime novels, Walters has deliberately written strong women into central roles in her novels to give "everyone, men and women, equal nastiness, equal goodness" (Berlins). In fact, her strong women characters are often more dominant than the male detectives investigating criminal activity and murder; but even strong women, in particular Phoebe Maybury in *The Ice House* and Mathilda Gillespie in *The Scold's Bridle*, are centered in the home. Well known for her long-standing habit of weekly prison visits with violent felons, Walters understands full well that the prisons sanctioned by the justice system are not the only prisons in society. The home and the family can be every bit as much a prison for women and children, especially those who suffer abuse or neglect. They are captives bound not by shackles, bars, and walls, but by marriage between men and women and by the bond between children and parents. In *The Ice House, The Sculptress, The Scold's Bridle,* and *The Breaker,* children in particular are captives in families that sacrifice love and care for conformity to social convention, house predators who molest their own children, or inflict other forms of neglect upon a child. In *The Echo* and *Fox Evil,* children who have no parents are held captive in other insulated communities — the homeless and caravaners — chiefly through their fear of authority such as the police or the foster care system, or through fear of physical harm. An important distinction among these children, however, must be made. While all of them may be viewed as victims of parental failures, the teenage girl in *The Scold's Bridle* and the two young boys in *The Echo* and *Fox Evil* rise above their victim status, display great personal courage, and are oddly able to mend schisms in broken families other than their own. Walters' view of children and their plight is not entirely without hope.

Since very few authors of detective or crime fiction create important child characters (American writers Martha Grimes, Dennis Lehane, Carol O'Connell, and Robert Parker come to mind) and make them central to the narrative action or themes of their novels, Walters' focus on children is unique. Munt observes that "children of any age rarely occupy more than a cameo role in traditional crime fiction, being presented at most as objects of exchange in cases of kidnap, or victims of abuse in the more sensationalist stories. In virtually all cases their appearance is highly stylized and idealized, their function merely as adjuncts to the adults' manoeuvring" (166–67). Further, Christopher Routledge notes that children are rarely a presence in crime fiction written for adults:

> Where children do appear in adult detective narratives ... they are either needful of sympathy, perhaps victims of crime or disease, or else they occupy a similar marginal space as the detective. Like the detective, they are told lies, denied access to certain things, and their opinions are ignored, although, interestingly, less often by the detectives than by other adults [65].

While Walters' child characters may indeed be viewed as victims deserving sympathy, they are not the murder victims at the center of the puzzle to be solved, and in no way do they occupy "marginal space." They are the collateral damage in the midst of failed families. The manor house is no safer than the council estate, families of the upper crust are as broken as those of the lower class, and children of the affluent are as neglected or abused as those who are homeless. Principally, but not exclusively, Walters' damaged children are young, powerless girls who naturally and rightfully — but often futilely — have relied upon a mother's love to protect them.

In their roles at the forefront of her novels, Walters' children have much in common with the children in the fictional world of Charles Dickens, who had a "profound understanding of the vulnerability of children" (Puttock 19). He understood the mental and physical cruelty to which children could be subjected and "its psychic consequences, in particular the confused feelings of shame, inadequacy, and guilt suffered by unloved, abused, or neglected children" (Puttock 19). In the nineteenth century, the Victorian view of the child was based on a somewhat uneasy blend of Calvinism and Romanticism, rendering the "child as a highly ambiguous figure in Victorian culture, a site of extremely conflicting attitudes for adults" (Schober 5). Children were meant to be managed; "child rearing discourse emphasized the malleability of children's minds, their willingness and eagerness to submit to adults.... Children are not inherently evil — simply empty-headed — and thus appropriately disciplined and instructed by their elders" (Jenkins). It is not a great leap from strict discipline to abuse, especially when it has become an established generational practice within a family, abuse begetting abuse. Further, children who act in ways that bring embarrassment of social judgment to the family would certainly be deemed in need of such discipline and instruction. Walters' depiction of children and their treatment by their parents continues to bear out the conservative view of the family and parenting established in late-19th and early-20th-century Great Britain.

Walters' view of the child's plight under the control of parents in dysfunctional households is indeed a dark one. In *The Ice House,* Jane Maybury has been sexually abused by her father; in *The Sculptress,* Olive Martin is used for what she can do to keep the household running and is neglected in favor of her prettier younger sister; in *The Scold's Bridle,* Mathilda's sexual molestation by her father and an uncle carries down through three generations to the emotional abuse of her granddaughter Ruth Lascelles. Walters' most disturbing child character is the toddler Hannah Sumner in *The Breaker,* who at three years old compulsively acts out extremely overt sexual behavior. While the home is no safe harbor, the outside world as well is predictably dangerous for children. In *The Echo,* teenager Terry Dalton's only home is, ironically, with the homeless. And the most memorable of Walters' children, little Wolfie in *Fox Evil,* lives in a bus among a group of gypsy-like travelers under the dominance of a brutal leader. These two young male characters have been set adrift in a society that offers them little nurture and expects them to fend for themselves for any kind of care.

Each of these children suffers from what Dr. Leonard Shengold describes as "soul murder," stemming from abuse that he asserts is criminal: "There is an inherent moral protest in the term" (536). Children are fragile beings, and the effect of physical abuse such as "torture, hatred, seduction, and rape — and even of indifference, of deprivation of love and care — is the devastating one of developmental arrest; for their souls — their psychic structure and functioning — are still forming" (537). Bearing out what is known about the effects of abuse and neglect, Shengold's theory of soul murder is especially applicable to the vulnerable children in Walters' novels. The children mentioned above can rely only on betrayal, not on love, from an abusive or abandoning parent — yet to whom *can* such children turn? According to Shengold, the need for parental love and children's hope to be worthy of it leads them to believe that *they* are bad; the shattering of self-image and identity leads to intense feelings of shame and worthlessness (541). The concept of soul murder is particularly applicable to Jane Maybury, Olive Martin, Ruth Lascelles, and Wolfie.

The majority of Walters' children at least begin their lives in the bosoms of their families. In several of her earliest novels — *The Ice House, The Sculptress, The Scold's Bridle,* and *The Breaker* — Walters depicts families as bound by conservative values and a desire to maintain the pretense of respectability and to shield the family from scrutiny by society. These families have bowed to social convention to conceal, or confer respectability upon, the pregnancies of young, unmarried girls or women. In *The Sculptress* and *The Scold's Bridle*, moreover, efforts are also made to avoid revelations of the fathers' homosexuality. If pregnancy outside marriage violates social mores, then a homosexual added to the moral mix is an even greater transgression that must be hidden. In each case, these social aberrations set into motion events that have lasting effects on the children in these families: Jane Maybury and her brother Jonathan in *The Ice House,* Olive Martin in *The Sculptress,* Ruth Lascelles in *The Scold's Bridle,* and Hannah Sumner in *The Breaker.*

In *The Ice House*, the family circle is, by village standards, an unusual one in that it comprises Phoebe Maybury, owner of the house and mother of Jane and Jonathan, and her friends Diana Goode and Anne Cattrell. Home and hearth in the novel are continually assailed by the villagers' shunning of these women, whom they irrationally — and inaccurately — fear and abhor as lesbians, and by the local police, who are investigating a second murder at the Maybury property. Phoebe not only wants to protect her home and children from the intrusive authorities, but she also wants to protect a dark secret deep within the home, especially now that she finds herself a murder suspect for the second time.

Like other Walters women, Phoebe did not enter into marriage willingly or freely. When she became pregnant at seventeen, Phoebe's parents forced her to marry David Maybury, a man twice her age; she bitterly describes the marriage as his reward for seducing her. When she discovered him raping their eight-year-old daughter Jane, much as he took advantage of her as a teenager, she certainly *wanted* to murder him but he fled from the home before she could do the deed. The children know only that their father has left them; the family unit is disrupted, the father is absent, and the children carry the burden of guilt and shame that they are somehow responsible for his abandonment.

The subsequent investigation by the police into David's disappearance, described by Phoebe as pure hell, harmed both her children; it damaged her son but nearly destroyed her daughter. Jane has been under psychiatric care and suffering from anorexia during the time following her year-long molestation; recently showing signs of improvement, by doctor's orders she is to be protected from undue pressure and stress. Unable to prevent the police from intruding into her home and into her children's psyches before, and facing another police investigation after the discovery of a body in the ice house in the present action of the novel, Phoebe fears the police invading her home yet again. She fears they will, as before, question Jane unmercifully until she breaks down, and at one point during the investigation, Jane does have a flashback to her father's sexual abuse. To a lesser, though still significant, degree, Jonathan was also hurt by being interrogated at the time of his father's disappearance. Then ten years old, he became a bed-wetter; he also was overwhelmed at the responsibility he had to assume beyond his years as the man of the house. Now twenty, he still feels inadequate as a result of his mother's continued protectiveness and his concern for his sister. For Jonathan, the second interrogation is far worse than the first one, and provokes him to feelings of impotence and uncontrollable outbursts of anger about what is happening to his family, to the point that he nearly shoots someone.

Despite Phoebe's fierce desire to protect them, Jane and Jonathan must relive the damaging experiences that followed the initial investigation into the disappearance and Phoebe's alleged murder of their father. They are forced to endure the dual trials, times two, of two deaths and two traumatic police interrogations. Phoebe and her housemates also suffer the indignity of the police bringing the community animus into the private realm of their home; as an institutional presence entering their lives, the police attempt to validate the community's misperception and vicious rumors about these three women. In her role as mother, Phoebe

Maybury stands out as an exception compared to other mothers in Walters' novels. Given what happened to her as a young girl, perhaps she should have been more vigilant about her husband's behavior toward her daughter; but when she did discover his molestation, she immediately stepped in to stop it. In many ways, Phoebe has since sacrificed her own life to safeguard her children, in particular Jane's privacy and well-being. While she was unable to prevent her daughter's abuse, Phoebe nonetheless is a loving parent who fiercely tries to protect her children from further harm.

Another family for whom the home fires do not provide warmth and safety, whose father is largely absent, and whose mother — unlike Phoebe Maybury — fails to mother is the Martin family in *The Sculptress*. As in *The Ice House*, social conformity, related both to unwanted pregnancy and the added embarrassment of homosexuality, is a precipitating factor in the damage to the Martin children. This family is run by the controlling, uncommunicative, domineering mother, Gwen, and the withdrawn, isolated, homosexually promiscuous father, Robert. Their daughters are Amber, pregnant at thirteen, pretty and well-liked, but also jealous, immature, and self-centered, and her older sister Olive, huge, unattractive, and deceitful. Olive also was pregnant and had an abortion and, as the novel begins, is imprisoned for murdering her mother and sister.

Although one of the most consistent elements of *The Sculptress* is its ambiguity about the actual facts, particularly who really murdered Gwen and Amber, it appears that Olive was desperate for love and therefore loved most those who had needed — not loved — her most: her mother and her sister. Her efforts to please them made her totally dependent on them, regardless of how they treated her. According to a neighbor, Olive did everything at home and her mother could not have coped without her; Gwen forced Olive to have an abortion because she feared Olive would marry and abandon her family. Olive's version is that Amber was so immature and jealous that she had to abort her baby to avoid upsetting Amber. No matter which, if either, of these versions is the true one, Olive's needs were not acknowledged in the family; Amber, on the other hand, was the center of attention. According to Olive, there were two Ambers: the socially pleasing Amber outside the home and the abusive, disruptive Amber at home — behaviors perhaps learned from her mother. In a play on the phrase idealizing the woman as the "angel in the house," Amber is described as a "street angel, 'ouse devil" (*The Sculptress* 210) whom both Gwen and Olive feared. She puts on a much different face for those outside the home than she does for those who should be closest to her.

Both Gwen and Robert Martin were parents in name and outward appearances only. Gwen is revealed as a drunk who assiduously maintained a façade of respectability to conceal her flaws and to pretend the reality of her husband's sexual orientation and his evening pub crawls for partners did not exist. Olive describes her father as a completely contemptible man who lived in self-imposed isolation in a single room in the house, with allegiance only to himself and without any sense of responsibility to his family. Described by acquaintances as a bad mother who cared more about what people thought than her own children, Gwen abdicated her parental obligations to a strict Catholic school where the requirements were discipline, structure, and results—a controlled, well-managed environment that reinforced society's expectations for young women in particular but that was quite obviously unsuccessful in shaping Olive's and Amber's behavior. Her children's pregnancies—their failures to live up to these expectations—drove Gwen into hysterical denial.

The Martin home exhibits none of the archetypal qualities of warmth, love, and safe harbor. Described as white, sterile, and cold (87), the Martin house, now empty after the murders, was simply a façade for a family in which the parents could not communicate verbally or emotionally and in which, as a child growing up, Olive was a prisoner of her love for a family that had nothing but disregard for her. She tells the journalist who visits her in prison, "No one loves me.... No one's ever loved me" (282). Olive epitomizes what Munt describes as the "bitter struggle between (mainly) mothers and children as implying the sickness at the heart of the conventional nuclear family, where each member vies for a limited resource of love and nurturance" (167). Perhaps the murders are the end result of that struggle, but while the judgment of her guilt or innocence in the murders remains ambiguous, Olive's choice to go to prison is understandable. She had lost the only two people who needed her, her affair was ended and her baby aborted, and she was left with only her indifferent father. She survives physically but remains an emotionally and now psychologically wrecked hulk of a human being. In prison, preferring to be feared rather than laughed at, with her imposing size and presence, she at last has some control — if not love — in her life.

In *The Scold's Bridle* the intergenerational effects of incest and yet another forced marriage sets off a chain of events that leads to three murders and nearly destroys three generations of women: the grandmother Mathilda Gillespie, her daughter Joanna Lascelles, and Joanna's daughter Ruth. Each of these women has been abused and controlled in ways detrimental to maternal family bonds and individual well-being. The central symbol of this control is the scold's bridle, a medieval device used to repress women who were outspoken or who resisted male authority. This metal contraption serves the same purpose in the novel, first put on Mathilda as a child when she threatened to tell the vicar about her father's abuse, which he "bestowed" upon her as a sort of perverted gift on the occasion of her tenth birthday. Further, her mentally ill uncle began to abuse her when she was thirteen, eventually impregnating her. Like Phoebe Maybury, Mathilda enters into an arranged marriage with an older man in exchange for her silence about the molestation; like Phoebe, she is forced to yield to social conformity to protect the family name. Her later abandonment by her husband, a physically abusive homosexual who wanted only the family money, shaped a life of murder, an inability to form healthy relationships with men, and the emotional abuse of her own daughter that included the use of the scold's bridle. The reader is privy to Mathilda's thoughts, before her death, about her marriage — a forced, unwanted arrangement — and the abuse of children: Mathilda understands better than most the difference between facile discussions of child abuse in the abstract and the reality of the harm parents can inflict on their children (29). First for Mathilda, later for Joanna, and then for Ruth, abuse is the trigger for their histories of damage and years of living in fear.

In retaliation for her father's sexual abuse and failure to protect her from her uncle's subsequent abuse over twelve years, it appears that Mathilda murdered both of them, easily enough because they were both drunks, and cleverly enough not to be accused of the crimes. The mother and daughter who should love and support each other harbor secrets that make each woman fear the other. Joanna comes very near to smothering Ruth as an infant and then for years lives in dread that Mathilda saw her and will kill her in turn. Mathilda knows that, years earlier, two-year-old

Joanna saw her smother her abusive father and fears that Joanna will kill her; Joanna's adult life as a woman who prostitutes herself to support a drug habit, much like the one that killed her husband, continues the family propensity for abuse. Like Gwen Martin, Joanna sends Ruth off to school, in this case a boarding school that actually becomes Ruth's safe haven from maternal neglect. Although Ruth's grandmother at least cared about her, with Mathilda's murder early in the novel, Ruth is set emotionally adrift, only to take up with a clever young man in his twenties who preys on her desperate need for love. Their "relationship" gets Ruth kicked out of school, her only remaining "family." His method of control is also abusive; in addition to his demands for sex with Ruth, he has his gang of low-life cronies gang rape her, and she ends up pregnant and alone. Her mother had already abandoned her, and Mathilda is dead. Unlike many of Walters' children, however, Ruth Lascelles unexpectedly finds herself informally adopted by Mathilda's doctor and her husband; for a while, at least, they become her surrogate parents, a circumstance that benefits all three of them and that will be addressed later in this discussion.

As Mathilda Gillespie's sordid family saga unfolds following her murder, and after Ruth recounts the horrors she has endured, a family friend's summary judgment of Mathilda reinforces the power of social mores; she was born at the wrong time and was compelled to live an adult life for which she was particularly ill suited. Although she was smart enough to do, or become, anything she wanted to, family and social conventions dictated that she be a wife and mother (151). Against her own best interests, and because of abuse and an early marriage to conceal the incest, Mathilda became a lifelong prisoner of conservative social values. Like Jane Maybury, but for different reasons, she was despised by her community and lived alone in her home. An embittered and imperious woman, she died wearing the scold's bridle. With her murder, the residual damage in the family falls heavily on Ruth, an unmarried pregnant teen contemplating abortion. Having lost the only person who cared anything about her, Ruth is left with a narcissistic mother whose principal parental talent is neglect. The horrible legacy of Mathilda's childhood sexual abuse aside, the power of the parent over a child cannot be underestimated. In this respect, Ruth is kin to Olive Martin, as she too had hoped for some small store of her mother's "limited resource of love and nurturance" (Munt 167). As a friend of Ruth's observes, "We all want to believe our mothers love us. It's supposed to be the one relationship we can depend on" (136).

As woeful as the childhoods of Jane Maybury, Olive Martin, and Ruth Lascelles are, Hannah Sumner in *The Breaker* is perhaps the most pathetic of Walters' fictional children. Found walking on the streets of a seaside English town, three-year-old Hannah has been left alone because her mother has been raped and murdered. Her physical abandonment is bad enough, but Hannah's bizarre emotional state and the causes of it that eventually unfold are appalling. Following her rescue, the police doctor's evaluation reveals a child in good health, well cared for, with no outward evidence of abuse; but she is unnaturally withdrawn, passive, silently observant, and uninterested in other people, including other children. Yet she becomes aggressive if approached and resorts to extreme tantrums if denied what she wants. Most revealing is that she shows a strong fear of men, screaming when one comes near her for the first time, and she has traces of some odd drugs in her system. The police doctor's report concludes, "She should not be returned to her family/guardians without exhaustive inquiries being made about the nature of the household" (*The Breaker* 39).

During the murder investigation, the facts that emerge about the Sumner marriage vary somewhat through the various interrogations of the father, William. What soon becomes clear, however, is that the Sumner marriage was, at best, one of convenience and that William's wife Kate is another of Walters' mothers held hostage by social conventions and aspirations to acceptability and position. Following her affair with a coworker and the resulting pregnancy, expectations of society regarding unmarried pregnant women precipitate Kate's pursuit of a husband and respectability. Having grown up in poverty, in a family abandoned by the father, Kate has no intention of living with a baby in that same predicament and cleverly manipulates William into marriage. Their union is strictly a calculated, pragmatic arrangement; the currency is security, social acceptance, and respectability for Kate and sex on demand for William, who can perform sexually only with certain unusual types of assistance. Assigned to the Sumner home to see to Hannah's well-being after her mother's death, WPC Griffiths engages William in a tense conversation about his marriage. As a husband, William says he was like a boarder in a rooming house whose landlady merely tolerated his presence (180). How could a child be expected to develop normally and thrive in such an environment?

In the Sumner family, Hannah is a small prisoner who has become virtually invisible in the midst of her parents' self-serving lives. Each of the parents wins in their marital arrangement, but baby Hannah is the ultimate loser emotionally and psychologically. Early in the marriage, while Kate kept her end of the bargain and was apparently a doting mother, William remained a workaholic and mostly absent father. Kate's virtual appropriation of the child made Hannah a wedge between her parents and taught the child to be a skillful manipulator who played the mother against the father, with the result that her tantrums for her mother's attention effectively threatened William's access to frequent sex. The solution, at William's insistence and with Kate's acquiescence, was to have sex in front of Hannah. If the methods used to address William's performance deficiencies were illuminated here, one would view the Sumners' self-absorbed behavior as abhorrent indeed.

The effects of inappropriate and damaging adult behavior on Hannah are graphically demonstrated in front of one of the investigators. Entering the room where he is waiting to interview William, Hannah begins to engage openly in sexual behavior. She masturbates quite energetically, her eyes focused on the man the entire time; he later describes her behavior to a colleague as extraordinarily creepy, because she knew exactly what she was doing and how to do it. He concludes she must have been previously exposed to graphic sexual behavior, obviously by her parents. During subsequent questioning, William admits that he and his wife had sex in front of Hannah, offering the lame excuse that Kate used Hannah as a shield and the child just would not leave them alone; having sex in front of her was the only way he could be gratified. Thus, once again a child's needs are subordinated to the needs of adults in the family. In this instance, Hannah's well-being was sacrificed for Kate's chosen lifestyle and status and for William's sexual needs. The investigation also ultimately reveals that Kate was far from being the perfect mother, as her infidelity during William's long workdays was facilitated by drugging Hannah to sleep in the front seat of Kate's lover's car so they could have uninterrupted sex in the back. Worse for Hannah, her parental future holds only William.

While Walters has made clear her concerns about the failures of various social institutions, specifically the family, and she consistently depicts children in dire straits, she also asserts her "great faith in the redeeming power of love" ("An Interview"). While many of her children are captives of abusive and neglectful families, some are cast out to live on their own in any way they can. In spite of their mistreatment and neglect, however, these throwaway children end up in a more supportive and loving environment than they ever would have within their own families. Ruth Lascelles in *The Scold's Bridle*, Terry Dalton in *The Echo*, and Wolfie in *Fox Evil* are as mistreated as the children previously discussed, but they differ in that they either find themselves taken in — or insinuate themselves into — substitute families that are much in need of their healing presence. These children, respectively, help save the marriage of a couple bent on divorce, mend a disaffected journalist's relationship with his estranged mother, and unite a widower with his grown illegitimate granddaughter. Somehow, the damage these children have suffered becomes a balm for others' pain; what has been lost in biological families can either be repaired or established anew in surrogate relationships. Whatever the means by which they join these newfound families, these children become a force for the restoration of love, acceptance, and understanding absent in their own families, but which they are unexpectedly able to provide for others.

In *The Scold's Bridle*, the investigation to bring to light the killer of Mathilda Gillespie also illuminates the marital problems of the Blakeneys, a childless couple unwittingly embroiled in the mystery. Sarah Blakeney was Mathilda's doctor, her husband Jack an artist who painted Mathilda's portrait; the Blakeneys are two of the very few people whom Mathilda liked and allowed into her home. While Sarah and Jack clearly care about each other, their marriage is crumbling, ostensibly because he appears to be a philandering dilettante content to live off his wife's income. His assumed dalliances, however, are only the surface problem; the real crux of their marital problems is their different attitudes about having a child of their own. In this relationship, even the *idea* of a child can disrupt the family unit to a significant degree. When they married, they made a "deal" not to have children; Jack's position is that they would not have them at all, while Sarah believed that once he became established as an artist the matter could be revisited. Coupled with Sarah's lack of trust in Jack over an alleged affair, this difference in understanding has eaten away at her love for him; they are at the brink of divorce. Sarah believes, wrongly, that he has had an affair with an actress and fathered a child with her; her referral of this woman for an abortion is the basis for her suspicion of Jack's infidelity. His love for her has been undermined by her lack of trust in him, since he did not, in fact, have this affair, nor did he father the child. Too quick to believe the other woman, Sarah never asks Jack the truth; too stubborn to tell her, Jack continues to flirt with other women to hurt her in return.

Beyond the alleged infidelity, it is the idea that he would have a child with someone *else* that hurts Sarah. Early in the novel, Sarah kicks Jack out; while she still believes in his artistic talent, she no longer believes in him as a person. Their marriage, and any potential for having a family, is imperiled by their mutual distrust. Her admiration has turned to dislike, her amusement to boredom, her love to pity. Sarah soldiers on as a well-respected doctor, and Jack's desire for her is stunted by her deliberate distance from him. At least no child of theirs is brought into this family already poisoned by distrust and damaging misperceptions.

In the course of Mathilda's murder investigation, the Blakeneys unexpectedly become surrogate parents to the teenage Ruth, who is trying desperately to maintain a façade of aloof sophistication but is living the nightmare of abuse and gang rape. Following Mathilda's death, Ruth's only inheritance, as noted earlier, is the family tradition of child abuse, her mother's rejection, the requisite lack of self-esteem leading to an unwanted early pregnancy, and the resulting shame that accompanies these experiences. Thanks to the "social engineering" talents of the chief investigator on the murder case, following Ruth's rape and newfound homelessness, Jack Blakeney is convinced to return home, with Ruth in tow. Her desperate need for support and safe haven facilitates the reconciliation between the Blakeneys and provides, through her need for help and nurturing, a mutual purpose for them. Taken aback by the unexpected and rapid turn of events, Sarah fully realizes that the presence of this child in her home has changed both her marriage and her life in a positive and unanticipated way (156).

Like Sarah, Jack too is changed by Ruth; he is privileged to become her confessor, a role he thought would have been bestowed upon Sarah. He comforts Ruth as a loving parent would, "holding her tight and stroking her hair as her father would have done if he lived" (169). The story of Ruth's rape so horrifies and enrages him that he charges off as the avenging angel/vengeful father; in this act of vigilante justice, he endangers himself, rescues yet another child victim, and gets arrested for appearing to be a pervert of just the sort he is trying to stop from hurting other children. Sarah tells the police investigator that Jack has belatedly realized that he can feel like a parent: " He is acting in lieu of Ruth's dead father" (301) so she will know *someone* loves her. Jack quickly makes clear that two people care about her, surprising Sarah with his inclusion of her in this newly formed family.

The centrality of the Blakeney marriage and the importance of family and children are clear, as the narrative ends not with the exposure of Mathilda's killer, but afterward, with the focus back on the Blakeneys' relationship, where the novel began, with their discussion about having their own child and Sarah's pain over his alleged aborted baby. Saying she is no longer hopeful about having children of her own, Sarah continues to protect herself by agreeing with what she believes Jack still thinks — that having babies brings only problems which she would rather avoid. When he replies that he is rather getting used to the idea of having a baby, Sarah reveals her hurt and bitterness, throwing Jack's alleged affair and illegitimate child in his face (322). If he refused to have a child with her, how could he then get his mistress pregnant? Further, Sarah may herself have been dodging the issue of having a baby because of a lack of confidence in her marriage and her obviously painful memory of what she endured as a child during her own parents' divorce. Jack makes clear that the effects of her lack of trust about the assumed affair and her apparent indifference to it undermined his faith in their marriage and, with baseless allegations and faulty assumptions finally cleared up, the two of them seem to come to a new understanding (322).

Whether the Blakeneys will ever have a baby together or not, Ruth's courage in helping the police, her need for guidance and support, and her involvement in their lives have compelled them to face the challenges in their relationship. Through her terrible ordeal, Ruth has brought them to the point that they can shift their myopic focus from themselves to the welfare of a helpless child; they have been able to restore their mutual honesty and trust, and they can now at least see the possibilities for their future. In all probability, Ruth's coming into their lives has saved their marriage and perhaps has even made it possible for them to consider having a child of their own at some point. If so, they will be better parents for having had Ruth in their lives.

In contrast to Ruth Lascelles, who at least knows who her family is, Terry Dalton in *The Echo* is a homeless teenager who has been in and out of foster care since he was six. He thinks his mother went to prison, and has no idea of who his father might be; he was probably "anonymous and therefore irrelevant" (*The Echo* 58). Only fourteen, he now lives among a group of homeless men in an abandoned warehouse: "Reality was Terry's shit-hole of a warehouse where dereliction ruled and the manner of a man's death was the most interesting thing about him" (124). Although it is not the most nurturing environment, he finds living with the homeless safer than his stay in foster care, where he feared being sexually abused had he not run away. Parentless himself, Terry has, oddly enough at his tender age, become a father figure to a homeless, mentally ill alcoholic, Billy Blake; Terry looks out for him, takes good care of him, and protects him to the extent he is able, until Billy's death. When journalist Michael Deacon probes Billy's story, he is drawn to Terry's spunk, his outspoken defense of his homeless "family" and their rights, and his intelligence, all of which have made him the unofficial leader of the group of homeless men. In no time, Deacon finds himself the temporary surrogate father of this boy.

As homeless as Terry is, figuratively speaking, Deacon is even more homeless. Estranged from his family for years and twice divorced, he has no one else in his life, he is grinding away at a job he hates, and he is drinking too much. As he works on his story about Billy Blake, he wonders if he too could die alone, forgotten, discovered by a stranger — who would look for him if he disappeared? Daily, he dreads going home to his barren flat; he has sunk into "maudlin gloom, indulging himself in ... inspired self-loathing" (48); and he blames himself for his father's suicide, his failed marriages, his lack of friends, his family's bitterness toward him, and his lack of children. He has not spoken to his mother in five years because, he says, he is punishing her. While Deacon's many failures are real, the true cause of his estrangement from his family is much more mundane: quarrels over money and inheritance.

After he invites Terry home with him for a few days over Christmas, the dreaded anniversary of his father's death, Deacon's rapid evolution into the parental role leads him to clean Terry up, give him money in exchange for information about Billy, buy him food and clothes, and begin to teach him to read. Terry is manipulative as only the most streetwise can be; he is also friendly and witty, homophobic, and politically incorrect. These traits, as well as Terry's stories of homeless life, deepen Deacon's paternal feelings and his awareness of what the boy is lacking in his life; Deacon wishes "there had been a woman there to hear his story, one who would have wrapped him in her arms and petted him, and told him there was nothing to worry about" (157). As surrogate father and newly found son, Deacon's and Terry's interactions begin to reflect typical family give and take, including irritations and disagreements, between a father set in his ways and a fourteen-year-old who is full of energy, chatter, and self-centeredness. Terry jokingly calls Deacon "Dad," and their relationship allows Deacon to enjoy the role he realizes he has always wanted but has never had a chance to play.

Even as the child in this newly formed "family," Terry brightens Deacon's drab existence and helps re-establish his communication with his family. Chiding him about the barrenness of his flat and noting that he (Terry) is *homeless* and has nicer things, he selects art posters and other decorative items to add life to Deacon's flat. But by far the most important influence Terry has on Deacon is to light the way for him back to his relationship with his mother Penelope. Deacon's decision to visit her on Christmas Eve and drag along a reluctant Terry has less to do with obligation and the possibility of familial détente than getting Terry out of London and away from police suspicion in an arson. To Deacon's astonishment, Terry displays a savoir faire uncommon in one so young and in his circumstances, when he behaves as if he is very much a part of the family. His animated conversation with Deacon's mother Penelope, his informed appreciation of her artwork, and even his kindness to the senile family cat all charm the socks off her.

Not the least bit shy about stepping into any situation as though he rightfully belongs, Terry assumes a role as one of the family and through his presence and his actions begins to draw Deacon and Penelope closer. Speaking his mind and freely offering Deacon and his mother advice on getting along better, he says they should hear themselves argue, that both are wrong about the other; he defends Deacon's goodness to Penelope, telling her that he is good and kind, that she should show him she is glad to see him (228). His advice sounds a maternal chord in Penelope which points out Terry's lack of real family: "What a pity your mother is lost to you, Terry. She'd be proud of the man her son is becoming" (228). Back in London, Deacon hears a phone conversation between Terry and Penelope that is a revelation to him; Terry tells her, "*We'll come to see you ... next weekend? ... we'll have a New Year's Eve party*" (291), sounding as though he has been a member of this family all along. Penelope's pleasure with Deacon's taking Terry in is tempered by her concern about his ability to follow through and she expresses skepticism about his reliability: "*That child deserves better than to be tossed aside when something more attractive comes along*" (292). While the reconciliation between Deacon and his mother is far from complete, Terry's presence in their lives and wisdom beyond his years have at least gotten them together face to face, and he now have the two of them talking with each other again. Perhaps the Deacon family is on the mend, thanks to young Terry.

Predictably, the father-son relationship between Deacon and Terry is short-lived, though its effects on the Deacon family will endure. Terry's ingrained street ethics are revealed in his good-bye note, which justifies his departing theft of the art posters, stereo, television, and Deacon's stash of cash, saying he has earned these things by learning to read and write and promising to be in touch. But Terry's innate goodness is also evident, as leaves a gift for Deacon more valuable than anything he took; in the note he tells Deacon to free himself, to ditch his editor at the magazine and focus on writing books: "*Do your own thing, mate ... like Billy always said: any man who dies in chains deserves to*" (338). What Deacon may or may not do with the advice Terry bestowed upon him is beyond the scope of the novel, but events suggest that Deacon becomes more open to friends and family, that he is much less miserable and self-absorbed, and that his work may once again be rewarding. His temporary assumption of fatherhood of Terry has given him back his life; this wise young homeless boy has freed him from the chains of unsatisfying work and, more importantly, from the pain of estrangement from his family.

Unlike Ruth Lascelles and Terry Dalton, Wolfie in *Fox Evil* is a mere waif who is the most touching and irresistible child in all of Walters' novels. Like a small, abandoned animal cub left to die in the wild, the aptly named Wolfie is a starved, neglected, drugged, motherless child living in a bus among a group of traveling caravaners. Struggling to survive after his mother and brother disappear, Wolfie is left with the brutal Fox, called Fox Evil, a clever manipulator who he believes is his father. In the midst of this community of nomads in the caravan camp, Wolfie is really alone; only the motherly Bella, an unofficial leader of the group, shows him any kindness. Wolfie spends most of his time in abject terror, afraid of what the razor-wielding, cruel Fox will do to him next. Even in his terror, he seems quite aware of needing something parents might give him that he is missing now. He wishes he "knew more about parents" (*Fox Evil* 174); his very limited knowledge is based on movies, in which moms said "love you" and "pumpkin," words he never expects to hear uttered to him (174). The terrible knowledge he does have is that he cannot escape from his miserable existence. Wolfie is afraid of everything, especially Fox — but his "fear of authority was far greater than his fear of Fox. In any child's mind, a bad parent was better than no parent at all" (253). With these words, Wolfie personifies Shengold's concept of soul murder. His fear of authority stems from his tremendous fear of being found without a parent and being turned over to the police or to "strangers," his term for the child welfare people.

The location of the caravan camp places Wolfie in fortunate proximity to the home of James Lockyer-Fox, whose wife Ailsa has recently been found dead. The Lockyer-Foxes are another of Walters' families constrained by social convention and concern with appearances. Their now grown children have been lost to them for years, their promiscuous daughter pregnant at eighteen and cast out of their home, only to die later from drug use, and their wayward son a compulsive gambler and assumed thief. Yet another absentee father, James was away in the army; and because she was more concerned about the family name than her daughter, Ailsa demanded that her illegitimate baby granddaughter be given away. Depressed following his wife's death, James, like Phoebe Maybury and

Mathilda Gillespie, is isolated. The village gossips are in full throat, accusing him of Ailsa's murder and incest with his daughter; the anonymous, nasty, threatening phone calls have rendered him virtually helpless, alone, a prisoner in his own home.

Unlike most other parents in Walters' novels, James is burdened with guilt about the past and his failures as a parent, and he has managed to locate his granddaughter, Nancy Smith, now an army captain. In a letter to her, he acknowledges these failures and the bitter lessons he has learned; if he had been a better parent, he writes, "My children would have grown up to be stable members of society and you would have been welcomed for who you were, not banished for what you were" (43). Perfectly content in the only happy family in the novel, Nancy at first rebuffs James's overtures, but she later relents and agrees to meet him. Their way back to each other is not a smooth one, and Wolfie plays a key role in Nancy's decision to establish a relationship with her grandfather.

Wolfie's happenstance acquaintance with the Lockyer-Fox family results from his ranging about the grounds of the manor searching for his missing mother. When Wolfie hears and misperceives Lockyer-Fox as "Lucky Fox," he thinks they may be related and James will know where his mother is. But Wolfie is also afraid because he has heard James called a murderer. Unaccountably drawn to James and Nancy and desperately wanting to ask them for help, he decides they don't look like murderers, and he likes their voices, especially Nancy's because it reminds him of his mother. When James and Nancy finally meet Wolfie face to face, he is immediately drawn to Nancy because she is warm and kind. Equally drawn to Wolfie, James admires his good sense; he treats Wolfie carefully, like a little wild animal, and lets him know his door is always open to him. Wolfie interprets James's hospitality to mean he will "always have a hiding place" (197), which he knows he will need with Fox around. Nancy's and James's kindness toward Wolfie change him, giving him hope he has never felt: "He felt braver than he had for weeks.... They [James and Nancy] spoke to him of a future. Alone with Fox, he thought only of death" (215).

Wolfie's newly formed bond with James and Nancy has not only given him a form of parental comfort but has also lessened his fear. While his lot in life is significantly improved through his acquaintance with the

Lockyer-Fox family, Wolfie will eventually be able to reciprocate and bridge the gap between grandfather and granddaughter. Their reconciliation has been disrupted by James's sudden decision to break off contact with Nancy because he fears his own dissolute son may have been her birth father. When she returns to the manor to sort out the confusing communication with James, Wolfie further endears himself to her when he intervenes in Fox's ambush. Wolfie's recognition of the imminent lethal threat to her forces from his subconscious the repressed memory of what had happened to his mother and brother. He remembers their fates, and he is consumed with shame that he had been too paralyzed by fear to intervene for them. This shame over his inability to act then compels him, at great personal risk to his own life, to warn Nancy, as if *she* is his mother: "With a sob of fear ... Wolfie race[s] toward the terrace with all his turmoil and anguish for his lost mother pouring out in a high-pitched 'NO-O-O!'" (288). Following her terrible encounter with Fox Evil, Nancy's relationship with Wolfie evolves into one of surrogate mother, as she counters his fears of being sent away to foster care with promises of protection and care. In debt to Wolfie for her life, for the moment, at least, she does for him what his dead mother cannot.

Events that follow emphasize Walters' focus on the importance of family and parental care. When Wolfie is later brought into the manor for his safety, he and Nancy are inseparable under their new mother-child bond, which precipitates an argument with a member of the household staff about parenting. Having now heard that Fox could be her real father, Nancy is horrified at the prospect; she argues with the staff member who defends Fox as a parent and questions Nancy's relationship with Wolfie. Nancy sums up what Walters depicts as lacking in so many children's lives when she says, "Parenthood isn't about ownership, it's about duty of care, and Fox has failed to show this child any care at all" (312). The desire she has had all along to protect Wolfie is even more heightened now that she realizes they may be related.

At the end of the novel, Nancy and James are brought together back at the manor, in large part through Wolfie. Their mutual concern and affection for this child have helped bring about their permanent reconciliation. Nancy's earlier concerns about her birth parents that had caused a rift between her and James have been replaced with her desire never to know the truth about the past but instead to have a relationship going forward with her biological grandfather. As James stands on the terrace with his arm around Wolfie, telling him about the manor and the surrounding grounds, Nancy and Bella ponder the child's future, undoubtedly foster care — a fate Nancy had impetuously promised Wolfie he would not have to face. Knowing what they know about Fox's crimes against women and children, they marvel at Wolfie's ability and good fortune in surviving at all. Thanks in large part to Wolfie's need for them, and his bravery in protecting Nancy against Fox, the relationship between Nancy and James has been restored. The conclusion of the novel brings together, a year later, a happy gathering of extended family waiting for Nancy to arrive for a visit. James is in reasonably good health and on good terms with her visiting adoptive parents. Now thriving in foster care with a good family nearby, Wolfie is there for the day on one of his regular visits to see James. Blood kin or not, Wolfie is indeed part of the Lockyer-Fox family. Together, he and Nancy have given James a second chance to be a good parent, and the family is restored, as intact and harmonious as it could ever hope to be.

In Minette Walters' worlds — both real and fictional — community, relationships within the family, and connections with other people are crucial. In her words, "The building block of society is the family.... If the family doesn't work ... the knock-on effect is huge.... The people who are set adrift at an early age go off the rails" (quoted in Foley 14). Further, she observes that "women are a very powerful force in family life. The mother is absolutely the linchpin around which families operate" (quoted in Sibree). When community fails, when a mother does not mother, when a father does not father, when a family fails, the children are left to fend for themselves in a society that holds them as beneath, or beyond, regard. More critically, when children are abused or neglected, when they cannot get the love they have a right to expect from a parent, they may suffer shame that cripples because of the "implication that one is at core a deformed being fundamentally unlovable and unworthy of membership in the human community. It is the self regarding the self with the withering and unforgiving eye of contempt" (Karen 3). Jane Maybury, Olive Martin, Terry Dalton, Ruth Lascelles, and Wolfie are damaged souls who certainly have viewed themselves through that "withering and unforgiving eye." Only little Hannah Sumner has thus far escaped such harsh self-judgment because of her young age. While the lives of these children are undoubtedly made miserable by the failures of social systems that should protect and nurture them, Walters' ultimate view of children's futures is not entirely negative. *The Scold's Bridle* and *Fox Evil* best illustrate the possibilities for hope, as Ruth and Wolfie are both cast down by lack of parental love and then raised up by other caring, though flawed, adults outside these children's nuclear families. The key to such a future is the one thing these children were missing in the first place: love. Walters says simply, "Love is redemptive, if only you can make contact" (quoted in Thomson).

Works Cited

Berlins, Marcel. "Crime Pays." *Hot Air* Jan/Mar. 1998. 13 Feb. 2007. http://www.minettewalters.co.uk/about_minette/articles/hotair2.htm.

Deats, Sara Munson and Lagretta Tallent Lenker. *The Aching Hearth: Family Violence in Life and Literature.* New York: Plenum Press, 1991.

Foley, Catherine. "Motives That Drive a Life of Crime." *Irish Times* 26 Nov. 2002: 14. Proquest. Embry-Riddle University Hunt Library, Daytona Beach, FL. 13 Feb. 2007. http://www.proquest.com.

Gardiner, Jean. "Women, Recession, and the Tories." *The Politics of Thatcherism.* Eds. S. Hall and M. Jacques, London: Lawrence and Wishart Limited, 1983, pp. 188–206.

Hall, Stuart and Martin Jacques, eds. *The Politics of Thatcherism.* London: Lawrence and Wishart Limited, 1983.

"An Interview with Minette Walters." *BookBrowse.* 13 Feb. 2007. http://www.bookbrowse.com/author_interviews/full/index.cfm?author_number=387.

Jenkins, Henry, ed. *The Children's Culture Reader.* New York: NYU Press, 1998.

Karen. Robert. "Shame." *The Atlantic* Feb. 2002: 40. Proquest. Embry-Riddle University Hunt Library, Daytona Beach, FL. 7 Mar. 2007. http://www.proquest.com.

Morrell, Martin. "Crime Pays." http://minettewalters.co.uk/about_minette/articles/hotair2.htm.

Munt, Sally R. *Murder by the Book? Feminism and the Crime Novel.* London: Routledge, 1994.

Patrick, Bethanne Kelly. "Acid Reign." *Pages Magazine* Jul/Aug. 2002. 13 Feb. 2007. http://www.minettewalters.co.uk/about_minette/articles/acid_rn.htm.

Puttock, Kay. "'The Fault ... of Which I Confusedly Felt Guilty Yet Innocent': Charles Dickens' Evolving Championship of the Child." *Children's Literature Association Quarterly* 17:3 (Fall 1992): 19–22.

Reddy, Maureen T. *Sisters in Crime: Feminism and the Crime Novel.* New York: Continuum, 1988.

Routledge, Christopher. "Children's Detective Fiction and the 'Perfect Crime' of Adulthood." *Mystery in Children's Literature: From the Rational to the Supernatural.* Eds. Adrienne E. Gavin and Christopher Routledge. Basingstoke, England: Palgrave, 2001. pp. 64–81.
Schober, Adrian. *Possessed Child Narratives in Literature and Film: Contrary States.* Basingstoke, England: Palgrave Macmillan, 2004.
Segal, Lynne. "The Heat in the Kitchen." *The Politics of Thatcherism.* Eds. S. Hall and M. Jacques. London: Lawrence and Wishart Limited, 1983, pp. 207–15.
Shengold, Leonard L. M. D. "Child Abuse and Deprivation: Soul Murder." *Journal of the American Psychoanalytic Association* 27 (1979): 533–59.
Sibree, Bron. "Mind of Minette." *The Saturday Mercury* 18 Nov. 2000. 13 Feb. 2007. http://www.minettewalters.co.uk/about_minette/articles/mind2.htm.
Spelman, Judith. "Minette Walters: An Intelligent Approach to Crime." *Writers News* June 1994. 13 Feb. 2007. http://www.minettewalters.co.uk/about_minette/articles/winternw1.htm.
Sturrock, June. "Murder, Gender, and Popular Fiction by Women in the 1860s: Braddon, Oliphant, Yonge." *Victorian Crime, Madness, and Sensation.* Eds. Andrew Maunder and Grace Moore. Aldershot, England: Ashgate Publishing Limited, 2004. pp. 73–88.
Swanson, Jean and Dean James. *By a Woman's Hand: A Guide to Mystery Fiction by Women.* New York: Berkley Books, 1994.
Thomson, Liz. "Crime and Compassion." *Publishing News* 12 Oct. 2001. 13 Feb. 2007. http://www.minettewalters.co.uk/about_minette/articles/pubnews.htm.
Trodd, Anthea. *Domestic Crime in the Victorian Novel.* New York: St. Martin's Press, 1989.
Walters, Minette. *The Breaker.* New York: G. P. Putnam's Sons, 1999.
_____. *The Echo.* New York: G. P. Putnam's Sons, 1997.
_____. *Fox Evil.* New York: G. P. Putnam's Sons, 2003.
_____. *The Ice House.* New York: St. Martin's Press, 1992.
_____. *The Scold's Bridle.* London: Macmillan, 1994.
_____. *The Sculptress.* New York: St. Martin's Press, 1993.

Body of Evidence / Body *as* Evidence in *The Sculptress*

CAREN J. TOWN

Our bodies, no less than anything else that is human, are constituted by culture.
— Susan Bordo, *Unbearable Weight* (142)

In Minette Walters' second novel, *The Sculptress* (1993), body image and body politics are at the center of the story. Walters' apparent murderer is the grotesquely fat Olive Martin, who has been imprisoned for killing her mother and much prettier (and thinner) sister Amber. Olive is dramatically overweight, and the size of her body directly affects the judgments people make about her, evoking either complete disinterest in her plight, or eagerness to believe her capable of such brutal crimes, or, if they think she might be innocent, quickness to let her take the fall for someone more attractive. Olive, with her large body, greasy hair, and offensive body odor, is someone most people in the novel consider to be dangerous, disgusting, or simply disposable, in large measure because of her physical appearance.

Amateur detective Rosalind "Roz" Leigh is no exception to making these superficial judgments at first, but her personal exposure to tragedy leads her to overcome an initial revulsion. A journalist who lost her daughter in a car accident, Roz is urged by her agent to interview Olive, as a last-ditch effort to save her career — and possibly her life. Roz has been unable to write (or enjoy eating, sex, or any other pleasures) since the death of her daughter, which was caused by her drunken ex-husband. In the course of her research on and meetings with Olive, Roz starts to sympathize and eventually to identify with Olive's helplessness and anger, and her conviction that Olive is innocent gives her life a new focus. Thin, edgy, angry Roz becomes the perfect foil for heavy, passive, and (apparently) helpless Olive. Through her twin protagonists, Roz and Olive, Walters manipulates the conventional equation made between body size and morality (especially for women) and turns her novel into an astute commentary on gender, girth, and guilt.

Much of what Walters is attempting to say in this novel about gender has affinities to Judith Butler's conception of the performative and transitory nature of sexual identity. In her early work, *Gender Trouble*, Butler says that gender is "a set of repeated acts within a highly rigid regulatory frame that congeal over time to produce the appearance of substance, of a natural sort of being" (33). If certain actions are performed enough times, Butler believes, they become indistinguishable from the reality: one can act one's way into becoming a man or a woman. The same thing may be true for guilt and innocence, and Walters is clearly exploring the ways in which appearance can lead observers to make (possibly false) assumptions about guilt or can be manipulated by the guilty to appear natural — and innocent. In *Bodies That Matter*, Butler comments, "To the extent that gender is an assignment, it is an assignment which is never quite carried out according to expectations, whose addressee never quite inhabits the idea s/he is compelled to approximate. Moreover, this embodying is a repeated process" (231).

In spite of one's best efforts, then, the performance of gender is never entirely successful and must be repeated many times in order to appear compelling. This is not unlike the process of investigation in a murder, as Walters knows. The guilty (and the innocent) must repeatedly enact the behaviors and attitudes of innocence, until they are either believed — or uncovered. Gender is, Butler says, "neither a purely psychic truth, conceived as 'internal' and 'hidden,' nor is it reducible to a surface appearance; on the contrary, its undecidability is to be traced as the play *between* psyche and appearance" (244). As with gender performances, so with criminality; there comes a point in many investigations where it becomes impossible to separate the truth of the murder from what either the investigator or the criminal believe — or want very badly — to be true. This is especially the case in *The Sculptress*, in which the personal demons of the investigators (Roz in particular) make it difficult to determine whether they are capable of correctly distinguishing between guilt and innocence. Both gender and innocence in the novel are thus incompletely controlled, necessarily repeated, and fully invested performances.

As well as directly addressing the slippery nature of both gender and guilt, the novel also comments on the relationship of gender to body size, a subject Susan Bordo explores in *Unbearable Weight*. Bordo says that female bodies have been historically more vulnerable to "cultural manipulation.... Perhaps this has something to do with the fact that women, besides *having* bodies, are also *associated* with the body, which has always been considered woman's 'sphere' in family life, in mythology, in scientific, philosophical, and religious ideology" (143). Women's bodies are, traditionally, the signs and symbols of their moral standing in society, and in the case of *The Sculptress*, extremes of weight are seen as signs of instability and culpability. Both Roz and Olive represent these cultural stereotypes and, especially in Roz's case, have absorbed the related shame. As Bordo says, "Women and girls frequently internalize this ideology, holding themselves to blame for unwanted advances and sexual assaults. This guilt festers into unease with our femaleness, shame over our bodies, and self loathing" (8). The more the shame, the more the desire to control those unruly bodies, she says, although these attempts are often doomed:

> The attempt to subdue the spontaneities of the body in the interests of control only succeeds in constituting them as more alien and more powerful, and thus more needful of control. The only way to win this no-win game is to go beyond control, to kill off the body's spontaneities entirely, that is, to cease to *experience* our hungers and desires [146].

Clearly what Roz has done is subdue the desires of the body. Her sadness and anger have led her to deny herself both physical and psychological sustenance.

Olive is another case entirely. Her body, which appears to be "out of control," is a reminder to others of the dangers of the body, of its excesses. To Roz — and everyone else involved in the narrative — Olive's fatness has a moral component. Olive's body reminds readers as well of what crimes their bodies might be capable. Olive, though, doesn't accept the shame that people are quite willing to heap upon her. In fact, she seems to revel in her offensiveness and uses it to manipulate people. She violates the stereotype of the guilt-ridden (and unhappy) fat woman and seems content with her size. Roz, on the other hand, is the one punishing herself with her body. Minette Walters clearly wants readers to question the traditional values Western culture has placed on the body, making her very thin detective perhaps more troubled than her very heavy murderess/victim.

The genre of detective fiction is a highly appropriate place to confront such issues of body image and gender. As Sarah Dunant points out, "More often than not, the body in some shape or form begins the story. Without the body, without the murder, there would be no fiction" (12). While there are dead bodies (two, in fact) in the prologue to *The Sculptress*, there is a third body, a living body that confronts readers on the first page, the living body of Olive Martin that Roz Leigh finds impossible to confront "without a shudder of distaste" (1). From the very beginning of the novel, Walters is proving Dunant's point that "the body — especially the female body — has become a cultural battlefield over which men and women are, albeit obliquely, facing and confronting each other in print" (4). Dead bodies open nearly every murder mystery, but, especially with contemporary mysteries written by women authors, the living bodies of the detectives and the criminals become the real "battlefield," the true contested space. In *The Sculptress*, the mutilated bodies of Olive's mother and sister are finally less compelling than the large living body in the jail cell.

As has been alluded to earlier, there is another body of importance in this story, the liquor-soaked, anxiety-ridden, and shockingly thin body of Roz, the self-appointed investigator in this story. Despite attempts to pull herself together, Roz is falling apart, and each time she meets with Olive, she discovers just how fine the line is between victim and criminal, between positively taking charge of one's life and making irrevocable mistakes, between seeing justice served and exacting revenge. Over the course of the novel, Roz becomes aware that she is, as Robin Woods says, "part criminal, part community," and she discovers that in many ways Olive is her "double: someone who, with a slight moral alteration, or the merest touch of 'criminal infection' might actually be her" (21). An additionally fascinating aspect of *The Sculptress* is that Roz, unlike most detectives, is not trying to prove the guilt of the main suspect but is set on finding a way to set her free. She does not "restor[e] a disrupted community to its original state, and the protagonists to their original guilelessness," as Woods says, by definitively exposing the murderer. Instead, Roz is instrumental in helping Olive re-enter the community, even though her innocence remains in question; Roz's own demons may have led her to set a murderer free.

In this, Walters epitomizes what Maureen Reddy calls the "feminist counter-tradition" in crime novels:

> Feminist crime writers accept few of the givens of traditional detective fiction. By calling into question that which is taken for granted in other crime novels — the value of detecting, the know-ability of the truth, the detective's commitment to solving the crime, the reader's interest in deciphering clues and solving the puzzle, the detective's superior authority, the primacy of reason — feminist writers push readers to question their own assumptions about the genre [176].

For contemporary feminist writers of detective fiction, the detective's confidence in his or her ability to uncover the truth about a murder through rational detection says more about the culture's confidence in masculine notions of guilt and innocence than it does about any inherent truth. Walters raises these questions in *The Sculptress* by making the investigator nearly as troubled as the "criminal." Roz is like other contemporary female sleuths, whose "private worlds interweave and intersect with those of the perpetrator of the crime in ways that serve to blur the distinction between the two and, consequently, the polarization of 'right' and 'wrong'" (Clark and Zyngier 148). Throughout *The Sculptress*, the dichotomies between innocence and guilt, indulgence and self-denial, proper and improper women are systematically dissolved. Minette Walters insists that how a woman appears to the world, how she is read by that world, may be tragically wrong. In fact, Walters tells interviewer Charles Silet, "One of my major themes is that what we perceive, first impressions, are generally lousy" (184). Certainly, the first impressions people have had about Olive may prove to be false, although their final judgments (especially in Roz's case) may be equally "lousy."

The novel opens with a brief description of the murder from a newspaper clipping,* and then the narrative begins with Roz's first meeting with Olive. Interestingly, Walters tells Silet that she based this encounter on a meeting with a very large *man* in the course of her volunteer work in the prison system. The "total exposure" she felt at that meeting was the genesis for the book, she says (184). Roz feels equally exposed and vulnerable when she meets Olive for the first time. Walters' changing of the male inmate to a woman is significant, however. As Bordo has shown, a woman's size has a much more complicated set of resonances than a man's; rather than simply indicating power (or menace), Olive's fatness also has a moral component — her gluttony being merely the gateway to the other deadly sins. Roz says that Olive is "a grotesque parody of a woman, so fat that her feet and hands and head protruded absurdly from the huge slab of her body like tiny disproportionate afterthoughts" (1). Olive's size renders her femininity "grotesque," especially to tiny, damaged Roz. Not surprisingly, Roz is afraid of Olive, afraid "of being shut up in a confined space with this monstrous creature who stank of fat woman's sweat and showed no emotion in her grotesquely bloated face" (3). Roz is afraid in quite a different way than she would be afraid of a man, however; she fears what Olive will reveal about her own weaknesses, her insecurities, her fatal flaws.

As on the first page, the "grotesque" is mentioned again on page three, which seems to indicate that Roz considers Olive to be not completely human, and yet her confrontation with Olive's grotesque face and body begins to reveal a great deal about Roz. Indeed, Olive almost immediately starts to snip away at "the barrier of barbed wire that Roz had erected around herself" (4) as a result of the tragic death of her daughter. Aware from the beginning of Roz's loss of her daughter, Olive expresses (possibly feigned) surprise that Roz is willing to take on her story, given her own victimization by the tabloids. Roz responds by saying that it may be time

---

*A common device of Walters is to bring in extra-fictional documentation — newspaper articles, psychiatric reports, police documents, and, recently, e-mails — into the narrative. The primary purpose of this seems to be to lend a sense of "authenticity" to the narrative, but it also has the effect of showing the reader the wide variety of ways in which a particular story can be interpreted. In a work like The Sculptress, it is especially important for Walters to emphasize that truth is very often shaped by the perspective of the observer.

for them to learn to treat tragedy in a dignified way (5). Even early in their meetings, Olive has led Roz to find parallels in their situations, which, of course, will make the journalist a more sympathetic listener and possibly an ally in her bid for release. Roz, for her part, is torn between finding it difficult to look at Olive and impossible to look away, watching Olive's fat finger "with a horrible fascination" (6). One wonders if food- (and love-) starved Roz isn't about ready to take a bite out of round and salty Olive.

Rather quickly, Roz discovers psychological and ethical connections between herself and Olive, none of which are particularly comforting. Under Olive's relentless questioning, Roz starts lying, thinking that if she tells enough lies they will come to feel like the truth (7). This is, of course, what everyone thinks Olive has been doing all these years — convincing herself (and others) of the lie of her innocence. Roz also tells Olive that she hasn't been psychologically analyzed because she's "*too frightened of what they might find*" (9), which makes her sound much more like the possibly homicidal Olive than the successful journalist she is and the confident, in-control woman she pretends to be.

As the interview continues (with Olive doing much more interviewing than being interviewed), Roz finds that she begins to share Olive's cynical outlook (10), and she begins to reconsider her decision not to write the book. Although she and Olive are dramatically different, Roz is intrigued (11). The alleged murderess Olive is, paradoxically, bringing Roz back to life, reawakening her curiosity and the concomitant desire to write. Where Roz is mistaken, though, is that she and Olive are actually that different. From the first pages of the novel, Walters is showing that, regardless of how society views them, excessive thinness and fatness are in themselves not revelatory; they are not obvious signs of control (in the case of the thin person) or lack of it (in the case of the fat one), nor do they indicate the relative degrees to which a person values herself — or deserves value from the world. Both Roz *and* Olive are damaged, as their extreme physical appearances indicate, but Walters suggests they are also both entitled to respect and attention, instead of quick and thoughtless judgment.

While the story progresses, Roz's already tenuous grip on sanity becomes even looser. Driving back from a visit to Olive's lawyer (to obtain background for the book she is tentatively moving toward writing), Roz realizes she didn't remember the drive and speculates that she could have hit and killed someone on the road without recalling it (10). Roz recognizes that it is possible, for her, like Olive, to have killed someone without knowing or remembering having done it. In fact, Roz's life on the outside bears a striking resemblance to Olive's in prison. She "was living in a twilight world where so little mattered that day followed day with nothing to distinguish their passing" (24). Roz is starting to realize both that she has the potential to be a murderer and also that she has created her own prison out in the world. Her life as it is now would not change substantially if she were convicted and imprisoned for just such a vehicular homicide.

As she explores the connections between Roz and Olive, Walters reminds readers of the connections between body image and self-respect. She has Roz's agent attempt to manipulate the reluctant Roz into doing the book by mentioning a rival's new work (and suggesting that Olive's story might have a place in it): This conversation, as it was meant to do, leads Roz to make a final commitment to tell Olive's story. Roz, as her editor knows, won't allow Olive to be exploited for a "disgustingly tasteless" (25)—an appropriate oxymoron for this novel—work of pseudo-psychology. She is, however, perfectly willing to use Olive's story to rebuild her shattered career (and life). Much of this conversation is simply moving the plot along; in order for the novel to go forward, Roz has to agree to write the book and look into Olive's story. However, this glimpse into the world of celebrity body image also directs readers to a thematic concern of Walters': the far-too-easily assumed relationship between obesity and damaging behaviors (especially for women).

Continuing her research into the murders of Olive's mother and sister, Roz visits Olive and Amber's Catholic school teacher, Sister Bridget, who calls into question the idea "that beauty is a surface quality" when Roz suggests it: "Beautiful people are prized," Sister Bridget says, and as a result they "have less reason to be spiteful, less reason to be jealous, less reason to covet" (47). In other words, they become better people because their beauty means they are treated better. In this particular case, Olive's sister Amber has had fewer emotional and moral challenges because of her beauty, Sister Bridget believes. As a result, she is a "better" person than her sister. Fletcher and Whip say about this scene that "[T]he argument is explicitly made that beauty is a moral asset that cushions people, allowing them to be more likeable and even to be 'better' than they might otherwise be. In this sense, physical appearance influences the inner self just as the inner self is assumed to affect the body" (105). Although this is what Sister Bridget believes, the relationship between external appearance and internal culpability is far more complicated for Walters. A lovely exterior, as she well knows, can hide various sorts of crimes, and an "ugly" one may well hide true innocence.

Even Sister Bridget undercuts her argument by her behavior toward Olive. For unattractive people like Olive, Sister Bridget says, "the tests are harder" (49). Unlike her sister, Olive was difficult to like (49). Nevertheless, Sister Bridget did come to like Olive (for her evident love and concern for her sister, as well as for her superior intelligence); she visits Olive in prison and, although she is uncertain about Olive's innocence, is instrumental in helping Roz get her freed. Clearly, the ability to find the good inside the unattractive exterior, as well as a certain degree of Christian charity, has made Sister Bridget Olive's ally. Sister Bridget may have found Amber more appealing but she, like Roz, is powerfully drawn toward Olive.

As always, though, Roz's motives for sympathizing with Olive are more complex than most people's. When she is told by Sister Bridget that "[t]he only certainty about Olive is that she lies about almost everything" (51), Roz understands completely, thinking that it is simpler to lie (52). Like Olive, Roz has a variety of secrets and depths of emotion that she keeps hidden even from herself, and certainly from others. Lying, after all, is often easier than admitting that one has lost control of one's life.

One of the difficult truths that Roz is reluctant to face is that the loss of her daughter and the destruction of her marriage have made her suicidal — and perhaps homicidal as well. She fantasizes about killing herself (53), and she also wants to hurt others, as she tells Olive, although she is "shocked by the admission" (67). Roz certainly has trouble keeping her temper, and this leads to a violent physical argument with her ex-husband. After the fight, Roz feels "her murderous anger assuaged ... as if she had exorcised her own guilt in some way" (121). Roz obviously understands that violence is one way to assuage her anger. After the incident she admits she could have killed him, if she had had a weapon (264). Once again, she realizes that she is not so different from the Olive who has been convicted of a violent crime; she is driven by "murderous anger" and can only find peace through destructive acts.

Not surprisingly (to readers at least), the only person Roz can confide in is Olive, although Roz is initially puzzled about why she wants to confide in a prisoner, rather than a trained psychologist. She talks to Olive because Roz believes they have experienced a similar blow (and the subsequent desire for retribution). As they continue to meet, Roz and Olive become quite simpatico. As a corrections officer breaks off one of their conversations, "tearing the fabric of their precarious intimacy," Roz sees "her own irritation reflected in Olive's eyes" (70). Two women, each with their respective pain, respond in the same negative way to the intrusion of the male voice (and authority) that is effectively judging and silencing them both. Although one is in prison and the other is "free," they both feel the injustice of their respective situations.

The final message that Olive gives Roz at that meeting is an empowering one: "We are all masters of our fate, Roz, including you" (70). This is a surprising comment from someone who is in prison for a crime she claims she hasn't committed. It isn't exactly clear what "fate" Olive has mastered, whether she has chosen prison as a way to escape her demons, even though she is innocent, or whether the "fate" she controls involves manipulating Roz into helping to set her free, despite her guilt. Regardless, Olive seems poised to help Roz, who is both innocent and guilty, take charge of her life once again.

The course of the investigation (both legal and literary) is convoluted, in keeping with the genre's tradition of leading the reader down various blind alleys before finally revealing the killer. Roz continues her research for the book while the "real" detective, Sergeant Hal Hawksley, a former policeman who initially investigated the murders, is drawn back (despite his own problems) into the case. He remains convinced that Olive is guilty, although he recognizes that, despite her revolting exterior, Olive can be charming. He warns Roz not to be taken in by superficialities, telling her that monsters do not always look like monsters (91). Hawksley rightly recognizes the multi-leveled nature of appearance and reality. Roz first was frightened and mistrustful of Olive (primarily because of her large body), but Hawksley sees that she too-quickly trusts Olive's intelligence and (apparent) vulnerability.

Still, he may also be prone to superficial judgments. Assuming Olive's guilt in the initial investigation, Hawksley fails to realize that he might have contributed to a false confession when he offers the hungry (and food obsessed) Olive something to eat if she finishes her statement (209). Once again, the truth is often difficult to find when it is disguised by other motivations.

As is the case with Hawksley, the other people Roz interviews seem equally convinced of Olive's guilt, although they are quicker to make a connection between her fatness and her culpability. The mother of Geraldine, Olive's closest friend at school, says about her: "I didn't take to her. She was a clumsy girl, slow, impossible to talk to, lacking in humour, and, frankly extremely unattractive ... a sad, unloved, and unlovely child" (80). *She* has no problem believing that such an "unloved, and unlovely child" could commit murder, as if clumsiness and a lack of humor could be equivalent to homicidal impulses. Olive's neighbors seem to feel the same way. Hawksley remembers that when Olive was arrested and had her head covered in a blanket to hide her identity, one of her neighbors shouted: "You'd need a bloody marquee [a canopy or tent] to cover that fat cow. I'd recognize her legs anywhere" (99). Once again, Olive's bulk gives her away and reinforces the disgust and distrust her neighbors feel toward the "fat cow." Being as fat as she is, she must have done something to justify her arrest in their minds.

In fact, nearly everyone Roz interviews has the same response to Olive. She tells one of Olive's former coworkers that everyone thought of Olive only in terms of her size (132). Roz says she could write a whole book on "how social ostracism led a lonely, unloved girl to turn in a fit of frenzied anger on her teasing family," but she says she isn't going to "because I don't think it's true" (132). For various reasons, including her own situation, Roz is convinced that simply being "lonely [and] unloved" did not lead Olive to murder. Based on her own experience, Roz knows that people need some other (more earth-shattering) motivation to lash out in anger.

Perhaps some of the foundation for this belief comes from Roz's ideas about the relationship between body size and anger. Being a nervous, painfully thin person, who is filled with a lot of anger, Roz may not be able to see the potential for violence in someone Olive's size. Roz asserts to Hal that Olive cannot be guilty because her size will render her calm and peaceful (107). Fat people, according to Roz, are too "stolid" to lose their tempers. Roz may be wrong about Olive (and fat people in general), but the novel seems to support this position, as the apparent murderer, Mrs. Clarke, is much "smaller [and] daintier" (302) than Olive. Walters seems to be telling us that the thin ones may be the ones we need to watch.

Roz's thinness catches Hal's eye as well. He believes Roz is far too thin and tense for him (105). Readers know that Roz does "liv[e] on her nerves," and as the courtship progresses, Hal (who now owns a restaurant) spends most of his time with Roz feeding her. Clearly, the assumption made by Hal (and by implication by society) is that thin women are nervous and probably incapable of the generosity of spirit necessary for love. Just as there is too much of Olive, there is too little of Roz — too little softness and comfort, both for herself and for others. As they do with Olive, people are willing to make assumptions about Roz based on body size, assumptions that may prove completely wrong.

Roz's twin weaknesses, her physical and psychological vulnerability and inability to make meaningful connections with others, suggest that Walters may be operating under an essentially conservative pattern outlined by Kathleen Klein: Detective fiction is designed to raise emotions of both fear and pity only to assuage them through the agency of the sleuth who solves the mystery, captures the criminal, and restores order. When that detective is a woman, a similar, equally strong response is raised. Like the criminal, she is a member of society who does not conform to the status quo. Her presence pushes off-center the whole male/female, public/private, intellect/emotion, physical strength/weakness dichotomy. Therefore, her facade of normal respectability — like the criminal's — must be stripped away. If she can be shown as an incompetent detective or an inadequate woman, readers' reactionary preferences are satisfied; their second catharsis is achieved (4–5). According to Klein, the appropriate catharsis is not realized unless the detective (in this case Roz) is shown to be inadequate. Certainly, Roz appears inadequate in a variety of ways, both as an objective journalist and as a "real" woman, but the "moral tale" of this novel seems to be moving in an entirely different direction from the one Klein suggests.

Body of Evidence/Body as Evidence in The Sculptress (Town)

What happens in *The Sculptress* is far more disturbing than Klein's scenario: Olive and Roz — criminal and investigator — come to seem like two parts of the same person. Roz's friend and editor Iris (with whom Roz is staying after the fight with her husband) suggests that Roz "break out of this prison" of her current life and, as Olive has done, "[l]et someone else in" (128). Roz, as we have already seen, is as much in prison, as isolated, as Olive. After spending some time recuperating from the fight at Iris's apartment, Roz realizes that a "solitary life was emotionally, mentally, and spiritually deadening. There was, after all, only so much that one mind could encompass, and obsessions grew when ideas went unchallenged" (129). Thus, the one brooding dangerously in this novel is not the convicted murderess but the journalist writing her story. Later in her investigation, Iris wonders why Roz "picked on a bloody murderess to fill the void that her daughter had left in her heart?" (167).

Further on, Roz tells Sister Bridget that Olive has given her a sense of purpose (226). Sister Bridget says that Roz has become a surrogate sister or mother for Olive, and Olive has given Roz back her old confidence and helped her move on from the past. Clearly, these two women support each other, although Roz may need Olive more. Roz is not "inadequate," as Klein puts it; instead, she has developed sympathies for the villain and has turned to the alleged criminal for her emotional support. No easy answers here.

These emotional connections, however, don't allow Roz to transcend judgments based on Olive's body. When Olive tells Roz that she had an abortion and then denies it, Roz is quick to believe the denial. Sister Bridget cautions her to be aware of her subconscious prejudices that prevent her from believing that fat, repulsive Olive could have had sex with a man (169). Because Roz finds Olive physically unattractive, she cannot imagine Olive having sex and thereby becoming pregnant. Consequently, she is quick to believe that the story about the abortion is a lie. At one of their final interviews in prison, Roz describes Olive "at her most unattractive, unwashed hair hanging limply about her colourless face, a smear of tomato ketchup ground into the front of her shift, the smell of her sweat almost unbearable in the small room" (280). In this interview, Roz tells Olive, "You adored your mother, didn't you? You always adore the people who need you.... I needed you. That's how I know" (282). To the end, Roz remains at least partially unaware of the emotional comfort she receives from Olive. Olive, on the other hand, is quite astute about why Roz needs her: "You wanted to know how it felt to kill someone, that's all you needed me for." Roz insists that she "needed someone to love" (282). Each of these explanations may be true. Olive may need to help someone, and Roz may need to love someone; but Roz also wanted to explore the violence in her nature, and Olive wants a way out of prison.

Roz's investigations eventually disclose the apparent killer. The evidence mounts but remains "desperately thin" (302), because the witnesses are either dead or demented. The truth about this case may never be known. "Desperately thin" is an appropriate way to describe much in this novel, including Roz's size and especially the case Roz is building for Olive's innocence.

Given Roz's rather speculative conclusions, readers are left uncertain about Olive's guilt. Olive's fiscally dishonest lawyer says that Olive is a "clever monster" (305) who set the whole thing up, but he is not particularly trustworthy (even if he may be right). As Olive is released from prison, readers are disturbed by the last paragraph of the novel. Hal sees a "look of gloating triumph" on Olive's face, and he recalls a quotation he had on his desk: "*Truth lies within a little and certain compass, but error is immense*" (308). It is never clear what prompts the look directed at Hal. Olive may simply be telling him that while he could not uncover the truth and clear her name, the women in her life were able to help her. Of course, she may also be taunting him with having gotten away with murder. The quotation at the end of the passage is from Henry St. John, Viscount Bolingbroke, in his 1716 *Reflections Upon Exile*, and it clearly suggests Hal's anxiety about whether he and Roz have allowed the real murderer to escape; but it also raises rather disturbing notions of the possibility of ever getting close to the "little and certain compass" of the truth.

The Sculptress violates several conventions of the traditional detective novel: the murderer is not definitively revealed, the (perhaps) wrongly accused person is released only to remain under a cloud of suspicion, and the investigators (or at least one of them) are left no more certain than when they began. Walters has said that she deliberately constructed the ambiguous ending because she feels that in the British judicial system "nobody is interested in finding out the truth; they are only interested in pitting one story against another" (Silet 185). Truth, she says, "is what I am trying to write about" (185). This does not necessarily mean, though, that she is trying to discover a definitive truth about guilt or innocence in her novels; she may merely want to ask readers to consider how we come to know — and to believe in — a particular version of the truth.

In *The Sculptress*, Minette Walters is writing about people's inability to know for certain whether they have found the truth in any given situation, but she is also asking readers to concentrate on the judgments they make about guilt and innocence based on the external reality of the body. Glenwood Irons says, "Female authors who have chosen to create a woman (and sometimes a feminist) detective have altered the male prototype to the extent that their detectives speak from a woman's perspective and address the problems which women face in modern society" (xii). The problem that Walters is addressing is the moral equation people make between fatness and several of the deadly sins — gluttony and sloth, obviously, but also by implication envy and anger, which might possibly lead to violence. Olive Martin is judged by her family, her neighbors, the police, and the legal system to be guilty in large part because her fatness renders her repulsive in their eyes. To them, her guilt is written on her extremely large body.

Rosalind Leigh is writing the story of her life on her body as well, paring it away through guilt and anger so that she can eventually cease to exist and be free from the pain caused by the death of her daughter and the negligence of her ex-husband. For Roz to grow strong she has to draw sustenance from Olive's story; for Olive to have people believe in her innocence (whether she actually is innocent or not), she has to nourish Roz and help her find the strength to tell the right story. Both women's bodies provide the evidence needed for their guilt — and their innocence.

As Kimberly J. Dilley says, "[M]ystery novels by women have provided a fertile venue for women's discussions about their own lives and their place in a society where gender prescribes behavior, expectations, and limitations" (xix). In *The Sculptress*, Minette Walters has tackled these issues directly. By having a massively overweight female "villain" paired with a self-destructively thin "heroine," Walters asks readers to consider how women's bodies help to construct their relationships to their families; their love interests; their friends, neighbors, and coworkers; and even the judicial system. Had Olive been conventionally attractive, and less physically repulsive, the detective on the case might not have been so quick to believe that she was capable of such a particularly disgusting crime. On the other hand, her large size, and the interpretation the person attempting to vindicate her puts on it, may have caused an altogether different miscarriage of justice.

In Minette Walters' mind, weakness (or strength) — either physical or moral — has no inherent connection to bodily dimensions, regardless of how frequently society wants to link the two. A 98-pound weakling like Rosalind Leigh might be perfectly capable of physically destroying her ex-husband and incapable of attracting a man; a 264-pound "monster" like Olive Martin might have been too passive to lift a finger to defend herself from abuse and also attractive enough to cause a man to disrupt his home and his wife to go on a murderous rampage. "Some persons who appear very ordinary on the surface," Walters reminds readers, "are underneath very, very interesting individuals" (184). Olive may be fat, and not particularly likable, but she may also be a complicated and finally inexplicable individual. Roz may be thin and tense, and apparently complex, but finally she ends up being the simpler of the two women. The effect of this reversal of expectations is uncanny. At the end of *The Sculptress*, readers are left, like Hal Hawksley, shivering "for no apparent reason" (308) as Olive either achieves her much-deserved freedom — or gets away with murder.

Works Cited

Bordo, Susan. *Unbearable Weight: Feminism, Western Culture, and the Body.* Berkeley: University of California Press, 1993.

Butler, Judith. *Bodies That Matter: On the Discursive Limits of "Sex."* New York: Routledge, 1993.

_____. *Gender Trouble: Feminism and the Subversion of Identity.* New York: Routledge, 1990.

Clark, Urzula and Sonia Zyngier. "Women Beware Women: Detective Fiction and Critical Discourse Stylistics." *Language and Literature* 7 (1998): 141–58.

Dilley, Kimberly J. *Busybodies, Meddlers, and Snoops: The Female Hero in Contemporary Women's Mysteries.* Westport, CN: Greenwood, 1998.

Dunant, Sarah. "Body Language: A Study of Death and Gender in Crime Fiction." *The Art of Detective Fiction.* Eds. Warren Chernaik, Martin Swales, and Robert Vilain. New York: St. Martins, 2000, pp. 10–20.

Fletcher, M. D. and R .J. Whip. "Minette Walters's Feminist Detective Fiction." *Clues* 18 (1997): 101–12.
Irons, Glenwood. "Introduction." *Feminism in Women's Detective Fiction*. Ed. Glenwood Irons. Toronto: University of Toronto Press, 1995, ix–xxiv.
Klein, Kathleen Gregory. *The Woman Detective: Gender and Genre*. Urbana: University of Illinois Press, 1988.
Reddy, Maureen T. "The Feminist Counter-Tradition in Crime: Cross, Grafton, Paretsky, and Wilson." *The Cunning Craft: Original Essays on Detective Fiction and Contemporary Literary Theory*. Eds. Ronald G. Walker and June M. Frazer. Macomb: Western Illinois University Press, 1990, pp. 174–87.
Silet, Charles L. P. "An Interview with Minette Walters." *The Armchair Detective* 27 (1994): 182–85.
Walker, Ronald G. and June M. Frazer, eds. *The Cunning Craft: Original Essays on Detective Fiction and Contemporary Literary Theory*. Macomb: Western Illinois University Press, 1990.
Walters, Minette, *The Sculptress*. New York: St. Martins, 1994. (1993)
Woods, Robin. "'His Appearance Is Against Him': The Emergence of the Detective." *The Cunning Craft: Original Essays on Detective Fiction and Contemporary Literary Theory*. Eds. Ronald G. Walker and June M. Frazer. Macomb: Western Illinois University Press, 1990, pp. 15–24.

Shakespeare, Scolds, and Self-Fashioning: The Making of Mathilda Gillespie in *The Scold's Bridle*

RHONDA KNIGHT

Stephen Greenblatt's *Renaissance Self-Fashioning: From More to Shakespeare* (1980) documents an important moment in the modern understanding of identity. He shows that in the sixteenth century there was an increased awareness that identities could be formed, or fashioned, through a "manipulable, artful process" (2). Using anthropologist Clifford Geertz as a guide, Greenblatt shows that the impact of culture on identity comes not through custom and tradition but through "control mechanisms — plans, recipes, rules, instructions" that summarize and codify custom and tradition (quoted in Greenblatt 3). The Early Modern period abounded in visual and written texts that sought to explain, teach, and guide. Courtesy books, emblem books, pamphlets, along with more obvious legal and governmental texts, all aimed to codify behavior. Ballads, plays, masques and other performative texts also modeled forms of behavior. Greenblatt shows that while the concept of identity was both fluid and malleable, individuals demonstrated limited autonomy in fashioning their identities in relation to these culturally prescribed texts and codes.

This concept of self-fashioning informs the character of Mathilda Gillespie in Minette Walters' crime novel *The Scold's Bridle*. At first glance, the connection between a crime novel written in 1994 and a scholarly study of early modern literature and history might be surprising; however, historical associations dominate Walters' book. The title itself refers to an instrument of punishment used during the period on scolds — women who disrupted society with their speech. Furthermore, Shakespearean texts form an important backdrop to the mystery. The text abounds with passages from Shakespeare, most of which appear through the diary of Mathilda Gillespie, the murder victim, whose "entire education was based on learning chunks of Shakespeare by heart."[1] Even the murder scene has Shakespearean overtones, as we will see below.

Greenblatt's concept of self-fashioning relates directly to the culture of the Early Modern period, while the self-fashioning of Mathilda Gillespie bridges the gap between the artifacts of that time — Shakespeare's texts and the scold's bridle — and the codes of her own society. Mathilda's family, the Cavendishes, is the local gentry in the village of Fontwell, Dorsetshire. Her father was an MP, and the family lived in the manor house. The book portrays the gap that still existed between manor and village in the early twentieth century, even though the villagers would not have been as dependent on the local gentry as they would have been three generations earlier. Changes in the English economy in the late 1800s and early 1900s caused the breakup of most large family estates, and much of the gentry's power dissipated with this loss of land. Walters tells us that Mathilda was over sixty when she died; therefore, she was probably born during the 1920s or 1930s, a transition period representing the faded glory of the gentry's old customs and traditions. Mathilda moved in a world of society weddings, dowries, and boys with public school educations and posh accents. The codes of the gentry changed more slowly than they did for the other classes. Therefore, class-consciousness and the social mores associated with keeping up appearances and separating herself from the village governed the young Mathilda's actions. One of the villagers, Mrs. Graham, recalls Mathilda's class bias, saying that even though Mathilda had known her family she would not speak to them because they were of lower class. However, she would speak to Mr. Wittingham because he made a living from his financial and real estate investments (21). In the span of her life, Mathilda saw a great change in the way "commoners" like Mrs. Graham treated the gentry. During her youth, the gentry demanded respect simply because they were gentry. The older Mathilda still feels entitled to this automatic respect, but that time has passed.

While class codes certainly inform Mathilda's self-fashioning, the institution of the family is its largest contributor. The book reveals a history of sexual abuse from both her alcoholic father and his mentally handicapped brother; but this issue is complex, and we will untangle it below. At this point, we should note that the abuse provided the catalyst for Matilda's self-fashioning. Just like the early modern gentlemen who followed Castiglione's *The Courtier* and other courtesy books as guides for masculine behavior (Kutcha 235–37), Mathilda, through the influence of her family heirloom, a scold's bridle, grasps the image of the scold as a behavioral model. In one sense, Mathilda's act of self-fashioning follows Greenblatt's formula, as she acts within the antiquated codes prescribed for the country gentry; however, in another sense, hers is an act of negative self-fashioning. Her object choice, the scold, is a model of proscribed behaviors, actions that were reviled and punished throughout the Early Modern period. Yet, it is those very behaviors that gave women power and made them objects of fear and derision. Those behaviors give Mathilda power to overcome her abuse and gain control of her life.

Mathilda's unconventional self-fashioning is only part of the "fashioning" that dominates *The Scold's Bridle*. The mystery hinges on a staged murder scene that depends on Matilda's propensity to reference Shakespeare. The murderer and his victim manipulate and fashion their worlds in relation to these two early modern figures — Shakespeare and the scold.

Shakespearean Murder

The opening scene of the book — the murder scene — inextricably joins Shakespeare and the scold. Mathilda is found dead in her bath, her wrists slashed with a utility knife. She wears a scold's bridle on her head, but this instrument of torture is not the only strange feature of the crime scene. Plants adorning the bridle increase the scene's ghastliness: "Nettles and Michaelmas daisies sprouted from the awful contraption that caged the bloodless face, its rusted metal bit clamping the dead tongue still in the gaping mouth" (3). The stems of the daisies and the nettles form a veil anchored in the headband of the bridle, the daisies pointing up and the nettles pointing down. Although this mise-en-scène is fraught with symbolism, neither the police nor Dr. Sarah Blakeney, Mathilda's physician, can read the symbols (53). Dr. Blakeney explains that the usual place for Mathilda's scold's bridle was in a pot of geraniums, as a decoration, calling them "her coronet weeds" (4). The attending pathologist provides the first Shakespeare connection when he responds to "coronet weeds" and explains that the phrase is from *Hamlet*. He completes the passage:

> There with fantastic garlands did she come,
> Of crowflowers, nettles, daisies, and long purples,
> That liberal shepherds give a grosser name,
> But our cold maids do dead men's fingers call them:
> There, on the pendent boughs her coronet weeds —[Walters 4].[2]

Since the passage describes Ophelia's suicide, for the investigating party, the pathologist's words immediately associate Mathilda with Ophelia and suicide. The policeman acknowledges this connection, saying they should stop staring at the body, "[u]nless Ophelia was murdered" (4). The pathologist assures him it was "[d]eath by drowning, ... while of unsound mind" (5). What goes unsaid at the end of the pathologist's sentence is "just like Ophelia."

The murder scene creates the two dominant questions of the mystery: Why was a scold's bridle found on Mathilda's head, and why did the murderer stage her death to resemble Ophelia's? The generic question of whodunit is less interesting than these questions because Walters makes Mathilda the central character of the novel. In most crime novels, either the personality of the detective or the personality of the murderer dominates; but in this case the personality of Mathilda intrigues the readers: we do not care who killed her as much as what she did to cause someone to kill her.

Walters employs a strategy that allows the readers to understand both the public and private Mathilda: she produces two simultaneous texts. One is the dominant text — a third-person narrative of the murder investigation. In it Dr. Sarah Blakeney, her husband, Jack, and Detective Cooper ask questions, follow clues and perform all the tasks expected in a crime novel. The second text is Mathilda's diary, from which a short entry, written in the first person by Mathilda, precedes each chapter of the dominant text. These diary entries appear in reverse chronological order, with the final page of the novel consisting of the first page of the diary. Since the murderer burns the diary when he kills Mathilda, none of the characters in the dominant text, except he, knows its contents.

The murderer ostensibly kills Mathilda because she plans to sell a large parcel of her land to a housing development which will build within ten feet of his yard. When he opposes her, she threatens to blackmail him by publishing the details of her diary, which implicate him, for the whole village to see (350). After this confrontation, the killer begins reading the diaries and realizes that destroying them will not solve his problem. He had to destroy her because the diaries were only an "outward manifestation" of her "poison" (350).

The murderer plans the murder, hoping that he can make it appear as a suicide. He attempts to stage Mathilda, who knew and loved Shakespeare so well, as a suicidal Lear (299). In this case, the killer's knowledge causes him to create a visual text that the others, who do not have his knowledge, misread. Because he has read her diaries, he knows that Mathilda believes that Sarah Blakeney is her daughter whom she gave up for adoption. Mathilda bases her beliefs on Sarah's resemblance to Mathilda's other daughter, Joanna, and the fact that Sarah shares the exact birthday with the child Mathilda gave up. Mathilda is mistaken because Sarah was not adopted; but because she never let Sarah know her beliefs, Sarah could not correct her error. The police learn this from Sarah's husband, Jack, to whom Mathilda had revealed her ideas. In his elaborate murder scheme, Sarah is positioned as one daughter, with Joanna, the other daughter, and Ruth, the granddaughter, rounding out Lear's trinity.

The pathologist's seemingly appropriate comment on "coronet weeds" (4) sends the investigators in the wrong direction, looking for Ophelia and *Hamlet* connections. D. S. Cooper's boss, D.I. Jones, finally reminds him that it was "King Lear [who] went mad..., wandering in the fields near Dover with a crown of weeds on his head because his daughters had deprived him of his kingdom and his authority" (298). The murderer had intended to reference *King Lear* 4.4.1–6 instead of *Hamlet* in his decoration of Mathilda. In *King Lear*, Cordelia describes her father's wandering:

> Why he was met even now
> As mad as the vexed sea, singing aloud,
> Crowned with rank fumiter and furrow weeds
> With hardocks, hemlock, nettles, cuckooflowers
> Darnel, and all the idle weeds that grow
> In our sustaining corn.[3]

Once the police realize that the murder scene refers to *King Lear*, they must determine who Cordelia is in the murderer's scheme of things. In his plan, Cordelia — the favorite — murders Mathilda's Lear for the Cavendish family fortune. The frontrunner, of course, is Sarah Blakeney, to whom Mathilda has left all her money.

Sarah is implicated in other ways, as well. The second question of Mathilda's death addresses the scold's bridle, a Cavendish family heirloom that functioned as a multivalent symbol in Mathilda's life. When the bridle was not in the pot of geraniums, Mathilda was wearing it, claiming that it took her mind off her arthritis, which she called the "Resident Scold" because of its nagging pain. When Dr. Sarah Blakeney took over Mathilda's case and changed Mathilda's pain medication so that the pain was controlled, Mathilda began to call the doctor "her little scold's bridle" because she had "harness[ed] the Resident Scold." (28)

Walters is careful in her novel to provide the readers with the tools to understand the scold and the scold's bridle through historical contexts. In an epigraph, Walters first prepares the readers through two definitions. The first is from *Chambers English Dictionary*, which defines a scold as "a rude and clamorous woman." The second definition, from the *Oxford English Dictionary*, is for "branks," the Scottish word for a scold's bridle: "an instrument of punishment used in the case of scolds, etc., consisting of a kind of iron framework to enclose the head, having a sharp metal gag or bit which entered the mouth and restrained the tongue." In chapter two, Walters reinforces her epigraph in a conversation between Dr. Blakeney and Mrs. Graham. Mrs. Graham asks, "Scold, as a woman with a vicious tongue?" and Sarah explains how they were used hundreds of years ago to silence women, "Any women. Women who challenged male authority, inside the home *and* outside" (20, her emphasis).

Throughout the dominant text, examples of Mathilda's scolding behavior are plentiful. D.I. Jones characterizes her as "a bloody-minded, mean and vicious old woman, who ... [sowed] nothing but discord for sixty years" (273). Her estranged husband, James Gillespie, admits to the police that he used to hit her to scare her into ceasing her vitriolic talk. Dr. Blakeney's patient, Mrs. Graham, representing the voice of the village, believes that when Mathilda chose to wear the scold's bridle during her apparent suicide she was expressing contrition for her "vicious tongue" (21). Walters never elaborates further on Dr. Blakeney's description, but historical accounts provide a vivid picture of not only the ways in which women challenged male authority but also the methods of punishing this behavior.

The Historical Scold

The term *scold* and its corollary *shrew* have existed since the Anglo-Saxon period. Sandy Bardsley shows that from the late medieval period *scold* was more than a name for an unruly woman: it was a category that held its own set of punishments, ranging from being fined to being ducked in the community cucking stool (141–46). In her study of women's speech in the Early Modern period, Pamela Allen Brown notes that there was an important distinction between *shrew* and *scold*. While shrews were "garrulous, domineering and intractable [wives]," their speech generally did not harm social harmony beyond the walls of their homes (1). Valerie Wayne categorizes the power of the shrew's tongue as such:

> Her behaviour was unregenerate from a religious point of view because she made excessive and sinful use of her speech. It was inordinate from a social point of view because she challenged her husband's position as head of the marital hierarchy. Good wives were advised to be silent during these periods in history, and too much talking was not merely annoying; it was an illegitimate exercise of power [161].

On the other hand, a scold was a threat to social order; her speech disrupted the neighborhood. A 1686 study of the scold contends that she is "her Neighbours perpetual disquiet, her Families Evil Genius, her Husbands Ruine, and her own daily Tormentor," "who calls her Neighbours *Heathen Edomites*"[4] and "cares not a straw for the Cunstable not [sic] Cuckingstool" (*Twelve* 22, 23).

David Underdown's study of the early modern scold indicates that she was more than a threat to neighborhood peace; she was deemed a threat to patriarchal authority. Underdown argues that from the mid-sixteenth century to the mid-seventeenth century, there was a "public obsession with scolding women, domineering and unfaithful wives" ("Taming" 116–17).[5] He argues that this "public obsession" stemmed from anxiety over the fragility of patriarchal authority ("Taming" 117; see Amussen). In the introduction to her article, "Civilizing Subordination: Domestic Violence and *The Taming of the Shrew*," Emily Detmer catalogues the "discursive sites" in which this "public obsession" or, in her terms, "anxiety about disorderly women" appear (273). They include literary sources, such as plays and ballads, and legal sources, such as treatises and calendars of crimes, as well as conduct books and sermons (273).

Susan Dwyer Amussen shows that "the goal of marriage" in the early modern period was "quietness" (i.e., an absence of fighting, arguing and nagging) (77). Because domestic space in villages was rarely private, the neighbors knew what happened in other households. While a man might be married to a woman called a shrew or a scold and the whole neighborhood or village knew of their fighting, her actions were rarely punished unless her scolding extended beyond the familial and presumably private space. When this happened, she was usually accused of being a "common scold," a legal term that carried punishment. *A Grand Abridgment of the Common and Statute Law of England* (1675) defines a scold as "a troublesome and angry woman, who by her brawling and wrangling amongst her Neighbours, doth break the publick Peace, and beget, cherish and increase publick Discord" (Sheppard, quoted in Boose 186). Similarly, in 1620, the records of Langridge in Somerset accuse Anne Weeks of being "a common scold, a raiser of idle report s and fames, and a common sewer and breeder of discord between her neighbors" (quoted in Underdown, "Taming" 119). Martin Ingram acknowledges their "quasi-public power as brokers of gossip, makers and breakers of reputation" ("Scolding" 49). These descriptions emphasize the scold's presumed threat to social order and harmony.

Lynda Boose argues that the loose or chiding talk of scolds opened them up to accusations of other crimes, such as being a whore. The conflation assumes that if a woman cannot control one orifice, she cannot control the other. According to Patricia Parker, garrulity and lust "are ranged against Obedience" in the measure of a woman (26). She notes the husband's complaint from *Curtaine Lecture* (1637) that he could "neither governe her tongue, nor—"(quoted in Parker 26). This idea stretches as far back as Chaucer, whose Wife of Bath says, "A likerous mouth moste han a likerous tayl [A gluttonous mouth must have a lecherous tail] (*Wife of Bath's Prologue* 466). While the Wife of Bath is commenting on the drinking of wine, she connects excess with excess — gluttony with lust. In the case of the scold, garrulity proves lust. LaRue Love Sloan further points out this connection in her study of *The Taming of the Shrew*. She cites several sixteenth- and seventeenth-century pamphlets that "equate female volubility with sexual indiscretions." For example, Richard Brathwaite in the courtesy book *The English Gentlewoman* (1631) writes that the sins that emerge through excessive speech are "the wanton heart" and the "rancorous heart" (88–89). In *A Bride-bush, or a wedding Sermon* (1617), William Whately says that scolds are "next to harlots, if not the same with them" (39). The 1540 translation of Juan Luis Vives "De Institutione Feminae Christianae" (The Instruction of a Christian Woman) contains a warning to maidens "if thou speake muche, they reken the lyght" [If you speak much, they reckon you loose] (Vives 38).[6] The "looseness" of the scold's various body parts meant "control of women's speech becomes a massively important project ... imagined as a defense of all the important institutions upon which the community depends" (Boose 196). And control necessitates punishment.

Punishments of the scold in the sixteenth and seventeenth centuries were vivid displays that, to modify Michel Foucault's words, were "art[s] ... rest[ing] on a whole technology of representation" (104). In *Discipline and Punish*, Foucault outlines the circumstances through which punishment operates. Two of these are important for our reading of the punishment of scolds. First, the punishment "must be as unarbitrary as possible"(104). Second, the punishment must present a "complex of signs" that renders the crime unattractive and "makes the penalty be feared" (106). The disciplining authority must subvert the pleasure of the crime into a mockery of that pleasure (106–7).

In early modern England, shaming rituals, which subscribed to these Foucauldian categories, were grassroots punishments directed against individuals whose actions did not conform to societal norms. A common shaming ritual called the skimmington was directed against adulteresses, cuckolded husbands, henpecked and abused husbands, or other married couples who exceeded presumed marital norms. Much has been written on these rituals[7]; however, my purpose here is to provide a short description to contextualize the punishing of scolds. The ritual of the skimmington varies according to location, but the basic procedure involved

> surrogates for the offenders (preferably the next-door neighbours) act[ing] out the proscribed behaviour; the "husband" in the position of humiliation, riding backwards on horse or donkey and holding a distaff, the symbol of female subjection, while the "wife" (usually a man in women's clothes) beat him with a ladle [Underdown, *Revel* 102].

This ladle gives the skimmington its name because it is the skimming ladle used in the production of butter and cheese and is thus a sign of womanly work (Underdown, *Revel* 102). Accompanying this display was "rough music,"[8] provided by bells, musical instruments, and household implements, such as kettles, pots, and pans (Ingram, "Ridings" 86, Cunnington 287; Thompson 3). *Chamber's Book of Days* vigorously sets the scene that the shamed couple could expect:

> In a country village, [they] will probably soon be serenaded with a concert of rough music. This harmonious concert is produced by the men, women, and children of the village assembling together, each provided with a suitable instrument. These consist of cows' horns, frying-pans, warming-pans, and tea-kettles, drummed on with a large key; iron pot-lids, used as cymbals; fire-shovels and tongs rattled together; tin and wooden pails drummed on with iron pokers or marrow-bones [2.511].

This passage shows that during the skimmington the villagers were not mere onlookers but active participants in the event of punishment.

The carnivalesque atmosphere of the skimmington shaming ritual mirrors the legal punishment meted out to the scold.[9] *A Grand Abridgment* outlines the punishment she should incur:

> And for this she is to be presented and punished in a Leet [a court], by being put in the Cucking or Ducking-stole, or Tumbrel, an Engine appointed for that purpose, which is in the fashion of a Chair; and

herein she is to sit, and to be let down in the water over head and ears three or four times, so that no part of her be above water, diving or ducking down, though against her will, as Ducks do under the water [Sheppard quoted in Boose 186].

This punishment, however, entailed more than just the dunking. Usually, the woman would have been previously ridden in a cart throughout the town. An early seventeenth-century ballad, "The Cucking of a Scould," describes such an event. The scold is brought to the cucking-stool in a "wheele-barrow," wearing only her undergarment and with "Neats tongues about her necke," which were probably cow tongues. The scold in the ballad is guarded by "an hundred armed men," who take her through the market "With piercing Pikes and Spears: / and Trumptes sounding sweete." They are accompanied by "a company most orderly / With pleasant Phifes and Drums." Music, however, is not the only festive element:

> And forty Parrats [parrots] then,
> On sundry pearches hie,
> Were carried eke before the scould,
> Most fine and orderly
> And last of all a mighty wispe
> Was borne before her face.
> The perfect tokens of a Scould
> Well knowne in every place.

The *OED* provides one definition of "wispe," which means a small bundle of hay or straw, that shows its connection to the scold: "a twist or figure of straw for a scold to rail at." The ballad characterizes the parrot as another "perfect token" of the scold; the parrot is a mimetic symbol referring to the scold's chatter and verbosity (Impelluso 302; Jobes 1239).

While this elaborate display of parrots, fifes, and drums is the work of a seventeenth-century balladeer, we can see similar displays in historical records. In the Norfolk records for 1597 the following appears: "Margaret Grove a common Skould to be Carried with a Bason rung before her to the Cucke-Stool at Fyebridge & there to be 3 times ducked" (quoted in Spargo 14 n. 19). "Bason" refers to "hollow metal dishes clashed together to produce sound" (*OED*).[10] An account from the *London Evening Post* of 1745 attests to the popularity of such events, estimating that 2,000 or

3,000 people witnessed the female keeper of the Queen's Head alehouse ducked in the Thames for scolding (Chambers 1.208–9).

As noted earlier, the association between scolds and whores was common. Further evidence of this tie comes through the similarity of their punishments. Again, in Norfolk, thirty-five years earlier than the punishment for Margaret Groves, a punishment was prescribed for "A Woman for Whoredom." She was "to ryde on a Cart, with a Paper in her hand, & Tynklyd with a Bason, & So at one a Clock to be had to the Cokyng-Stool & ducked in the Water" (Spargo 14). The only difference in the punishment is that the woman charged with "whoredom" holds a paper in her hand that presumably says "whore." Therefore, to any inattentive early modern onlooker, a woman ridden in a cart to the cucking stool, accompanied by rough music, could be charged with being either a scold or a whore.

Rarely mentioned in these references to punishment for scolds is the bridle, because it was an illegal form of punishment.[11] T. N. Brushfield, a nineteenth-century antiquarian from Cheshire, notes that

> no notice of their use is to be found in the Corporation [town or city] books, several of which have been specially examined with that object in view.... [T]he magistrates were doubtless fully aware that the punishment was illegal, and hence preferred that no record should remain of their having themselves transgressed the law [quoted in Boose 196].

Thus, much of the evidence for the use of scolds' bridles survives through the device itself. Numerous scolds' bridles, like Mathilda Gillespie's, exist and thus confirm their use. Boose notes that precise record keeping often indicates its use in the community. For instance, the 1658 Worcester records show that four shillings were spent to mend "the bridle for bridleinge scoulds" and to supply it with "two cords" (Boose 197). The turn-of-the-century American antiquarian Alice Morse Earle reckoned that there were fifty bridles extant in England in "museums, churches, and town halls." She tells of a bridle in the church vestry in Walton-on-Thames engraved with the following verse "Chester presents Walton with a bridle / To cure women's tongues that talk too idle" (Earle). Legend holds that circa 1632 "Chester," from a nearby parish, expected his uncle in Walton-on-Thames to leave him his estate, but the gossip of a townswoman somehow deprived Chester of his windfall (Chambers 1.211).[12] There is no evidence that this bridle was ever used for its intended purpose.

Even though the illegality of scolds' bridles omits them from official records, there is one important first-person account documenting the experience of wearing a bridle. In 1656, the magistrates of Carlisle punished Dorothy Waugh for public preaching rather than scolding. Presumably since her offence was through speech, however, she was made to wear a scold's bridle. She writes in "The lamb's defence against lies" that she was placed in the mayor's prison; the mayor called for "the bridle" and told her that she would have to wear it three hours.

> And that which they called so was like a steel cap, and my hat being violently plucked off, which was pinned to my head, whereby they tore my clothes to put on their bridle, as they called it, which was a stone weight of iron by the relation of their own generation, and three bars of iron to come over my face, and a piece of it was put in my mouth, which was so unreasonable big a thing for that place, as cannot be well related, which was locked to my head, and so I stood their time with my hands bound behind me with the stone weight of iron upon my head, and the bit in my mouth to keep me from speaking [249].

During the three hours, the jailers charge two pence for people to see her. Afterwards the jailers remove the bridle, and Waugh is "kept in prison for a little season" (249) until the mayor returns and orders her to wear the bridle again. He then sends her to be whipped out of town, wearing the bridle (249–50). Waugh's experience reinforces the spectacular nature of the scold's bridle as an instrument of punishment, and she becomes a spectacle for both private and public consumption: the citizens pay for a private showing, and the mayor provides them with a public spectacle as she is whipped out of town.

The historical scold recalls an era in which most women were powerless in their marriages, in their churches, and in their communities. When they did speak up or out, trying to change their situations, they were tried in court, labeled as scolds, and punished by the cucking stool or the scold's bridle. Their punishments were public displays that served to persuade them to modify their behavior and to deter any onlookers from acting in a way that might incur similar punishment. The punishment guaranteed that women remained continual victims of any abuse legitimized by the patriarchal order. Many forms of such physical, emotional, and sexual abuse were condoned through marriage laws and the privileges of the class system.

Mathilda the Scold

The women described above share shocking similarities with the image of Mathilda, which appears on the last page of *The Scold's Bridle*. The final page represents the ten-year-old's first page in her diary. As the entry shows, the child surely begins writing as a means of therapy, but the fact that it is a document to be read by others controls the young Mathilda's discourse:

> *It is my story for people to read when I am dead. If anyone finds it they should take it to the police and make sure Father is hanged. He made me do something wicked today and when I said was going to tell the vicar, he locked me in the cupboard with the scold's bridle on my head. I WAS BLEEDING* [365].

The death of Mathilda's mother is the catalyst for her father's abuse. Her father tells her that her mother would understand. Like the patriarchal order of the sixteenth and seventeenth centuries, her father uses the bridle as a threat to keep Mathilda's tongue in check. She writes that if she tells anyone what her father has done to her, he will use the bridle on her at will (365). This first entry establishes an important context. The bridle and the threat of the bridle as a repeated punishment limit the agency of the woman, or the girl in this case, to control her body or her speech.

The great irony that Walters portrays through the diary is that Mathilda becomes the woman early modern patriarchy feared that women would become if not held in check through such devices as the cucking stool and the scold's bridle. As she matures, Mathilda scolds, commits incest and adultery, mentally and physically abuses the men in her life, and generally does as she wishes. Her first abusers/victims are her alcoholic father, William, and his mentally handicapped brother, Gerald. The young Mathilda uses all the tools available to her — her body, her speech, and the scold's bridle — to empower herself.

Walters signals this change in Mathilda through the second diary entry and demonstrates the culmination of her power in the third entry. Mathilda writes in the second entry, "*It is easy to manipulate a man if all he wants is something as worthless as love. Love is easily given when it is the body that's invaded and not the mind. My mind can withstand anything*" (351). By the time of the third entry, Mathilda has gained complete control of the men in her life through her use of sex and the scold's bridle. A desire to keep the family money is at the root of Mathilda's transformation. Her grandfather's will left the money in a trust to be inherited by Gerald's closest male relative, presumably Mathilda's father. The grandfather's assumptions present a problem Mathilda aptly sums up in her diary, and she alludes to Gerald's sexual relationship with a woman named Grace, whom Mathilda and her father see as a fortune hunter (329). Mathilda is afraid that Grace will marry Gerald and have a son who will inherit all the money. In order to keep Grace from controlling Gerald through sex, Mathilda begins a sexual relationship with him. She writes that Gerald begs her to end the relationship, fearing they both will burn in hell for their behavior. In an eerie reversal of the first entry, Mathilda now punishes her father by making him wear the scold's bridle, while Gerald cowers nearby, afraid that he will be next (329).

Mathilda soon dominates other men through her use of her body and the scold's bridle. The contraption becomes a sexual fetish in her relationship with Duncan Orloff; although Duncan aspires to marry Mathilda and her fortune, she will not marry him because he "*takes pleasure in his own humiliation*" (330). Her reasons do not center on her lack of respect for Duncan or his lack of self-esteem but on the elimination of her own satisfaction, since her only pleasure, she realizes, comes from humiliation and control. Through her encounters with her father, her uncle, and Duncan, Mathilda has taken the acts of punishment and shaming associated with the historical scold's bridle and inverted them to assume control of all the traditional symbols of patriarchy — the father, the head of the family, and the husband. She recognizes this herself, wondering if she is "unnatural" because she is so contemptuous of men (308).

Mathilda's next set of "unnatural" actions includes her getting pregnant with her uncle's baby and marrying a homosexual, James Gillespie, to give the child a father. She epitomizes the early modern fears of the uncontrolled scold — her loose tongue has yielded unchecked sexual behavior that challenges social norms. Like the wives punished through the skimmington, she has inverted the power structure of the household. In the fifth diary entry, Mathilda has given birth to her uncle's child and is pregnant again through an adulterous affair. Her description of James is typical of the emasculated, cuckolded husband of early modern texts: "*He weeps and rants in turn, screaming insults at me like a fishwife, intent, it seems, on trumpeting my 'whorishness' to the entire building*" (286). Her choice of insult is important. Providing a dietary staple, fishwives played an integral part in the market economy of early modern Europe. They gained reputations as foul-mouthed cheats (Honig 305). Texts, such as ballads and pamphlets, portrayed them as loud women who shouted insults and curses at each other.[13] The fishwives' treatment of customers was scarcely better, as they approached them "in overly familiar tones, a mixture of insults and dangerously persuasive supplications" (Honig 305).

By calling James a "fishwife," Matilda not only categorizes him as coarse, shrill, and bad tempered (Taylor 189), but she also genders him female, which carries multiple ramifications. Of course, it is a reference to his homosexuality. This gendering statement also casts him as the weak, submissive partner in the marriage. She further compels him into this role, not through her body or through the punishment of the scold's bridle, but through her speech — in this case the language of blackmail. She hires a private detective to follow James and take photos of his activities. After seeing them, she writes, "'*The fitchew nor the soiled horse goes to't with such riotous appetite.*' ... *There'll be no more talk of divorce, that's for sure, and he'll go to Hong Kong without a murmur*" (287).

The passage is from *King Lear* (4.6.122–23). Mathilda again genders James as female, for Lear is speaking of women who pretend to be chaste and modest but are not. The next two lines, "Down from the waist they're centaurs / Though women all above," continue Lear's condemnation. Her gendering comments signal the competition that Mathilda places in marriage (and in all her relationships). She must be "the woman on top" (Davis). Because James tries to control her behavior through chiding and hitting her, she finds a way to condemn him to being a husband in absentia. The social codes of the gentry dominate Mathilda and James' blackmail negotiations. James prefers being deemed a man who forsook his marriage and family to being deemed a homosexual; Mathilda prefers the title of abandoned woman to divorcée. Both fear divorce because, as James tells D.I. Cooper, "you washed your dirty linen in public when you divorced in those days" (244). The higher the status of her father, the more closely she had to guard her reputation. So in aid of protecting her reputation, Mathilda learns that language (blackmailing and scolding) has benefits over using her body or the scold's bridle to control men. She reveals this realization at the end of her fifth diary entry when she chides herself for needing to be more effective in blackmailing her uncle and her father (286). Just as early modern men feared, marriage teaches the scold more methods to dominate and control men. Mathilda learns how to get rid of James, and then she turns her attentions to her uncle and father.

Mathilda's diary traces a trajectory of scold-like behaviors that reach their zenith with murder. Here, again, she follows the model of her early modern predecessors, whose anxiety concerning disorderly women even extended to husbands fearing their wives would murder them. Until 1640, ballads and chapbooks that related real crimes "focused almost exclusively on women who killed their husbands" (Amussen 75). Amussen particularly refers to the 1688 case of Mary Hobry, who not only murdered her husband but also cut his body into pieces so that she could hide it. Her case was a cause celebre, published in four separate texts. All portray her as an abused wife whose husband gave her venereal disease and "tried to force her to 'a compliance with him in villanies contrary to nature'" (Sharpe 42).

Mathilda Gillespie is a savvier version of Mary Hobry because she gets away with the premeditated murders of her abusers. In her plan to kill her uncle, Mathilda forces him to add a codicil to his will acknowledging that her daughter is also his daughter and leaving the Cavendish fortune to Joanna. She then gives him an overdose of barbiturates. Gerald's death is thought to be suicide, but because of the family position, the coroner is cajoled into returning the verdict death by misadventure. Mathilda's sixth diary entry exhibits her egoism; she confesses that having her brilliance underestimated is irksome to her (267). In the next entry, Mathilda recounts how she smothered her father with a pillow. What is especially telling is the confidence she shows as her second murder goes undiscovered. She writes, "*James was really very lucky. Had I realized how easy it was to get rid of drunks, well, well ... enough said*" (251). Although Mathilda never reaches the status of husband-killer, as a double parricide, she certainly reinforces the fears that early modern society placed on unruly, uncontrolled women.

Where's Kate?

In Mathilda, Walters constructs the archetypal scold, embodied with all the irrational fears of early modern patriarchy, yet in a book so dominated by Shakespeare, one wonders why Walters avoids Shakespeare's most famous shrew, Katharina or more popularly, Kate. Mathilda quotes *The Taming of the Shrew* only once in her diary: "O vile, intolerable, not to be endur'd" when writing of her granddaughter's crying (194; *Taming* 5.2.98).

While we do not expect Mathilda to understand the nuances between a shrew and a scold, as Brown has indicated above, she does know her Shakespeare. Kate would not be a role model for Mathilda because, simply, Kate is tamed. She begins the play as a woman whom Gremio would rather "cart" than "court" (1.1.54–55). These lines carry the allusions of the scold ridden through town on her way to the cucking stool. Kate and Mathilda do have much in common: they are both abused, but while Kate is tamed, Mathilda learns how to abuse.

Detmer reads Petruchio's abuse of Kate through the Stockholm syndrome in which hostages bond with captors (284). Dee Graham and Edna Rawlings explain the mechanism of the Stockholm syndrome:

> The abuser traumatizes the victim (who cannot escape) with threat to survival. The traumatized victim needs nurturance and protection. Being isolated from outsiders, the victim must turn to the abuser for nurturance and protection, as she denies her rage. If the abuser shows the victim some small kindness, the victim bonds to the positive side of abuse [quoted in Detmer 287].

Petruchio's strategy of withholding food and sleep from Kate "make[s] her weak and materially dependent on him" (285). As she continues to weaken, he challenges her ability to see and know. For example, he demands that she say that the sun is the moon, and when she finally relents and says what he wants, he reverses his position: "Nay then you lie. It is the blessed sun" (4.5.17). He has taught her she must "see" the world as he does, "even if it is absurd or contrary to everything [she] knows" (Detmer 288).

Thus, by the end of the play, Kate has become Petruchio's submissive wife. The play ends with her lecturing the newlyweds, Bianca and the Widow, on wifely comportment:

> I am ashamed that women are so simple
> To offer war where they should kneel for peace,
> Or seek rule, supremacy, and sway,
> When they are bound to serve, love, and obey [5.2.165–68].

The ending of Kate's speech addresses the women in the audience: "Come, come, you forward and unable worms" (5.2.173). She extorts them to "place your hands below your husband's foot, / In token of which duty, if he please" (5.2.181–82). Clearly, these are philosophies to which Mathilda will not subscribe. She must be the one who "seek[s] rule, supremacy, and sway," and she must be the one to whom submission is paid. Mathilda would never identify with Kate in *The Taming of the Shrew*; she is more like Petruchio, the abuser/manipulator, although her strategies are not as intricate.

The diaries show that King Lear is much closer to Mathilda's image of herself; she sees herself as a tragic figure, someone who "*learnt only to survive*" instead of learning to love (16). While *Hamlet* is the most quoted play in her diary, appearing at least ten times, her *King Lear* passages demonstrate more personal identification. As she reflects on her mother and on herself as a child, she writes, "*Forgotten wraiths, both of them, unloved, abused, neglected. Thank God for Sarah. She convinces me that like Shakespeare's sad old man 'I am more sinned against than sinning...'*" (69, her ellipses). This passage connects her abuse to her later actions and seeks to justify them; thus, she becomes a tragic figure like Lear. Additionally, she co-opts the play's words. For example, when Dr. Blakeney asks her how she is, Mathilda replies with words from *King Lear*: "*I grow; I prosper. / Now, gods, stand up for bastards*" (Walters 86; 1.2.21–22). In the last months of her life, Mathilda feels that Joanna is plotting to gain control of the family money. One of her last diary entries summarizes her relationship with Joanna through a passage from *King Lear*: "*Ingratitude, thou marble-hearted fiend, / More hideous when thou show'st thee in a child / Than the sea monster"* (1.4.257–59). These three examples show how Mathilda struggles to understand herself, her actions, and her relationships through the lens of *Lear*.

When the murderer killed Mathilda and fashioned her body as a hybrid of King Lear and the scold, he was more correct in his representation than he ever could have imagined. We can best interpret Mathilda's many attempts to understand and control her unfortunate life through her relationship to these figures. Unfortunately, in her death she was more Shakespeare's tragic Lear than the brazen figure of the scold, who cared neither for the constable or the cucking stool (*Twelve* 23).

Notes

1. Walters, Minette. *The Scold's Bridle*. New York: St. Martin's, 1994. All further passages are from this edition and are cited parenthetically in the text.
2. Shakespeare, William. *Hamlet. The Necessary Shakespeare*. 2nd ed. Ed. David Bevington. New York: Pearson, 2005. 4.7.169–173. All Shakespeare plays in this article are from this edition and are cited parenthetically in the text by act, scene and line.
3. Walters provides a shortened version of this quote on page 301.
4. This is an anti–Semitic slur.
5. Martin Ingram's "Scolding" revises much of Underdown's research. Ingram takes issue with Underdown's assertion that women were rarely prosecuted as scolds until the 1500s. Ingram shows that the number of prosecutions in the 1300s is not significantly less. However, during Underdown's period of interest, the punishments were more public and tended toward spectacle.
6. See Sloan, paragraph 5.
7. See Underdown, *Revel*; Ingram, "Ridings"; Davis; and Thompson.
8. Ingram notes that this term was probably not used before 1700, although the practice existed ("Ridings" 86).
9. See Boose 189.
10. While most of the persons punished by cucking or ducking stools were women labeled as scolds or whores, community leaders used it to punish other offenders as well. Evidence shows that men who scolded and men or women who brewed small ale (use too little grain) or gave short measures of ale were subjected to cucking (Spargo 40).
11. For a summary of the variety of punishments used on scolds, see Ingram, "Scolding," especially 58–59.
12. The original bridle was stolen in the 1960s; a replica hangs in St. Mary's vestry in its place.
13. See, for instance, the seventeenth-century ballad, "The Bloody Battle at Billingsgate, Beginning with a Scolding bout between two young Fish-women, Doll and Kate." *Early Modern Center English Ballad Archive, 1500–1800*. Department of English, University of California-Santa Barbara. www.english.ucsb.edu/emc/ballad_project/ballad_image. asp?id=FILLIN.

Works Cited

Amussen, Susan Dwyer. "'Being Stirred to Much Unquietness': Violence and Domestic Violence in Early Modern England." *Journal of Women's History* 6 (1994): 70–89. *JSTOR.* James Lide Coker III Memorial Library. 1 Feb. 2007. www.jstor.org.

Bardsley, Sandy. *Venomous Tongues: Speech and Gender in Late Medieval England*. Philadelphia: University of Pennsylvania Press, 2006.

Boose, Lynda E. "Scolding Bridles and Bridling Scolds: Taming the Woman's Unruly Member." *Shakespeare Quarterly* 42 (1991): 179–213. *JSTOR.* James Lide Coker III Memorial Library. 13 Oct. 2006. www.jstor.org.

Brathwaite, Richard. *The English Gentlewoman*. London, 1631. *Early English Books Online*. Proquest. James Lide Coker III Memorial Library 24 Feb. 2007. http://eebo.chadwyck.com.

Brown, Pamela Allen. *Better a Shrew Than a Sheep: Women, Drama, and the Culture of Jest in Early Modern England*. Ithaca: Cornell University Press, 2003.

Chambers, R., ed. *The Book of Days: A Miscellany of Popular Antiquities*. 2 vols. London: W. & R. Chambers, n. d.

Chaucer, Geoffrey. *The Wife of Bath's Prologue*. *The Riverside Chaucer*. Gen. ed. Larry D. Benson. 3rd ed. Boston: Houghton Mifflin, 1987.

"The Cucking of a Scould." Early Modern Center English Ballad Archive, 1500–1800. Department of English, University of California-Santa Barbara. www.english.ucsb.edu/emc/ballad_project/ballad_image.asp?id=20029.

Cunnington, B. Howard. "'A Skimmington' in 1618." *Folklore* 41 (1930): 287–290. *JSTOR.* James Lide Coker III Memorial Library. 5 Feb. 2007. www.jstor.org.

Davis, Natalie Zemon. "Women on Top: Symbolic Sexual Inversion and Political Disorder in Early Modern Europe." *The Reversible World*. Ithaca, NY: Cornell University Press, 1978, pp. 147–190.

Detmer, Emily. "Civilizing Subordination: Domestic Violence and *The Taming of the Shrew*." *Shakespeare Quarterly* 48 (1997): 273–294. *JSTOR.* James Lide Coker III Memorial Library. 7 Feb. 2007. www.jstor.org.

Earle, Alice Morse. "Branks and Gags." *Curious Punishments of Bygone Days*. www.getchwood.com/punishments/curious/chapter-8.html#TOC9.

Foucault, Michel. *Discipline and Punish: The Birth of the Prison*. Trans. Alan Sheridan. New York: Pantheon Books, 1977.

Greenblatt, Stephen. *Renaissance Self-Fashioning: From More to Shakespeare*. Chicago: University of Chicago Press, 1980. rpt. 2005.

Honig, Elizabeth Alice. "Desire and Domestic Economy." *The Art Bulletin* 83 (2001): 294–315. *JSTOR.* James Lide Coker III Memorial Library. 9 Feb. 2007. www.jstor.org.

Impelluso, Lucia. *Nature and Its Symbols*. Trans. Stephen Sartarelli. Los Angeles: The J. Paul Getty Museum, 2004.

Ingram, Martin. "Ridings, Rough Music and the 'Reform of Popular Culture' in Early Modern England." *Past and Present* 105 (1984): 79–113. *JSTOR.* James Lide Coker III Memorial Library. 5 Feb. 2007. www.jstor.org.

———. "'Scolding Women Cucked or Washed': A Crisis in Gender Relations in Early

Modern England?" *Women, Crime and the Courts in Early Modern England.* Eds. Jennifer Kermode and Garthine Walker. Chapel Hill: University of North Carolina Press, 1994, pp. 48–80.

Jobes, Gertrude. *Dictionary of Mythology Folklore and Symbols.* Part 2. New York: Scarecrow Press, 1962.

Kuchta, David. "The Semiotics of Masculinity in Renaissance England." *Sexuality and Gender in Early Modern Europe. Institutions, Texts, Images.* Ed. James Grantham Turner. Cambridge: Cambridge University Press, 1993, pp. 233–246.

Parker, Patricia. *Literary Fat Ladies. Rhetoric, Gender, Property.* London: Meuthen, 1987.

Sloan, LaRue Love. "'Caparisoned like the horse': Tongue and Tail in Shakespeare's *The Taming of the Shrew.*" *Early Modern Literary Studies* 10.2 (2004): 1–24. http://purl.oclc.org/emls/10–2/sloacapa.htm.

Sharpe, J. A. "Domestic Homicide in Early Modern England." *Historical Journal* 24 (1981): 29–48. *JSTOR.* James Lide Coker III Memorial Library. 7 Feb. 2007. www.jstor.org.

Spargo, John Webster. *Juridical Folklore in England Illustrated by the Cucking-Stool.* Durham: Duke University Press, 1944.

Taylor, Gary. "Touchstone's Butterwomen." *The Review of English Studies.* n.s. Vol. 32. No. 126 (1981): 187–193. *JSTOR.* James Lide Coker III Memorial Library. 7 Feb. 2007. www.jstor.org.

Thompson, E. P. "Rough Music Reconsidered." *Folklore* 103 (1992): 3–26. *JSTOR.* James Lide Coker III Memorial Library. 5 Feb. 2007. .

Twelve Ingenious Characters. London, 1686. *Early English Books Online.* Proquest. James Lide Coker III Memorial Library 23 Feb. 2007. http://eebo.chadwyck.com.

Underdown, David. *Revel, Riot and Rebellion: Popular Politics and Culture in England 1603–1660.* Oxford: Oxford University Press, 1987.

_____. "The Taming of the Scold." *Order and Disorder in Early Modern England.* Eds. Anthony Fletcher and John Stevenson. Cambridge: Cambridge University Press, 1985. 116–136.

Vives, Juan Luis. *A very frutful and pleasant boke called the Instruction of a christen woman.* Trans. Rycharde Hyrde. London, 1547. *Early English Books Online.* Proquest. James Lide Coker III Memorial Library 24 Feb. 2007. http://eebo.chadwyck.com.

Walters, Minette. *The Scold's Bridle.* New York: St. Martin's, 1994.

Waugh, Dorothy. "The lamb's defence against lies." *Renaissance Woman: A Sourcebook. Constructions of Femininity in England.* Ed. Kate Aughterson. London: Routledge, 1995, pp. 249–250.

Wayne, Valerie. "Refashioning the Shrew." *Shakespeare Studies* 17 (1985): 159–187.

Whately, William. *A Bride-Bush, or a Wedding Sermon.* London, 1617. Early English Books Online. Proquest. James Lide Coker III Memorial Library 24 Feb. 2007. http://eebo.chadwyck.com.

A Wounded World: Victim/Victimizers in *The Scold's Bridle*, *The Dark Room*, and *The Breaker*

Lois A. Marchino *and*
Deane Mansfield-Kelley

A victim is the necessary component of detective fiction. Without one there would be no crime and no reason to investigate. In the mystery genre a victim is defined as the person upon whom a crime is perpetrated. Yet the role of victim and importance of that role are the least discussed in detective fiction criticism. Initially, this lack is due to Edgar Allan Poe and his establishment of the concept of the victim as "object." In "The Murders in the Rue Morgue" (1841), there is little information on Madame L'Espanaye or her daughter, Mademoiselle Camille L'Espanaye, the victims. Their deaths are necessary, so that Monsieur C. Auguste Dupin can illustrate his superior powers of inductive and deductive reasoning and solve the crimes. Everyone remembers the name of the detective; few remember the names of the victims.

This viewpoint continues through the writers of the Golden Age of detective fiction, who emphasize the detective and challenge their readers to solve the intricate puzzle of the crime. Agatha Christie, the best known writer to emerge from this period, clearly demonstrates this lack of interest in the victim. In "The Puzzle Game," from their critical book on the works of Agatha Christie, Patricia Maida and Nicholas Spornick comment on Christie's victims:

> Who is likely to be murdered? According to Christie, anyone — male, female, adult, child — anyone who in some way crosses the wrong person. The potential victim, Christie believes, is a person who could be killed — someone who is vulnerable. Given the closed society which Christie portrays, the victim is frequently a member of the inner circle who poses a threat to another person in the group. Although occasionally the innocent suffer, most often the victim is someone who has brought the event upon himself. No matter how well placed the victim is or no matter how sterling his character may be, Christie does not engage the sympathy of the reader; her focus is on the solution of the murder. By developing means of emotional distancing for the reader, she makes the puzzle solving all the more challenging. The focus then shifts from the victim to the murderer [71].

Likewise, S. S. Van Dine, creator of Philo Vance, emphasizes the victim in his "Twenty Rules for Writing Detective Stories" (1928), in which he states as Rule 7: "There simply must be a corpse in a detective novel, and the deader the corpse the better" (190). Readers of Golden Age mysteries could expect brilliant detectives, complex puzzles, and intriguing murderers, but the victims remained objectified.

Beginning in the 1960s, however, authors of detective fiction more consciously shaped their writing to parallel social reality. In this era of protest, issues of gender, race, class, and religion were made more relevant. The extent of victimization in our society became more apparent, and studies on victimization and victim involvement in crime evolved. In "Understanding Theories of Victimization," Robert Meier and Terance Miethe discuss basic victimization theories including lifestyle; exposure theory, which is based on routine activity and exposure to risk; proximity theory, which deals with connections to subcultures of violence; and environmental theories, which include the expectations of crime (459–99). By the 1990s, there was a new cultural awareness that anyone could be a victim.

According to Mark Seltzer in his book, *True Crime: Observations on Violence and Modernity* (2007), we now exist in a "contemporary wound culture" (57). We are part of "a victim culture — the new victim order," or as it has also come to be called, "the world risk society" (97). Seltzer writes,

> It is a world in which society as a whole comes to be understood, in the idiom of the insurance industry, as a global risk group. It is the experience of everyday life in terms of the perpetual emergency state of generalized alert and unlocatable, uninsurable threat. It is the exposed world in which the grey zone between ordinary and terrorized life keeps expanding, such that it defines the "new normal" [97].

He observes that it is crime fiction "that schools individuals (that is, readers) in the counterfactual riskscapes of modernity" (97).

Beginning in the 1990s, the detective fiction writer who most enhances the role of the victim and vividly portrays our wounded world is Minette Walters. In her novels she creates hermeneutic, claustrophobic settings in which her characters struggle in an atmosphere of fear and violence. Her plots extend the patterns of victimization into a complex web from which few characters are exempt. Her major characters play the dual roles of victim and victimizer. They are victims of society because of gender, race, class, religion; they are victims of others because of fear, hatred, anger, jealousy, revenge. They victimize themselves because of emotional and psychological flaws, and they retaliate by victimizing others. The intricate strands of victimization found in our contemporary world are clearly exemplified in three novels from Walters' early-middle period: *The Scold's Bridle* (1994), *The Dark Room* (1996), and *The Breaker* (1998). All three novels are international best-sellers praised by reviewers, and *The Scold's Bridle* won the Gold Dagger Award from the United Kingdom Crime Writers Association (CWA) for Best British crime novel in 1995.

In *The Scold's Bridle*, the title itself is a clear foreshadowing of the gender issues, especially the victimization of women, which becomes a theme in this and other Walters novels. This instrument of punishment is a key element of the murder scene in which Mathilda Gillespie, the extremely wealthy matriarch of the elite Cavendish family, is found dead in her bathtub. With Mathilda, the single most important character in the novel, Walters breaks the rule of the traditional detective novel. No longer is the detective or the murderer the most fully developed and complex character; now it is the victim.

A Wounded World (Marchino and Mansfield-Kelley)

Following Mathilda's death — it is unclear initially whether it is murder or suicide — the police begin the customary thorough investigation of her life; but the reader's knowledge of her is enhanced by the literary device of letting her speak for herself through interspersing the chapters with passages from her personal diary, giving both external and internal glimpses of her nature. In an interview with Dean James, Minette Walters talked about this manner of presenting her victim:

> In *The Scold's Bridle* I decided to give my murder victim a real voice, so I used extracts from Mathilda's diaries to allow her to speak for herself. This was particularly relevant because of the way she died with "the rusted metal bit [of the scold's bridle] clamping the dead tongue still in the gaping mouth." However, it is not just the murdered person who is a victim, but also everyone closely associated with him/her and that well may include the murderer. The idea that violent death can happen within a family or a close community without huge trauma being suffered by everyone concerned seems to me to be absurd [196].

In the death of Mathilda, suspects and suspicions abound. In the typical Walters' microcosmic setting of the small village of Fontwell, Dorset, Mathilda is a powerful antagonistic force. Having lived all her life in Fontwell, she has a reputation for snobbery, intolerance, spite, and manipulation; the townspeople share an intense dislike for her. However, Walters shows Mathilda in the dual role of victim and victimizer; she is not only the primary murder victim, but the reader later learns that she is herself a murderer. Through Mathilda, Walters personifies the major issues of victimization: gender, class, race, and religion. Mathilda Cavendish Gillespie is a victimizer par excellence. There is not a more destructive female manipulator in the Walters novels except for Olive Martin in *The Sculptress*. In her youth, Mathilda was the extremely lethal combination of great beauty, exceptional intelligence, and strong will, using sex to control the men of the village, both married and unmarried. Mathilda is also noted for her snobbery. Always conscious of class distinctions, she runs a house where professionals enter through the back door (27). The people in Fontwell dislike her because she disparages them constantly. She is an atheist, believing religion is for the masses; she is an anti–Semite, temporarily disowning her daughter Joanna when she marries a Jewish rock musician, and later trying to force her granddaughter Ruth to change her name to Elizabeth, so she will not show any Jewish connections. The village considers Mathilda a complete bitch (27).

Although the villagers hate her, they do not really know or understand her. But the reader is made privy to the full extent of Mathilda's victimization through her diary entries, particularly the final one, which reveals the despicable social reality of child sexual abuse. As a consequence of her childhood experiences, Mathilda grew up hating her close relatives for their behavior toward her. Her diary underscores her distrust of both men and women, her inability to give love, and the underlying motives for the murders she commits.

According to current victimization theory, Mathilda also fits the profile of abused children who often become abusers themselves. She verbally abuses and physically mistreats her daughter Joanna, forcing the child to wear the scold's bridle whenever she cries. As an adult, Joanna nurtures a love-hate relationship with her mother. She is monetarily dependent on Mathilda and clearly has co-dependency problems in other areas. Likewise, Joanna mistreats her own daughter, Ruth, coming close to smothering her when she is an infant. Ruth is an excellent example of the new "victim culture." Psychologically and emotionally abused by her demanding grandmother and her narcissistic mother, she is starved for attention and affection. She therefore becomes the victim of Dave Hayes. Although Ruth steals things from her grandmother's house to please Dave Hayes, she is mainly victimized by her own emotional and psychological needs. As a contemporary teenager, her world is the "wound" world, filled with uncertainty, fear, and "the unlocatable threat" (Seltzer 57, 97).

Only one woman has a different view of Mathilda, and that is Sarah Blakeney, a young doctor who attends Mathilda the year before the murder. An outsider, unaware of Mathilda's history in the village, Sarah enjoys the older Mathilda with her scathing wit and flashing intelligence. She becomes Mathilda's confidante, and realizes, as a professional woman herself, that the villagers would never like Mathilda because she refuses to conform to the role that Fontwell expects her to fulfill. She is not a benign sponsor of the village activities, but a rich, powerful woman who insists on doing things her way. She refuses to be society's victim any longer. In making Sarah her heir, Mathilda unintentionally places her in the role of victim, as the villagers turn against her and shun her medical practice because they suspect Sarah has had her own motives for financial gain. Sarah learns what Mathilda already knew, that the modern world is a risky and treacherous place.

Although the dominant victim/victimizer characters in *The Scold's Bridle* are women, the male characters share these qualities as well. Mathilda's father and uncle were both victimizers, but they were also her victims. James Gillespie, Mathilda's husband, married her for her money and position, but was her subject too. Dave Hughes, however, is the consummate predator, and represents the random threats and violence of the "victim culture." As Susan Brownmiller reminds us throughout *Against Our Will: Men, Women, and Rape*, rape is the sine qua non of men's control of women under patriarchy. In an essential sense men rape women because they can, to keep them under control. Hughes has no remorse about what he does, and, because he has a pathological hatred of women, he believes they should be victimized to serve his needs.

When he is finally arrested, Hughes defends himself by implying that he is a victim of class distinction. Ironically, although it is no excuse for his behavior, Hughes recognizes the built-in victimization of the class system and how it both hurts and helps him. However, Detective Chief Charlie Jones, who is much aware of victimization theory and predator profiling, provides another reason for Hughes' behavior. He tells Hughes that he shows evidence of a psychopathic personality (205).

The police in *The Scold's Bridle* are knowledgeable, competent, and even empathetic characters. They apprehend Hughes and his gang and also discover Mathilda's murderer. The victim world is their world, the reason their profession exists, and they are prepared to cope with its violence and terror. Nevertheless, they are not major characters in the novel, and the emphasis remains on the victims.

In her interview with Dean James, Walters tells us that one of those victims could be the murderer, and in *The Scold's Bridle*, it is. Hearing of Mathilda's thoughts of selling the land behind their houses for a new development provokes him to decide to get rid of her. While the sale of land is a financial motive for killing Mathilda, all the years of her rejection, degradation, and ridicule add impetus to the murderer's actions. As first a victim and then a victimizer, the killer has experiences that mirror Mathilda's; and thus, according to Walters, the cycle of victimization continues in the modern world.

Following *The Scold's Bridle,* Minette Walters created another novel, *The Dark Room*, which continues the pattern of featuring the victim, and whose title seems to have a triple meaning. The major character, Jane Imogene Nicola Kingsley, nicknamed Jinx, is a fashion and pop culture photographer, spending a lot of time in the photographer's "darkroom." As the novel begins, Jinx has been in a car accident, suffers from amnesia, and fears the "dark room" of her memory and what might lurk there. Further, the "dark room" also refers to the mind of the psychotic killer, who in his last note writes, "I understand that sacrifice is necessary if the dark rooms of the mind are to be cleansed" (*The Dark Room* 319).

Jinx is a prime example of a single woman trying to maneuver the "riskscape" of the modern world. Ten years earlier, trying to escape her dominant and manipulative father, Jinx married Russell Landry, an older man of whom her father did not approve. After they are married, Jinx finds Russell's body in his art gallery, bludgeoned almost beyond recognition. Because of the trauma of his death and her discovery of the body, Jinx loses her unborn child. Russell's death is considered a random killing, an act of violence without explanation, found too often in contemporary times. As *The Dark Room* begins, Jinx awakens to find herself in the Nightingale Clinic in Salisbury, a hospital that specializes in addiction therapy but offers convalescent care as well. Her father has placed her there presumably for her own protection; she is confined with head injuries and is suffering from amnesia. The reader discovers, however, that Jinx has been the victim of two attempts on her life. She was knocked out and almost asphyxiated in her garage, and placed unconscious in her car, which was then run into a cement pillar. She knows who has done this and why, but the perpetrator's identity and motive are locked in her lost memory. Although Jinx is ill, anyone can come to see her; and the reader knows that one of the visitors must be the murderer, checking to see that she does not remember. As Jinx's amnesia slowly recedes, the area of her "dark room" decreases, but her fears and dangers increase when she learns that her ex-fiancé, Leo Wallander, and her best friend, Meg Harris, who were running off to be married, have been found murdered in a manner similar to that of Russell Landry.

Jinx's realization that she must know something about the murders and the murderer prompts her to feign nearly total amnesia while she helps the police with small pieces of information she says she can recall. Even with all her losses — a husband, her unborn child, her ex-fiancé, and her best friend — she does not intend to become the ultimate victim — a murder victim. At the hospital, even with a shaved head and bandages, Jinx manages to attract more than the medical attention of Dr. Alan Protheroe, the head of the hospital, create a protective group around her, and convince the police to follow her advice in their investigations. Through her subtle manipulations, everyone ends up doing what Jinx wants.

Although victimized multiple times, Jinx is still a survivor. In the past she had defied her father, who is obsessed with her, and rejected his money. She has supported herself with her photography and surrounded herself with people who care about her. But she is also an accomplished manipulator, and her frequent victim is her father. She knows her father adores her because she looks exactly like her mother, who died when Jinx was eight. She uses this resemblance to her advantage, and she counts on it to make him let her lead her own life.

Jinx's father, Adam Kingsley, has a well-deserved reputation as a victimizer. From a lower-class background, he became involved with the mob; he has made millions by buying cheap property, then frightening the tenants away and reselling the land at a huge profit. At present he is the C.E.O. of Franchise Holdings, a multi-million pound company, and has achieved respectability; but he has not lost his image as a dangerous man. Adam is ruthless and brutal to those around him except for Jinx; he physically abuses his two grown sons and his second wife, Betty, whose alcoholism is largely the result of this mistreatment. Adam, however, is also made a victim by his own family whose chaos ruins Adam's chances of maintaining his much-valued respectability.

Like the Kingsley family, all three major murder victims are part of the victim/victimizer cycle. Russell Landry's long affair with Meg, his wife's best friend, while he is married to Jinx leads to his murder. Leo Wallander and Meg Harris, who are also killed, are self-centered, manipulative, and deceitful. Leo takes money from his parents and lives off Jinx when they are engaged, yet he owns millions in property that he never tells anyone about except Meg. Although he is engaged to Jinx, he has an affair with Meg and then decides to marry her. Extremely promiscuous, Meg has no qualms about having affairs with her best friend's husband, and then her fiancé. Walters truly creates a warped world where there is little difference between the murderer and the murdered victims in terms of guilt; both are victims and both create other victims.

As in *The Scold's Bridle*, the murderer in *The Dark Room* is a victim himself, but in a second plotline is revealed as a serial killer, or at least a dangerous serial molester of prostitutes. His first prostitute victim's condition when she is admitted to hospital epitomizes his brutality. When questioned, the prostitute refuses to identify her attacker, fearing retribution; the policewoman tells her, "You've got two fractured cheekbones, severe bruising of the throat and larynx, a dislocated wrist, and internal bleeding from having a hairbrush rammed up your back passage.... You're lucky to be alive. The next woman may not be so lucky" (32).

Both groups of the murderer's victims are chosen because of his sexual psychosis, since he sees women as degrading, needing to be punished or sacrificed. The number of women injured or killed in this novel certainly supports the comment of Glenwood Irons in *Feminism in Women's Detective Fiction:* "Without doubt, the majority of murder victims who meet their deaths between the covers of mystery fiction paperbacks, in mystery movies on the small and large screens, and even in the daily news are women" (ix). Again in this novel, the police are well aware of the psychological profiles of murderers, since the killer is diagnosed as "dangerously psychotic ... with an extreme paranoid disorder, probably of sexual origin, either centered on his mother or his sister, or both" (328). Failing to kill Jinx, the murderer dies a horrible death, leaving a suicide note that looks as if he might have been forced to write it. Is he his own victim, or has someone murdered him to protect Jinx? Knowing the carnage that he has created, the police prefer not to examine his death too closely. The setting, plot, and characterizations in *The Dark Room*, with the Walters' touch, all function together consistently to portray the modern world as one in which, to reiterate Mark Seltzer's phrase, "the grey zone between ordinary and terrorized life keeps expanding" (97).

Another dark novel, *The Breaker*, features severely flawed central characters who are also simultaneously both victims and victimizers. In this novel, the most violent and damaging victimizers are males, and their victims are females. The novel begins with the discovery of a dead body on the pebbled shore of an isolated coastline in southwestern England, in West Dorset. Stephen Knight, in *Crime Fiction 1800–2000*, has pointed out that the story reads, almost deliberately, like a modernized version of Dorothy L. Sayers' 1932 Golden Age classic *Have His Carcass* (151), which opens with Harriet Vane discovering a dead body along England's western coast. There are other parallels, but the updated aspects in *The Breaker* include making the victim a woman who was raped and murdered, and centering the interest on what kind of person she was rather than on a central detective, as Sayers does with Lord Peter Wimsey.

The reader develops a very different attitude toward the victim in Walters' novel even before the body is found, for on a page before the start of the novel we are told, "She drifted with the waves ... waking to renewed agony every time salt water seared down her throat.... During intermittent periods of lucidity ... it was the deliberate breaking of her fingers that remained indelibly printed on her memory, and not the brutality of the rape" (unnumbered page). This image influences not only the degree of sympathy for the victim, but the interpretation of the title of the novel as well. As in *The Dark* Room, Walters' title again suggests multiple meanings. With photos and drawings of the rugged, ragged, isolated coastline and a book cover showing restless waves pounding against a steep cliff, this is no resort area with peaceful wide beaches. The title might logically be "the breakers," with all those powerful waves, but since the word is singular, it could refer to the breaker that tossed up the drowned body. But the breaking of all the victim's fingers suggests yet another interpretation. The investigation begins: Who is the breaker?

Another "modernization" of the earlier Sayers novel is evident when the body is first discovered by two young brothers on a cliff who spot it through binoculars. Totally engrossed, they salaciously look at the naked body for quite some time. In fact, the older brother, age twelve, masturbates while looking, before he begins to suspect that she is so immobile because she is dead. The boys' voyeurism is interrupted by hiker Stephen Harding, who calls emergency services to the scene on his cell phone. The local Police Constable, Nick Ingram, who places the body on a stretcher, may be the only one among the onlookers who suspects murder; he feels anger, because "death had stolen a pretty woman's dignity. As always, the victory belonged to the thief and not to the victim" (*The Breaker* 91). It was a "victory" for the murderer, whose victim's forensic evidence establishes that she has been raped, her fingers broken and, naked, drugged, but still alive, her body thrown from a boat into the cold, dark sea.

Three likely victimizers, all of whom are guilty of other crimes if not this one, attract the attention of the police as they investigate the murder. It is no surprise that Steve Harding becomes a prime suspect. He was on the scene when the body was found and the one to make the report. Later the younger brother tells PC Ingram that Harding had been "rubbing his willy with his telephone" when they were talking, "all the time the lady was being rescued" (91). He definitely becomes a suspect when the police find out that Harding knew the woman quite well, something he had not mentioned when the body was found. Identification of the body is determined in a roundabout way, when a little girl two or three years old is found alone along a street in Poole, the nearest village to where the body was found. Her picture is publicized as a lost child, and a woman who sees it calls her son to say it might be his daughter, Hannah. William Sumner then identifies both his daughter and the dead body of his wife, Kate Sumner. He too becomes a suspect, since husbands are usually the first ones to be suspected in the death of a wife (66). The suspicion increases when there are questions about his marital relationship that he refuses to answer; and, even more tellingly, little Hannah ignores him or screams at him when he tries to touch her. A third suspect is Anthony "Tony" Bridges, a close friend of Steve Harding from the time they were schoolmates and delinquent teenagers. Tony has become, incongruously, a high school chemistry teacher; but he is also a "druggie," and worse, is prone to slipping the "date rape" drug Rohypnal into the drinks of his girlfriend, Bibi. Interestingly, traces of Rohypnal were found in Kate Sumner's body. It is Tony who reveals that Steve Harding was having an affair with Kate; furthermore, Tony is jealous of Steve and worries that Bibi may be having an affair with him. Given this unpleasant male trio, the various police working the case realize that they not only must learn more about each of the men, especially their relationships to Kate Sumner, but also more about Kate's personality and history. The victim then becomes the focus.

Age twenty-nine or thirty when she is murdered, Kate has lived as what might be seen as a modern woman who has chosen to do as she pleases, but it is more accurate to see her as trapped by her gender and her own inadequacies. She is alone in the world, without a supportive network of family and friends, and no interest in others in general. While working in a desultory fashion in a dead-end job at a pharmaceutical company, she had had an affair with her much older boss. When she became pregnant with his child, she looked around for a husband, and married another employee, William Sumner, ten years her senior. Sumner has money, and he is quite satisfied with their arrangement, that he will support her and the daughter Hannah, who he knows is not his, and Kate will provide sex on demand and play the role of little housewife and mother. She also assumes he would prefer not to know about her affair with Steve Harding. Kate presumably would like to believe she is using Steve, and Steve, certainly egotistically, feels that he is using her.

Walters gives enough background on the suspects to show the psychological damage done to them when they were young. Each, in his own way, was a victim of parental abuse. Steve's parents did not want to acknowledge that he was a wayward boy and disowned him when they learned he was involved in making pornographic films. Tony's parents thoroughly disliked their troublesome boy, and he learned early to be sneaky, mean, and unfeeling. The two worked together, using Steve's boat to engage in preying on young women, smuggling, and human trafficking; but when questioned by the police, each sells out the other hoping to save himself. William was a spoiled and unsociable child who lived alone with his mother until he married at age thirty-seven, and he had never learned to care about people or relate well to women. Although all these traits are not enough to justify their behaviors, they do indicate why they all three adopt self-centered attitudes, and, like Dave Hughes in *The Scold's Bridle*, they have no remorse or guilt over their predatory actions, especially against women.

In addition to the brutal rape, broken fingers, and murder of Kate and the triad of basically psychotic suspects, *The Breaker* also provides another significant look at victimization and its aftermath in the character of Maggie Jenner, who is introduced early in the novel when the body is found on the shoreline. Maggie comes from a rich family, and PC Nick Ingram has secretly been in love with her for years, although he has not spoken to her much since her ill-fated marriage. She had married an "outsider" who was a con man interested only in the family money, which he promptly made off with. After this experience, Maggie has become a woman for whom "isolation and its attendant solitude was becoming an obsession" (13), and "she was all too aware that her distrust of men had now reached pathological proportions" (19). Maggie's victimization has damaged her self-image, thrown her into financial straits, and made her resentful of others who blame her as much as she blames herself. She turns her anger on those around her, which makes it difficult for Nick Ingram to pursue his romantic interest. That the novel details the romantic subplot is perhaps another nod to Sayers' *Have His Carcass,* but more to the point, it demonstrates that the circle of victimizer and victimized rolls on as relentlessly as the breakers roll onto the shore.

Perhaps the most symbolic of the myriad ways human beings participate in a seemingly endless cycle of victim and victimizer and grow up lacking compassion emerges in the novel in the form of the youngest character, Hannah Sumner. In retrospect, the reader recognizes that it was Hannah whom the murderer was describing in a second page prior to the Preface. Three hours after the murderer had raped Hannah's mother and dumped her into the ocean, he thinks of the child: "He had no feelings for her ... but he couldn't bring himself to touch her.... He could break her neck as easily as a chicken's but he fancied he saw an ancient wisdom in her concentrated gaze, and the idea frightened him. Did she know what he had done?" (unnumbered page). He abandons Hannah ashore in the grey dawn at the edge of the town of Poole.

When Hannah is found, a doctor's assessment is that she is psychologically underdeveloped for her apparent age of two or three, is overly passive, shows characteristics of mild autism, is unwilling or unable to use words, is uninterested in other children, and has a strong fear of men. The woman doctor who writes the report speculates that the child has been "taught dependence, which, while leaving her ignorant of her own capabilities, has encouraged her to be consciously manipulative" (40). Hannah has been abused physically with drugs and abused psychologically, even "trained," by both her father and her mother to be socially retarded. William Sumner accepts no responsibility for her upbringing, and he blames any "problem" on Hannah's mother. Although Hannah's case may be extreme, the novel suggests that she is not "unusual" at all: being victimized and learning to victimize can start very early. It is all too common: the "wounded world" applies to all ages.

The cycle of victimization is common among adults, although they may have learned to appear "normal." Detective Inspector John Galbraith perhaps puts it best when he is thinking about the murderer. He thinks to himself, "Sociopaths could be as charming and unthreatening as the rest of humanity, and it was always a potential victim who thought otherwise" (92).

Minette Walters is rare among most popular contemporary detective fiction writers in that her novels are all stand-alones rather than part of a series, and this writing style in itself may be a way of indicating the pervasiveness of the theme of everyone as a victim. In her novels she does not create a central detective, whether an amateur, a private investigator, or a law enforcement officer, much less have such a "hero" who continues throughout a series. In fact, the police play very minor roles. Walters is, instead, a master of the psychological thriller, each novel in its own microcosmic dysfunctional modern world. The emphasis in her novels is not on who solves the crime or even how it is solved. Nor is the emphasis on whodunit. The murderer is often a weaker or less discussed character. Indeed, one reason readers can seldom identify the murderer early in the book perhaps relates to Walters' claim that she never knows who committed the crime until she finishes the novel: "If I knew which one was guilty ... if I don't know then I still explore them [the characters] in depth. This joy, of going inside their heads, I'd be bored stiff if I knew what was going to happen" (Lawley). The emphasis in Walters' novels is precisely this "going inside their heads" of an extraordinarily inventive, complex, and unique cast of characters in each novel, with particular focus on the victim. What these characters reveal, over and over, is their participation in an intricate web of victimization. They have been victims themselves; if still alive, they victimize others. It is a world of dark rooms, where the presence of evil is a given, where any goodness is limited and temporary. It is the modern "riskscape" in which we all live.

Works Cited

Brownmiller, Susan. *Against Our Will: Men, Women, and Rape*. New York: Simon and Schuster, 1975.

Irons, Glenwood, ed. *Feminism in Women's Detective Fiction*. Toronto: University of Toronto Press, 1995.
James, Dean. "Interview with Minette Walters." *Deadly Women*. Eds. Jan Grape, Dean James, and Ellen Nehr. New York: Carroll & Graf Publishers, Inc., 1998, pp. 195–198.
Knight, Stephen. *Crime Fiction 1800–2000: Detection, Death, Diversity*. New York: Palgrave Macmillan, 2004.
Lawley, Sue. "Interview with Minette Walters." Desert Island Discs, BBC Radio 4. June 30, 2002.
Maida, Patricia D. and Nicholas B. Spornick. "The Puzzle Game." *Murder She Wrote: A Study of Agatha Christie's Detective Fiction*. Bowling Green, Ohio: Bowling Green State University Press, 1982, pp. 68–94.
Meier, Robert F. and Terance D. Miethe. "Understanding Theories of Victimization." *Crime and Justice* 17 (1993): 459–499.
Seltzer, Mark. *True Crime: Observations on Violence and Modernity*. New York: Routledge, 2007.
Van Dine, S. S. "Twenty Rules for Writing Detective Stories." *The Art of the Mystery Story*. Ed. Howard Haycraft. New York: Carroll & Graf Publishers, Inc., 1983, pp. 189–193.
Walters, Minette. *The Breaker*. New York: Jove Books, 2000.
_____. *The Dark Room*. New York: Jove Books, 1997.
_____. *The Scold's Bridle*. New York: St. Martin's Minotaur, 1995.

British Social Issues

Donna Waller Harper

The period after World War I marked a time of disillusionment as evidenced by the rise of modernism as a literary style that focuses on issues of alienation and isolation. Popular detective fiction in the 1930s and 1940s evolved from the logical, deductive reasoning of Sherlock Holmes novels and the cozy, deductive reasoning of Miss Marple to a unique American style. The American writers generated a significant change in the genre of the mystery novel and gave rise to the hard-boiled detective novel. In this genre shift, the setting becomes as important as the characters; this concept is exemplified in Raymond Chandler's description of the hard-boiled novel as taking place in the mean streets of an urban setting, where justice is not a clear dichotomy of black and white. Even though Chandler's Philip Marlowe continues to play chess with black and white pieces as he mulls the aspects of the crime he investigates, he recognizes that the complexities of chess are better indicators of the situations of the crime than the mere color symbolism of the chess pieces. Justice is not black and white like the chess pieces, but gray; furthermore, sometimes justice never prevails. The hard-boiled detective accepts this new development in solving crimes, and yet tries desperately to seek a just outcome in spite of the odds against it.

In the hard-boiled style, times are certainly different from those mysteries of Sir Arthur Conan Doyle and Dame Agatha Christie, in which the murder most assuredly occurs outside the pages of the novel so the reader never has to come to terms with the bloodshed. But hard-boiled writers know that bloodshed is all too prominent, especially in the more crowded setting of cities as opposed to cozy villages or mere sections of a city. They also recognize that happenings in the streets are not bland but are indeed more brutal, more demanding, and certainly less predictable. Hence the 1970s advent of the female hard-boiled detective revealed writers who recognized that not only has the world changed — the streets are even meaner — but also that the female detective also must be equally changed. She cannot be the Miss Marple who sits quietly knitting, observing the world around her, until the solution to the crime presents itself. Like her male counterpart, she has to be in the middle of the action. She has to be able to use her wits as well as her weapon; she has to be willing to make adjustments and accept a different world from that of her mother.

Writers who came after World War II had to make choices as to whether to accept the Christie cozy style or accept the mean streets of the hard-boiled writer. Some writers did indeed choose the cozy style and developed housewives, nurses, or teachers who happen on murder scenes and become involved — even helping with the solution; however, more and more writers, including women authors, chose to have private detectives in the same vein as Philip Marlowe and Sam Spade, or as members of the police force, or even as coroners who not only view the horrors of crime inflicted on the body but also use their skills to help solve the murders.

During that time period from the conclusion of World War I to the beginning of World War II — only twenty years — differences occurred in more than the genre of mystery fiction. Countries like Great Britain, deeply involved in having the wars fought on their home turf as well as in facing the economic impediment of two costly wars in such a short time, faced a series of economic and social adjustments, especially after the Second World War. In addition to the loss of manpower and money in fighting the war, Great Britain faced the loss of its empire after 1945. The mid-twentieth century saw the country facing the need for tremendous adjustments to its social structure. Immediately after World War II, Clement Atlee, a Labour Prime Minister, transformed Great Britain into a welfare state. Even though Conservatives like Winston Churchill, Anthony Eden, and Harold Macmillan eventually controlled power, they did little to adjust the health and social security programs initiated by the Labour Party. The

Conservatives favored private rather than public development of housing as well as the need to introduce some fees into the national health insurance program. Eventually, even Labour wanted to cut some public expenditures and attempted to further industrial expansion so as to increase exports in order to pay for her needed imports. The advent of Margaret Thatcher forced industry and labor to find ways to effect greater efficiency. By the time of her rise to power, poverty and unemployment had become widespread as a result of an influx of immigrants from former British colonies. All these developments added to new problems for Britain to face and address.

These myriad problems become the backdrop for many of Minette Walters' crime novels. Although her style is not exclusively hard-boiled, she recognizes the changes in society and the need to acknowledge and characterize those changes in her writings. She uses a unique style of traditional storytelling interspersed with letters, newspaper articles, interviews, and psychiatric and medical reports to showcase not only riveting stories of mystery and suspense, but also to reveal the social ills inherent in her country. Her novels reflect the multitude of issues facing an industrially developed First-World nation like Great Britain. She writes about the social service system, the medical — both physical and mental — system, homelessness, race, and crime. Topics in her novels reveal the layered social concerns that citizens of the United Kingdom face. In an interview on her website, she acknowledges, "All my books are political or sociological" ("Q and A"). The complexity of these challenges serves to reveal just how mean the streets have become and how the individual deals with the many problems that he encounters. Walters' revelations give the reader a sense of the majesty, complexity, and burden faced by both the British people and their government.

Sitting in Florence in 2000, I listened to a British citizen complain about the drain on the financial resources of his government by immigrants, many from former British colonies. Walters' novels address these same issues. Certainly, diversity has become a major concern in the 20th and 21st centuries. Citizens are now forced to interact with people whose skin color is different from theirs and whose theological, ethical, and moral systems are not Judeo-Christian. Beyond mere skin tone and theological relationships, the immigrants are also people whose customs and practices are different from those of the United Kingdom — although not necessarily different from the countries that Britain owned during the height of its empire in the latter 19th century and into the mid–20th century. By 2001, statistics by the British government acknowledged 4 percent of the UK population being Indian, Pakistani, and Bangladeshi, while 2 percent is black Caribbean or black African.

This forced interaction of people with those different from themselves is depicted in several of Minette Walters' novels. Again in an interview on her website, she acknowledges that all her novels deal with "different kinds of prejudice" ("Race"). Certainly, the inhabitants of the housing development Bassindale Row in *Acid Row* seem to have a propensity to distrust and hate blacks; yet Jimmy, the released criminal and father of Melanie Patterson's unborn child, is depicted against type and becomes a hero as he leads members of the community to freedom. Walters admits that her characterization of Jimmy is meant to portray him heroically as a balance to minorities in other novels (notably Annie Butts, the black Caribbean in *The Shape of Snakes*) ("Q and A"). Jimmy's girlfriend faces the crowd as it transforms into a mob seeking to do whatever damage possible, reminding them that they know her, know her reputation, and know her brother and mother. She asks whether, since they hate blacks, they will hate her child, who is the product of her relationship with a black man. Interestingly enough, Walters develops Jimmy as a hero — granted, a hero who is pressed into the status and who is initially uninterested in helping anyone but himself, his girlfriend, and his unwanted child. Jimmy reluctantly accepts his fate as does his child's mother, who fights to save the baby she carries and as well as to save the relationship with the man she loves.

In *The Shape of Snakes,* Walters also illuminates the issue of racism by drawing upon the true story of Stephen Lawrence, a black teenager who was beaten to death in London in 1993. While there was no justice in the real world of the Lawrence death, Walters can bring about a just outcome in her novel through her main character, the determined Mrs. Ranelagh. In portraying racial problems in this novel, however, Walters develops a case that is even less clear than the real-life incident of Lawrence's death, and she adds multiple layers of complexity by afflicting her black female victim, Mad Annie, with Tourette's syndrome and alcoholism. Because

Annie has more money and valuable possessions than most of her neighbors, and because she chastises the women for their promiscuity and the men for their infidelity, she is anathema to the neighborhood — with race being the deciding factor in their ongoing, often violent, conflict. She is banned from the local pub solely because of her skin color, and she is cruelly harassed by her neighbors; as a result, Annie is totally isolated from human interaction and must rely on her many cats for company and comfort. She and her neighbors are caught up in a vicious circle that continues to escalate until her death; the more aggressive and intense their harassment, the more objectionable — to the neighbors — her behavior becomes. While the people of the housing community are able to tolerate the brutality of the some of the neighbors and the promiscuity of other residents, they simply cannot tolerate a Caribbean black woman forcing them to face themselves.

In writing about race, Walters is able to demonstrate that difficulty dealing with the issue is not unique to those of British descent. She also develops situations in which members of the minority themselves face difficulties with their racial status in a country whose composite is more decidedly different from theirs. In *Disordered Minds,* Jonathan Hughes may be a brilliant writer, but he is unable to develop or sustain his true personality in part because he is unable to accept who is really is. He passes himself off as Iranian, he dresses as if he is more financially secure than he really is, and he affects a strong British accent. His race makes him self-conscious about slights, whether verbal or physical. When Hughes first goes to meet George (short for Georgina) Gardener, he encounters Roy — who is not only the owner of the Crown and Feathers but also later a suspect in the case at hand — as well as Roy's customer, Jim. The meeting erupts in finger poking and Roy calling Jonathan a "wog," a slur that to Jonathan is a "punch to the midriff" (77). Roy's apology leads to an interesting interaction when Roy admits that, seeing Jonathan gripping Jim's hand, he thought "he's dressed up like a dog's dinner and he talks like Laurence bloody Olivier" (87). Jonathan apologizes for the suit, saying he is wearing it in deference to meeting George Gardener; but then he verbally assaults Roy by alleging that he would dress differently had the pub been called the Pig and Wallow. When Roy admits that a pub's name frequently has nothing to do with the class of the place, Jonathan responds, "Being black and foreign does make the vagaries of English naming traditions difficult to understand" (88). Jonathan proceeds to assert that he is British, having been born in the United Kingdom and holding a United Kingdom passport; but he does shade the truth of his background by claiming that his father is Iranian and his mother North African.

Additional comments during the initial meeting in the pub have Jonathan citing the Celtic background of one of the patrons and alluding to the man's Welsh heritage. When the man responds angrily that he is not Welsh, Jonathan seems genuinely surprised that the man has an issue with being Welsh rather than the Celtic that he so readily embraces. The irony is not lost on the reader for long, as more of the interaction with Andrew, George Gardener, and Jonathan reveals his own discomfort with the true nature of his heritage. Although much of the novel centers on revealing the innocence of the convicted killer Howard Stamp, whom George feels may have been erroneously convicted of killing his grandmother, a subplot features Jonathan's own epiphany about himself and his ability ultimately to accept who and what he is. The final statement in the novel reveals his coming to terms with his heritage when he jokingly tells Wyatt that George is his mother who "had a one-night stand with a Jamaican road sweeper thirty-five years ago and she's been regretting it ever since" (*Disordered Minds* 533). Jonathan's ability to tease George with something akin to the truth of his own heritage shows the effect that the investigation has on him, not only in solving the death of Grace Jeffries, but also in finally accepting and being comfortable with who he is as an academic and as a person.

Walters' novels reflect the British struggle with racism inside its empire. Many citizens who have problems with the immigration of so many people from the various colonies may respond as the mob does in *Acid Row* or as the citizens do in *The Shape of Snakes,* but Walters is able to reveal the complex issues of race. Not only do the citizens resist the presence of people from backgrounds different from theirs, but the people they resist occasionally have their own challenges with trying to assimilate, as does Jonathan Hughes in *Disordered Minds.* Dealing with people who are different is a difficult task; Walters' novels show just how complex and how varied these interactions are.

People of different ethnicities are not the only ones who present a challenge for the population as a whole. Another problem that reflects society's difficulty in adapting to people who are different is homelessness, which has become a major social issue in many countries since the mid–20th century. The British government in its official documents recognized as early as the 1960s and 1970s the need to open homeless shelters. In 1977 the government initiated a Homeless Persons Act, which provided for those who were unintentionally homeless and whose needs were priority (although priority is not defined) ("Homeless").

Social programs, coupled with religious agencies, have tried to direct people to examine whether their beliefs are tolerant of a member of the human family who has fallen on hard times or whether they hold the person accountable for his own situation, and thus absolve themselves from the need to do anything. The attitude toward and the treatment of homelessness are most effectively revealed in *The Echo,* in which Billy Blake dies by starving himself in Amanda Powell's garage. Questions arise as to why Blake would seek to go to such a place, hide himself, and starve while he is within mere feet of a freezer full of food. The journalist Tom Deacon, a central character of the novel, covers the story; his investigation illuminates society's desire to relegate the homeless to non-persons, to pretend they do not exist, to blame them for any trouble. Deacon befriends a streetwise young man, Terry Dalton, who possesses an uncanny ability to recognize people's problems and whose insight into human nature helps explain some of the issues surrounding the final days of Billy Blake. With Terry's help, Deacon sees why Terry himself prefers to remain out of foster care and social services, and he sees firsthand how the police brutalize the homeless. He also recognizes through Terry the subculture that the homeless develop on their own. During one incident when the police roust the homeless after a fight between two of the men turns ugly, Terry reminds Deacon, "We have rights, Tom, same as everyone else" (118).

The development of Billy Blake's story shows the depth of psychological issues occasionally facing those who are cast into, or who revert to, a life of homelessness. Billy's life develops from situations that are not that foreign to many others not in his circumstances. He had instigated a crime in order to help a friend and romantic acquaintance; his involvement in this act has forced him to seek repentance, while his self-loathing causes him to subject himself to brutal punishment. This complex need to atone for past sins because he sees himself as an unworthy human is equally manifested in his humanity, which allows him to take the punishment for a crime Terry committed. In accepting jail time in Terry's behalf, Billy Blake punishes himself, but he also shows his greater love for his fellow man by keeping Terry out of the criminal justice system.

As Deacon's involvement in determining Billy Blake's identity and the cause of his suicide continues, he learns that few of the homeless use their real names. Despite never being told, readers can assume from the nature of the story that Terry never uses or gives his true identity. Billy Blake's name is an attempt to use the themes and religious issues associated with the works of the great English poet, William Blake. The choice of Billy Blake as his pseudonym reveals Peter Fenton's (Billy's real name) obsession with religion and repentance. As Billy Blake, he draws street portraits of the Holy Family and imitates the drawings of Da Vinci. Blake's talent is one he probably had or developed long before becoming homeless. Terry's experiences in living among the homeless have honed his instincts for self-preservation, as well as his ability to read people and intuit their inner thoughts and desires. These skills are best exemplified when he sets up Barry Grover, playing on Grover's homosexuality to affect a possible blackmail scheme. Although Deacon thwarts the plan, readers realize that Terry has learned more than any regular schooling would teach. His knowledge of human nature and street culture probably helped him manipulate Grover's insecurity about his sexual orientation. Clearly, Terry has survival instincts, as well as a pathological charm, that allow him to turn situations to his own best interests and advantage. His homeless status has compelled him to behave in this manner.

In *The Echo,* Walters is able to portray the many different reasons people choose or are forced into homelessness. Significantly, she creates characters that are charming and personable, but not necessarily socially upright. At the conclusion of the novel, Deacon has a genuine affection for Terry and chooses to keep him at his flat through the holidays. Yet Walters' narration advises the reader that Terry's acceptance of these conditions is not permanent; Terry is even mildly reluctant to be bound by any specific changes to his life. In part he likes the freedom of the street, but he also enjoys and accepts the possibility of the occasional foray into the comfort and luxury available in civilized living. He does not, however, necessarily want to embrace that lifestyle permanently.

Another different type of homeless community, the travelers in *Fox Evil* are the equivalent of gypsies. They travel in caravans, attaching themselves to one group or another as long as they choose. Yet they have a more acceptable social status since the government actually has a Traveler Liaison officer who seeks to enforce the regulations imposed on travelers. This officer ascertains that there is disposal waste, checks on the animals and their care as well as the general health and safety of the travelers, and ensures that travelers do not reoccupy the same land within three months. Because travelers use the technique of squatters' rights to travel by van and mobile home, they are then not bound by certain restrictions of the government, and never remain in one place long enough to come under the scrutiny of government officials. *Fox Evil* shows the efforts to circumvent the government agencies and laws by taking advantage of the Family Provision Legislation of 1938 and the Lockean property traditions. In Shenstead, the principal setting of *Fox Evil,* members of the landed gentry or new landed gentry community have failed to register certain parts of the land, and therefore have left it open for travelers to squat and claim the land. If this tactic were successful, they would cease to be homeless and instead would become part of the local community. Since none of the local residents has established a legal claim to the land on which the travelers reside, they threaten the nouveau riche community as well as the titled nobility — who seem removed from some of the issues not only because of their wealth but also because of personal trauma — with the prospect of their becoming neighbors. The established community definitely does not want to incorporate travelers into their social class.

Walters' research on the issues relating to travelers illuminates a lifestyle many associate with traveling gypsies of the Middle Ages, but she shows the various benefits and drawbacks of this unique lifestyle. Historically, gypsies' "refusal to settle or assimilate with the local population enables them to retain a separate identity. But it also provokes hostility and persecution" ("History"). The travelers, like the earlier gypsies and the present-day homeless, have different reasons for choosing to remain on the fringes of society. Their leader, Fox Evil, is unique in that he is a truly corrupt individual who manipulates the people around him while he is being simultaneously used by members of the landed nouveau riche who want more for themselves or want to prevent others from encroaching on their status. Like Terry in *The Echo,* the children in *Fox Evil* want to avoid social services and fear being taken from a lifestyle they know, even if that lifestyle has its own drawbacks. While the novel features a form of homelessness, the unusual nature of the travelers makes it difficult for the reader to care about them; their being gullible enough to be manipulated by Fox Evil makes sympathy for them a difficult task. Some of the social problems emphasized in *Fox Evil* are similar to those addressed in *The Shape of Snakes* and *The Echo.* While racism does not pervade *Fox Evil,* prejudice toward a subclass in society certainly is a major theme, just as it is in the other two novels.

Another important social structure that Walters features in her work is the British system of social services; in both *The Echo* and *Fox Evil,* an agency intended to be a support system for children in need of care instead becomes a threat to be avoided at all costs. The role and view of social services, in particular, is an important element in *Fox Evil,* in which despite his abusive treatment by Fox Evil, Wolfie, his son, would rather endure his abuse than submit to the treatment he fears at the hands of social services. The travelers have so maligned the social services system that the children quake at the thought that they might be subjected to their "care." School, however, is not one of the institutions the children fear; after all, one promise of Fox Evil is that the travelers will be able to secure schooling for their children if they are able to claim the land. Although the social services agency is not a direct character in the novel or a major part of the plot, the threat of social services here carries the same negative connotation that it carries in *The Echo.*

Also significant in this novel is the concept of legalities and how they can be used and abused by people who know the law. Those who believe that laws are made to instill and ensure justice may be surprised reading Walters' account of how Fox Evil manipulates the law to facilitate gaining access to the land. He is well read and recognizes the concept of property from Locke's viewpoint. He guarantees the other travelers that the land will become theirs and that they need never worry about the people who are their neighbors. In dealing with the concept of property ownership, Walters contrasts the different classes that exist in the community:

the nobility who inherit both land and honorary title; the nouveau riche like the Bartletts, who seek to move up the social ladder; and those who are not titled nobility but whose money goes back more than the few years than the nouveau riche have had theirs. The titled nobility and the nouveau riche participate in actual fox hunts, while ironically Fox Evil in essence hunts down their way of life and seeks to destroy it much as the hunters seek to destroy the fox. Fox Evil plans not only to use the issue of Lockean property rights but the 1965 Commissions Registration Act to secure the land for the travelers. Because the World Wars have thinned the ranks of the aristocracy and therefore upset the stability of the community, Fox Evil's plan is quite plausible and clever. Before the wars the landed nobility would have been more able to protect both their land and their neighborhoods; but the war has diminished those who could indeed hold onto their land along with their names and titles.

In addition to dealing with the issue of land inheritance and community change, *Fox Evil* also reflects a shift in attitudes about other British traditions. At one time the concept of the fox hunt was accepted as a right of those of the landed nobility. A subplot of *Fox Evil* centers on those who protest the fox hunt and thus distract the police while the travelers set up their organization in the neighborhood. The idea of animal rights and the barbaric nature of fox hunting are a minor theme in this novel that also connects it to *The Shape of Snakes* and the cruelty to cats depicted therein. Even though the nouveau riche are able to enjoy the luxury of owning horses and participating in the hunts, some of the public lump them into the same category as the wealthy who mistreat animals and violate their safety in much the same way they ride roughshod over the rights of the lesser people of society.

The problems of the lesser people in society are also shown in both *The Shape of Snakes* and *Acid Row* to be exacerbated by their housing situation. The changes in the types of council-owned housing built in the 1950s, 1960s, and 1970s were enormously detrimental to the lifestyles of those forced to live there. As *The Shape of Snakes* illustrates, large cities like London had streets like Graham Road where some of the houses were privately owned and others were rented at a pittance by low-income families. Although these council houses were often easy to identify, since their front doors were all painted a certain color, the actual houses were often quite pleasant, semi-detached and rather modern, or perhaps terraced with a small garden. They were a far cry from the "sink estate" described in all its horror in *Acid Row*. In an interview, Walters asserted that the real villain is in Bassindale: "We're all so *damned* [her italics] complacent, and the idea of shoving everyone onto a sink estate so we can all look the other way is crazy" (Thomson). As Walters says, the Bassindale-type estate was created with the best intentions; but instead of creating a village-like situation, the high-rise blocks ended up being lonely prisons. Walters describes the situation with irony: "Bassindale Farm had been put to the axe and replaced with concrete. It should have been idyllic. A worthy project in the postwar push for equality and opportunity" (*Acid Row* 8). Again, the war is a pivotal point for change, as explanations reveal that after the end of the war the "postwar baby boom" led to a need for houses. That these were built fast meant poor workmanship and design (8). Later these estates were only minimally maintained and the construction problems led to a general decay not only in the apartments but in the health of the families forced to live there through economic necessity (8). The novel revolves around the interaction of people placed together in a volatile situation as well as in shoddy, crowded housing in the council estate that provides virtually no way for the police to secure the neighborhood once the riot starts; the place is like a maze.

Complicating the situation involving the building construction of the neighborhood and the mixture of people present are the issues of health care for the lower socio-economic class of residents. While Dr. Sophie Morrison is a capable and caring medical provider, one of the other workers, Fay Baldwin, has little training and no empathy for the people she should assist. Thanks to Baldwin, gossip becomes a major aspect of social interaction and a major impetus to the violence in this novel. Vicious gossip, matched with the proximity of the homes and the incompetence and pettiness of the health workers, makes the novel vibrate with tension. Once Baldwin is chastised for her treatment of Melanie, her pettiness and desire for revenge lead to her inadvertently revealing the information that the community houses a pedophile. Baldwin's characterization reflects that "she [Fay] should have been working in the days when illegitimacy ... was frowned on.... That way her status as a virtuous woman would have counted for something" (7). Baldwin's sense of superiority makes it difficult for her to serve the people whom she so readily despises, and this disapproval makes her a less than empathetic and caring health professional. Changing times have made her a dinosaur: "Lecturing, scolding, and training the unwashed masses were probably what health visiting had been about when she started" (7).

Despite the health conditions and the poorly constructed housing, the people have a sense of community in this microcosm of society. Melanie and her mother make every effort to organize a protest about the placement of a pedophile in their neighborhood. Although their intentions are honest and well meaning — they want the people of the community to be informed and thus able to protect themselves — they quickly learn the danger of protests when the event spirals totally out of their control. While Melanie, with her mother, seeks to initiate the protest, she leaves her children unattended in the home that borders that of Zelowski, the pedophile. Once the mob takes on a life of its own, she struggles to return to them and eventually finds herself facing the very mob that her protest helped develop. She desperately needs to stop the firebombing of the Zelowski home in order to protect her own children, whose home would also be in peril.

In *Acid Row* blame does not rest with the police for the problems that arise in the neighborhood, as the action reveals they had little choice in relocating the pedophile to Bassindale Row, and they genuinely seem to want to assist in bringing an end to the protest. The culpability here falls to the planners of the housing community and to the government for their thoughtlessness in the design that is able to block off police access and thus make the inhabitants prisoners in their day-to-day lives, and even more so during events characterized by mob mentality. In general, the social services of police and health care seem to have the better interests of the people at heart in all their actions. Their agents appear selfless and genuinely concerned, and they have at heart the desire to protect families and the community — they just don't always have the means. Although this novel is bleak in its description of the estate as a cauldron of angry, disenfranchised youth, Walters also wants to show how the love that flourishes within the community is redemptive, and how some positive outcomes can evolve as soon as people make contact with each other

(Thomson). There are indeed forces that can counteract the failures of social institutions and services.

In the world of Minette Walters, gone is the society of landed nobility. Gone is the Britain of vast empire. These losses are replaced with a society in which people must face a life different from any life they knew in the past. Yes, social services are available, but not everyone wants those services because their help can be worse than the hurt they are designed to redress. Additionally, the services are not always able to keep pace with the needs of society, and new conditions arise that force the government and its social services to reassess where and how to spend whatever monies are available. Because modern life is complex and modern problems abound, people often become entrenched in their own concerns and close themselves to the needs of others. Offering keen insights into the British social structure, Minette Walters is aware of its changes as well as its flaws and imperfections. She seeks to establish what exists without attempting to develop any alternatives for what could have or should have been. The curtain is pulled back with all the flaws readily apparent, yet her picture is not exclusively bleak. Her novels reflect that human beings function within whatever aspects of human nature they choose to develop. In *Acid Row,* people may be unhappy with the housing environment, but they care for the community, the people, their families. Granted, some individuals seek to pursue self-serving ends, but many seek only to make a safe home for their families. In *The Shape of Snakes,* the families take advantage of the housing situation to upgrade their own personal existence. In *The Echo* and *Fox Evil,* some hope to exist outside traditional housing and family structures, although Fox Evil himself hopes to pervert the housing laws to his own purposes. While depicting the problems of race, homelessness, and the inadequacies of the social services agencies, Walters presents a balanced characterization of human nature functioning in and around these complex challenges despite it all. Some people fight the system; some work within it; some seek to change it. The people themselves need to assess what they want, need, and hope to change. Despite flaws in social systems and social orders, people are good or bad or most often a combination of these forces. They accept or reject the society in which they live. They can effect change or struggle along with society's inadequacies. Portraying British society with its successes and failures, Minette Walters enables readers to achieve a sense of what the social structure is, where it is weak, where changes need to take place, and what changes have been for the better.

Works Cited

"History of the Movement of Peoples." 22 August 2007. http://www.historyworld.net wrldhis/PlainTextHistories.asp?groupid=1289&HistoryID=ab18.

"Homeless." 22 August 2007. http://www.statistics.gov.uk/STATBASEproduct.asp?vinh=484.

"'Q and A' with Minette." 22 August 2007. http://www.minettewalters.co.ukabout_minette/mw_qa.htm.

"Race." 22 August 2007. http://www.statistics.gov.uk/cci/nugget.asp?id=455.

Thomson, Liz. "Crime and Compassion." *Publishing News* 12 Oct. 2001. 22 August 2007. http://www.minettewalters.co.uk/about_minette/articles/pubnews.htm.

Walters, Minette. *Acid Row*. New York: Putnam, 2002.

_____. *Disordered Minds*. New York: Berkley, 2004.

_____. *The Echo*. New York: Putnam, 1997.

_____. *Fox Evil*. New York: Putnam, 2003.

_____. *The Shape of Snakes*. New York: Putnam, 2001.

The Impenetrable M and the Mysteries of Narration: Narrative in *The Shape of Snakes*

TILDA MARIA FORSELIUS*

> *It's odd. Some people have very dear memories of their early childhood, but I have none at all. I used to think the stories my parents told me were real memories, but I've come to the conclusion now that if something is repeated often enough it acquires a reality.*
>
> —Minette Walters, *The Shape of Snakes* (359).

What is the role of narrative in memory and vice versa? Can retold remembrances ever be separated from the narrator's motives, subjective state, or power position—and if not, what is really the veracity of a narrative? Do readers of the popular crime genre expect reliability in a narrator, or has the postmodernist era deflated such expectations? Questions like these are raised by a popular crime narrative, Minette Walters's *The Shape of Snakes*. The plot of the novel revolves around a black woman's death in 1978 and the inquiry, twenty years later, regarding the cause of

---

"The Impenetrable M and the Mysteries of Narration: Narrative in Minette Walters's The Shape of Snakes*" by Tilda Maria Forselius, University of Gothenburg, first appeared in* Clues: A Journal of Detection, *volume 24, issue 2 (Winter 2006), 47–61. Reprinted with permission of the Helen Dwight Reid Educational Foundation. Published by Heldref Publications, 1319 18th Street NW, Washington, DC 20036-1802. . Copyright © 2006.*

the death. As the amateur investigator simultaneously takes revenge for a number of injustices that befell her at the time of the suspected murder, her motives are somewhat dubious.

By recapitulating the performed inquiry from the protagonist's first-person point of view, problems of memory, justice, and truth are raised. Although such themes may seem quite formulaic, the narrative is not a predictable one. Running parallel to the protagonist's struggle for fairness or revenge, the reading of the narrative gives rise to a struggle with genre conventions. This also has to do with memory, but on another level, namely, pertains to the reader's memory in the form of expectations of how a story like this one is likely to be told and his or her interaction with the narrative on these grounds.

Walters is one of the best-selling British crime fiction writers today. In the course of just over a decade — her first novel, *The Ice House*, was published in 1992 — Walters has written ten crime novels and has repeatedly succeeded on the market with books such as *The Scold's Bridle*, *The Dark Room*, *Disordered Minds*, and *The Shape of Snakes*. Her background as a pseudonymous writer of romance stories may provide a clue to her success with a large audience. It should be noted, however, that her crime novel writing seems to be moving toward a higher degree of narrative complexity.

One of the special features of Walters's authorial style is a technique of interpolating authentic-looking documents, whose narrative relevance the readers themselves must figure out. My own interest in *The Shape of Snakes* started in this way, as I was intrigued by the interpolated letters of the narrative. It is well known that the epistolary novel and the use of interpolated letters in literary narratives thrived in the eighteenth and nineteenth centuries, but, since then, these forms have led a more marginal life in the literary field. What, then, does the epistolary form add to a contemporary work of fiction?

In this essay, I aim to describe the narrative technique of the novel and relate it to the themes of memory, justice, and revenge carried by the protagonist's discourse. By referring to historically established interpretations of epistolary or semi-epistolary narratives, my purpose is to show that the letters in *The Shape of Snakes* problematize the sincerity of the writers' intentions. In the plot, this trait opposes the first-person narrator-protagonist's claims of presenting a course of action that leads to a solution of a crime case. The construction of the protagonist also raises questions, as it is gradually revealed that she embodies both the rational control of the hard-boiled detective and the elusiveness of a gothic character. Together, these aspects contest the reader's confidence in what is told, challenge the authoritative voice of the first-person narrator, and portray her narration as a mystery of its own.

Feminist Genre Readings with Certain Obstacles

As a contemporary writer working in a popular genre, Walters has not yet attracted much interest from scholars. In two journal articles, Fletcher and Whip thematically discuss four of her novels written before *The Shape of Snakes* in relation to the contemporary (sub)genre of feminist detective fiction or feminist crime fiction. Drawing on Klein and others, Fletcher and Whip describe how the view of crime in feminist crime fiction challenges the conservatism of the traditional detective genre. For example, violence against women and children often is comprehended and described as built into the societal structure, rather than seen as problems that can be solved within the context of law. In this way, the problems or crimes are not solved, at least not in full, within the narratives.

In the novels discussed (*The Ice House*, *The Sculptress*, *The Scold's Bridle*, and *The Dark Room*), Fletcher and Whip recognize this characteristic of the genre, as well as distinctive "feminist themes" such as incest, rape, wife abuse, and neglected children. Other patterns that Walters follows or relates to in the novels are that the obligatory murders are only loosely connected to the major themes explored and that the detectives are female amateur sleuths, whose achievements rely on intuition as well as reason. However, Fletcher and Whip also find conservatism insofar as the solutions offered are "specific rather than systematic" ("Feminist" 110) and argue that there is a "compulsive heterosexuality" to be found in the embedded values ("Exploring" 31).

Also from a feminist, albeit conceptually different, position, LeBihan discusses narrative in *The Ice House*. She uses appropriations of the critical categories identification, incorporation, and the grotesque to examine how the novel produces "a melancholic reading position that a feminist critic might want to resist" (288). This position can be attributed to the fact that the readers of the novel "find themselves thwarted in their attempts to forge the usual character identifications [...] through an introjection of the role of the detective, or even through an acceptance of the corpse" (294). The readers are hence both unable to come "face-to-face with death" and to terms with the secret in the heart of the novel, LeBihan argues (294).

In addition to these critical remarks, Molander Danielsson briefly mentions Walters in her thesis on the diversity of contemporary crime fiction. In view of the fact that Walters's novels do not display "a particular prosperity for change," which Molander Danielsson claims is characteristic of novels with "feminist interests," she concludes that Walters's "agenda is more generally postmodern than feminist" (110), which leaves these novels outside the scope of her study.

It seems, then, that these scholars, although approaching Walters's writing from different viewpoints, make similar observations: The novels display the signs of a feminist-oriented narrative, but this interpretation is weakened in the course of the reading. This notion also is crucial in my reading, as the features mentioned above — the feminist themes, the structural view on crime, the presence of value conservatism, and especially the obscurity of the narrative — also characterize *The Shape of Snakes*. However, my ambition is to consider whether the reading problems involved could be regarded as something else than a drawback. It appears to me that multiple clues pointing to older novelistic traditions are displayed in the narrative and that these may lead to interesting interpretations.

I wish to make a few observations on my use of terms such as feminist detective fiction and feminist crime fiction. Although Fletcher and Whip use these concepts as synonymous descriptive terms for the genre, I exclusively use the label feminist crime fiction, which seems broader, including narratives with female detectives as well as other characters as protagonists. When referring to Walton and Jones, I use their term, feminist hard-boiled detective fiction. For my purposes, however, feminist hard-boiled detective fiction also is part of the more general category of feminist crime fiction.

The Plot

I start my investigation into the narrative with a description of the plot and the narrative structure. It is divided into three temporally organized parts: the first about events in 1978, followed by the main section "Twenty Years Later," and finally a short epilogue. In the opening section, we are told how M or Mrs. Ranelagh found Ann Butts or "mad Annie" dead in the street in a London suburb and about her very strong reaction, when the mentally handicapped, black woman's death was dismissed by the local police as a self-induced traffic accident caused by alcohol consumption. M's conviction is that the accident was arranged and that there is some kind of racist motive behind it. When M tries to persuade people around her, among them her husband, Sam, and tell them her observations, she is harassed and accused of mental instability. These experiences lead to the breakdown of her everyday life, her marriage, and her professional life as a teacher.

In the second part of the novel, M tells the story of what happens when she, after twenty years abroad, returns to England with her family and continues to work on the case of Ann Butts. Looking up her former neighbors, she attempts to have them revise their witness statements and other narratives about what happened on Graham Road that night in 1978. On this mission in her old neighborhood, M finds a microcosm of Britain that has declined morally through greed, estate speculation, and a police force that is corrupt and incompetent. It is a society imbued with misogynist and racist offenses that the law in practice does not care about.

Although M's cause initially seems to be based on compassion for the dead woman, the reader soon becomes aware of the fact that there is something peculiar about her commitment. This is indicated by some of the interpolated letters and documents, which state that M has been hospitalized for mental health problems, has had problems with motherhood, has been diagnosed as manipulative and unforgiving, and has been in psychotherapy for many years. The view of her as mentally unstable, however, is not sanctioned by her own discourse. Instead, M brings up the disappointments of her life in connection with her cause. We are informed that motherhood was forced on her and that she, during the years abroad, had to give up teaching to serve her family. In one dialogue, it is revealed that her life as a wife and mother has been unsatisfactory and that her engagement in the death of Ann Butts pertains to this (80). Even though her social position and ethnicity are entirely different from the dead woman's, M obviously shares with her the exposure to structural subjugation based on gender. Because we also are made aware of the condition that any woman who is not content with her role in society may be regarded as mentally abnormal, we may understand the psychiatric diagnosis as a part of the societal hegemony.

The Narrative Organization

The story is communicated in the voice of M, whose first name remains an initial throughout the narrative. She also is the key subject of the plot, which means that she is a character-bound narrator, mediating between the reader and the other characters and also conveying her own actions, thoughts, morals, and motives. We do not know to whom she is telling her story; as readers, we are invited to share an implied receiver's position. Ostensibly true to the rhetoric of autobiography, all events are told in the past tense as the narrator is looking back on her previous experiences. The basic illusion of this rhetoric is that of a coherent personal memory, capable of righteously estimating and structuring events retrospectively. Scrutinizing such a narrative, however, like all first-person narratives, requires that we distinguish between the first-person narrator who remembers, evaluates, and reconstructs and the subject representations that are presented as the memorized "I"s in the various recapitulated situations. To clarify this situation, I will make a distinction in the following between the narrator/M (telling at the scene of the narrating) and M (retold at the scene of the action) when necessary.

Crucial to my reading are the letters and documents that are interpolated in each chapter, always after M's narration. These personal letters, e-mails, official statements/correspondence, cuttings from newspapers, and pages from photo albums are visually distinct in the novel, being placed on gray pages and looking quite authentic. Some of the personal letters are handwritten, others typed with fonts typical of typewriters or computers, and official documents and letters have letterheads and are signed by hand. They are all addressed or contextualized, which gives the impression that they once had a primary receiver — mainly, but not in all cases, M. Although most of them are dated between autumn 1978 and autumn 1999, the documents are not interpolated in any chronological order. They serve as temporal inversions creating suspense and adding disruptions to the narrator/M's chronologically ordered chain of retold events. How they should be interpreted and related to the retold events is up to the reader, as no direct references are made to them by the narrator/M. The connection is implicitly made about one-third into the novel (115), when M leaves her rucksack on the bed as an invitation to her husband to go through the contents. She informs him that it contains letters and documents that she has collected over a long period of time and that are of relevance to the murder case. The documents represent, as we come to understand, the substantial clues that she has gathered, the indicators that, together with her inquiries, are demanding hermeneutic interpretation. However, because this interpretation is not made clear by the narrator/M, we have to use the letters and documents as our own clues.

The First-Person Narrator Control of the Story

M's change of personality — from powerless witness to tough amateur investigator — is primarily explained in relation to her personal revenge motives and her own disappointments. At the time of the black woman's death, M herself was struck by a number of injustices and humiliations. Among them were rape and harassment, her husband's infidelity, and her mother's lack of understanding. After a dispute with her mother, M formed a self-sufficient strategy that enabled her to transcend this vulnerable state:

> All she'd really achieved was to prove to me how little I cared about anyone's opinion but my own. In an odd way her complete lack of sympathy was more liberating than distressing because it made me realize that control rests with whoever worries least about being seen to exercise it, and with cold deliberation I agreed to mend fences with my husband if only to keep a roof over my head [Walters, *Snakes* 8].

"Control" is a code word for the persona of M in the second part of the novel. The reference to the hard-boiled detective tradition is made explicit when M states that she, over the years, has grown "an impenetrable skin"

(80). Looking back on her former self, she mentions a personality "reconstruction" that is connected to her contemporary cause. "I didn't much like that person," she says about her younger self and explains that she was "too complacent by half [...] I decided to try lean and hungry instead" (334).

A crime investigator with personal problems or an eccentric personality is, of course, not unusual in the crime genre; this is, in fact, a powerful stereotype. The interesting complication here is the manipulative aspect that is gradually revealed and connected to the controlling, story-shaping aspect of M's narration. Although invited to engage in M's cause of action, the reader finds that the narrator/M is withholding information about her intentions and experiences in a confusing way. This is done not only in relation to characters at the scene of the action but also in relation to the reader at the scene of narration. One example is that M's sexual attractions in the past and their relevance for the case are merely hinted at but not explicitly stated. It is indicated in a letter from Libby, a former neighbor, that M had some kind of love affair with a police officer in 1978, and the narrator/M later confirms that there is a complicated attraction that persists to this day and nourishes her fixation on the murder (169, 190). Also, in a final confrontation, Libby brings up this affair and persists that M has cheated on Sam (412). This allegation is crucial, as Sam's infidelity is revealed to be a central part of the mystery. However, questions about the actuality of the sexual relation with the policeman are never answered in the narrative, controlled as it is by the narrator/M, who obviously does not want the reader to know for sure.

Numerous other things that could be expected to be explained are not clarified. For instance, when recounting certain events, the narrator/M may cryptically hint to the reader that she has been lying to or deceiving somebody in the situation without disclosing her reasons for doing so, or otherwise helping the reader understand why (for example, 108, 292). Commenting on her husband's bad memory, she states that this is advantageous for her, as he is easy to manipulate (20). He is naive in personal relationships, "ready to take people at face value," and has "no conception of the sides that exist in most people's natures," including M's (75) — she has managed to keep her engagement in Ann Butts's death concealed for years. Through sparingly offered self-reflections, it also is made clear that

M, in her reconstructive investigation of the murder (at the scene of the events), has played games with people, lied, used personal relationships to further false intentions, and so on. When the reasons for this behavior are not made clear, she also is playing with us, the readers (at the scene of narrating). Gradually, we have to realize that the "seductive" and "perilous" nature of the reader's "sustained intimacy with the [first-person] narrator," as Riggan puts it (34), may be seriously misleading.

The "Identification Reading"

A first-person narrator deceiving readers is not a new trick in crime fiction. Writers such as Charles Dickens, Wilkie Collins, and Agatha Christie have used such a technique. But, as is well known, the mainstream detective genre is based on the concept of a trustworthy investigator interacting with a past that is possible to explore and where truth can retrospectively be made to speak. In the theory of reading, the detective or the investigating protagonist often is described as "an agent of the reader" or a function through which the reader can project an interest piqued by the mystery (see, for example, Alewyn). When the detective is a first-person narrator, which is a signature of the hard-boiled tradition, an often-accredited theory is that he or she serves as "an important functional site of identification for the reader" (Walton and Jones 151). "Identification" is seen as fundamental to reading this kind of narrative: "The detective is our eyes and ears and mouthpiece too; the first-person narrative expects identification" according to Molander Danielsson (44). The rhetoric of autobiography and the "site of identification" are of special significance in the feminist-oriented part of the genre, Walton and Jones claim. The female protagonists are active subjects both in action and narration and this subverts the male objectifying gaze that was omnipresent in traditional hard-boiled detectives. The first-person narratives of the genre may even, they argue, be seen as a kind of role-playing and an empowering education of readers.

However, in line with the scholars referred to earlier (Fletcher and Whip; LeBihan; Molander Danielsson), I find that this kind of reading of *The Shape of Snakes* has to be modified. There is a narrative subversion going on when the author uses first-person narrator conventions typical of the feminist crime genre to influence the reader, which end up gradually destabilizing the constructed confidence or "identification reading," creating instead a distressing enigma in the reader. This divergence from genre conventions is in a way reminiscent of the emergence of feminist interests in hard-boiled detective fiction around 1980. Both cases serve as examples of how writers may use, in the words of Rabinowitz, a genre's "packages of rules that readers apply, as ready-made strategies for reading" (177) and still add new values and narrative interests to them. According to Walton and Jones, after the second wave of feminism in the United States, feminist hard-boiled detective fiction developed as a reaction to demands for "representations of strong women characters" (51). Because it is formula fiction developed from the pattern of controlled, masculine detectives such as Raymond Chandler's Philip Marlowe, there were subsequent narrative inconsistencies, and it has been debated whether the hard-boiled investigator in female shape really can give voice to so-called women's issues, or if the figure is by definition tied to a male hegemonic view on societal order. However, through a perspective of twenty years' development, it can be concluded that the feminist interest to a high degree has transformed this formula into a more soft-boiled approach to crime and crime investigation, including a new foundation of authority. Female "private Is" narrate their stories and attract the reader's interest by an authority based on "relatedness, empathy and care" that they have to conquer within the narratives and that is entirely different from the superior authority based on, for example, the "power to judge, power to command" inherent in male detectives, as argued by Reddy ("Counter-Tradition" 177). In a similar fashion, Klein stresses that women detectives have changed the crime genre toward a different ethic, "the ethic of responsibility" (235).

Influences from the Gothic Tradition

In their historical backdrop, Walton and Jones, as well as Klein, strangely enough, leave out the British gothic tradition, although it obviously is part of the genealogy of the crime genre. However, other scholars do remind us of the accuracy of the relation (for example, Day; Reddy, *Sisters*; Rowland). Initiated by Horace Walpole, Ann Radcliffe, and their contemporaries and further developed during the nineteenth century, the broad and long-lived gothic fantasy brings up the dark and elusive "underworld" of both society and the human mind. Exploring sexual aspects and redefining power relations between men and women and children and parents were some of the major themes from the start, which to a high degree included women's perspectives in what has been known as "the female gothic." The tradition also is renowned for eclectic use of other genre patterns and for narrative difficulties, especially with closure (Punter 19; Day 43–45).

Two decades ago, Day proposed that detective fiction emerged in the late nineteenth century as a "natural response to Gothic fiction" (50). Poe invented the detective, Day claims, to "provide within the world of the story a character who can explain and organize the events into a meaningful pattern"—a narrative with a closure (52). The chaotic, nonrealistic, and nightmarish experiences of the mostly passive gothic heroines and the active but self-destructive gothic heroes were thus given a counterpart in male detectives, who at the level of the story did have the mental strength and physical power to respond actively to events, mediate between the outlaw and law-abiding society, and serve as reestablishers of general order. Shaped as such, they also — as first-person narrators — were given the ability to control the narratives in a way that the gothic heroes and heroines never could, as their subjective voices were trapped in an irrational story/condition.

Looking at *The Shape of Snakes* from a gothic viewpoint is rewarding, as there are frequent references to this tradition. One example is the opening of the novel, where we find Ann Butts dead and M accused of psychiatric disorder when trying to define the case as a murder. In fact, the opening presents two victims, Ann Butts and M, suggesting the corresponding double of the gothic. Even if the setting is realistic, the corpse is a variation of the anomalous "other" (in the shape of the corpse, ghost, villain, and mad and deviant people) that pursues and haunts the heroine (see, for example, Delamotte). On closer inspection, the short overture presents a whole catalogue of classic gothic motifs: the deviant woman (the mentally handicapped Ann Butts) perceived by her neighbors as monstrous and disgusting; the exotic element in her background; drug addiction; the description of a house connected to a mystery; children's cruelty reflecting that of their evil parents; a confusing event leading to the breakdown of normal social routines and relations; and, finally, the heroine's (M's) escalating mental affliction.

Another aspect that further strengthens the association between the novel and the gothic is the many examples of interpolated letters and subjective journals, as well as the use of an unreliable first-person protagonist. In the gothic world, the modern concept of a dualistic split between subject and object, of a possible rational objectivity, is profoundly questioned. The protagonists are constantly deeply drawn into their own description of the problems that they experience. Through the veil of subjectivity, they can only find "a world created by the circle of their own fears and desires" (Day 4) and nothing outside themselves.

M's reflections on the quality of experience point in a circular direction back to the subjective, uncertain perspective. An example is her recounting of the return to the place where she once found the dying woman lying in the gutter:

> I found Graham Road changed beyond recognition.... The houses were smarter than I remembered, the pavements wider, the sunlight brighter and more diffuse. It had lived for so long in my memory as a dark, foreboding place that I found myself wondering what else my mind had poisoned over the years. Or perhaps it wasn't my memory that was at fault? [208–09].

Such gothic rhetoric creates a paradox in the logic of the crime-solving narrative, which, together with the other signs mentioned above, trigger the reader's uncertainty with respect to the narrator's reliability. Although M's intended project is to change a faulty or false collective memory of what happened to Ann Butts, numerous incorporated contemplations on her own memory, as well as on that of others, make one observant of the construction of memory as a narrative and hence the uncertainty of all retrospection, including M's own. In contemporary history studies, this notion is referred to as the formative or present memory and anticipates a change from the modernist ideas of personal, coherent memory and the ideals of a stable subject (Hutton 84). Normalizing a disruptive, unstable subjectivity as well as bringing up a multitude of possible pasts, the notion implicates epistemological problems of a new kind, as it makes concepts of truth elusive and multifaceted and the writing of history potentially deceptive. This predicament that is fundamental in the gothic world also finds empirical affirmation by present-day neurologists. Observations indicate that our memories are stored in the brain like pieces of a jigsaw puzzle. The prerequisite of all recollection is that missing pieces have to be made up to complete the picture, Saxby Pridmore argues. He concludes that with "this jig-saw model it is easy to see how the beliefs of trusted and authority figures, such as therapists, may influence memories" (128). Although appearing to look for so-called objective facts or truths of the past, the questions of the present generally involve and establish interests such as self-confirmation, power changes, reevaluation — and maybe even revenge. When the narrator/M reflects that she does not know if her childhood memories are her own or just stories made up by her parents and concludes that "if something is repeated often enough it acquires a reality" (Walters, *Snakes* 359), this is not only a clue to the collective lies covering the circumstances of Ann Butts's death. It also — as all concepts of authoritative truth may be questioned — reinforces the discomforting view on M's own project and sheds light on the power position of the narrator.

Epistolary Masks

The use of the epistolary form as such emphasizes these questions, as personal letters indeed are visible veils of subjectivity, lacking the illusion of containing objective description. In the epistolary multiple first-person narratives of the 1700s, such as Pierre Choderlos de Laclos's *Les Liaisons dangereuses*, the letter serves as a manner of performing personal intentions and creating intrigue. The letter often was compared to a mask in those days, allowing different roles to be tried out, including the role of the honest and pure heart. Also in classical rhetoric, the letter was seen as a speech act, with time-situated intentions, lacking pretensions of containing the full truth in a longer perspective, but still, of course, aiming to persuade.

Intentions toward the near future characterize the letter narratives in *The Shape of Snakes*, but there are, as always, levels in these intentions that depend on who the narrator is. When the letter writers are contradicting each other or M/the narrator, we have to draw the conclusion that what is presented as truth is relativistic, but who is consciously lying, who is merely improving reality slightly, and who is speaking in all honesty and sincerity? The reader cannot be sure. The narrators may all be potential snakes aiming to betray, just like the title of the novel indicates.

In the perspective of the complete author-narrative, however, the letters — as they turn out to be the property of M — are subordinated narrations. This also is suggested by the temporal difference between the two kinds of first-person narrations. While the narrator/M is telling her story in retrospect in an unknown present, the other first-person narrators (in the letters) are speaking the past in the present tense, and their narratives are displayed in a framework they were never addressing. Their words, lies, and truths are stuck just as they were written in their original historical contexts, but as letter reminiscences, they play a role in a game of information at another time. Only M as the subsequent narrator has the interpretive power over the perspective of the past. Thus, in a conventional reading, we could expect her narration to paint the full picture and help us evaluate the veracity of the subsidiary letter narratives. However, as we have seen, M's narration proves to be bound to antagonistic motives and to a problematic memory in ways that the reader had no reason to expect from the beginning. Thus, the conceptualizations of letter statements as dubious also both color and question her own discourse. Like many of the letter writers in the classic epistolary narratives, she appears to have duped us by using a facade, hiding her sincere self. This also is supported by the secrecy involving her first name. Alternatively, if she is not misleading us intentionally, she may, like a heroine of the gothic tradition, be unwillingly trapped behind a veil that she cannot cast off. In any case, from this reading perspective, the political correctness of her engagement for the black woman is merely a costume in a personal vendetta — or, at least, we suspiciously have to ask if this might be the case. Instead of collaborating with the narrator/M in establishing an illusion of a truthful recapitulation, we are made aware of the "artifices of narrative strategy," which, according to Day (46–47), is the romantic irony of the gothic model.

The Moral

The enigma of M does not, however, prevent her from being a justice seeker. Rather, the diverging aspects of her story compete along the way, so that different interpretations and reading strategies may be aroused. Through her investigation, M does arrive at an explanation of sorts for the crime, and she is able to persuade some of her fellow characters of its accuracy. However, police officials, although they investigate the allegations of robbery of Ann Butts's home, do not acknowledge any evidence of murder (415).

The structural nature of the murder accusation also seems to make charges difficult: "Ann Butts was murdered because a regime of racial hatred and contempt for handicap was allowed to fester unchecked in Graham Road," M states in her correspondence with the police (416). Lacking full success with legal authorities, M still seems content when she considers her revenge on a number of former friends and neighbors whose complacent lives, because of her investigation, have been deeply disturbed.

In the end, she initiates her next move of contacting the media. There is logic in seeing this as a satisfactory solution, grounded in the skepticism toward legal and other social authorities that impregnates the story. The morality of a comprehension of M's triumph as an acceptable answer, then, does not only reject the possibility of a trustworthy societal order and justice but also highlights personal morals in relation to political options. In this respect, M embodies the female knight, the lonely rider who accomplishes the goal of her cause, just like a detective hero from the hard-boiled school.

On the other hand, the haunted and ambiguous side of M's personality simultaneously makes itself seen. When she, within the logic of her understanding of the clues, ultimately does blame the murder on Libby, the very woman that had an affair with M's husband Sam twenty years earlier, the story seems to be a parody of a crime case and also genuinely gothic in the way that there is no real closure to be found, no illusion of a conception of truth to be communicated; instead, the story moves in circles as the projections of a paranoid and haunted mind. When the narrator/M in her last words in the narrative pictures herself "beside a river ... watching the bodies of Annie's enemies float by...," it seems like, in this frame of mind, she will not be satisfied with a single vengeance; it will have to be repeated over and over again (423). The "ethics of responsibility" or the mature authority based on "relatedness, empathy and care," attributes of the sleuth in feminist crime fiction according to Reddy and Klein, cited above, seem very distant.

Although a revenge act may be seen as transgressive, the questions implicitly raised and answered on the value level are, like the paranoid symptoms, indeed circular, as the morals seem to reinforce the same problems with which the narrative was launched. Whereas a large part of the narrator/M's determination initially appears to be built on dissatisfaction with the situation of women in relation to family and society, the outcome demonstrates her ambition to restore the nuclear family and repudiate sexual transgression. This has an obviously gendered and nonfeminist aspect, as the rejection primarily concerns the promiscuity in women that Libby is shown to embody ("her passionate nature could [not] be tamed by motherhood and a career" [403]), and mothers greedy for drugs and sex who neglect their children (such as Maureen [389]), although equivalent errors in men do not cause any final conclusions of that kind. Just like in the hardboiled tradition, including the feminist version of it, disruption is found in the female body. Paradoxically, it follows that thematized societal problems that we originally were to understand as sites of malevolence — misogyny and contempt for the lives of the unprivileged — impregnate not only the environment around M but also her own narrating self.

With this turn of the narrative, it is not surprising that M finally seems to prefer male companions. In the epilogue, she builds a pact of understanding with Sam (who initially cheated, raped, and forced motherhood on her) and Libby's former husband Jock (who has turned out to be a former patron of prostitutes). There is a transformation of personal power very strongly implicated in this ending, which is reminiscent of the older female gothic themes of vice "infecting" the domestic sphere, calling for the heroine's vigilance and restoration (Ellis 218–21). M's means of doing this, however, are quite different from those of the virtuous heroines of the past. It is through her skills at taking control of a narrative chain of events, through her hard-boiled guts to act and obtain revenge — in spite of all the ambiguities observed by the reader — that she (temporarily) repels the evil of infectious bad morals that threatened her family. Hence, the men in her domain have been transformed to a loyal and subordinate state, while women with an undomesticated sexuality still play the role of the "other" and offer a possible threat.

Then again, if these morals are produced by the narrator/M's discourse, how can we believe in them as anything but gothic distortion? Although the melodramatic final letter, written from Ann Butts to M, seems to normalize the anomalous woman to the extent that she — in a sentimental way — appears more human than anyone else, the heroine's mental disorder is not cured. This condition makes her interestingly related to the untamed and monstrous sides of the rejected women such as Libby. The final letter also might make us wonder whether, all along, there was, apart from the revenge and justice-seeking motives, a secret personal guilt-trap behind M's fixation on Ann Butts's death. More than anything else, however, M remains impenetrable and her story distressing, impossible to pin down in a singular genre description or to use for political empowering of the sort described by Walton and Jones. This enigmatic opacity and the narrative's rejection of an "identification reading" may be difficult to accept by some crime fiction readers, as well as its conclusive backlash values, but it does indeed provide a basis for contemplating questions of one's expectation about a narrative and one from the point of view of a female protagonist. The process of rethinking that the reader is obliged to undertake in the course of the reading makes a simple distraction like reading difficult and instead draws attention to narrative conventions as such and to the ongoing negotiations between the text and the reader.

To conclude, in *The Shape of Snakes*, Walters uses a formula from the feminist crime genre but radically bends the conventions by infusing the narrative with traits from the gothic and epistolary traditions, which serve as references to nonmodernist thinking. We find in the narrative the structural view on the crime; the female amateur sleuth; and themes such as family problems, abuse, and racism. There is an inquiry performed and an explanation of the crime presented in a context of social problems, but confidence in legal instances is disclaimed and not reestablished. Both thematically and in the way the story is narrated, the undercurrent from the gothic tradition and the interpolated letters problematize the rhetoric stability of the first-person narrator-protagonist. When the authority of M is implicitly questioned by her own way of narrating and through the context of the interpolated letters and documents, it becomes untenable to use her view as the only lens through which the facts of the murder case are revealed. Instead, M's own psyche comes to the foreground as a mystery, albeit not as a paradigmatic new way of reading. Through this ambiguity of the protagonist, the reader is obliged to reflect on the power aspects of the narrator, as well as on the contradictions and discontinuities of the narrative. Subsequently, we find no sustaining closure, nor is there any reassurance in the moral. As in the classic gothic model, these traits highlight the narrative artifices and the process of interpretation. Instead of coming to terms with the enigma of the narrative in the form of an unambiguous solution, the reader may feel cheated, as genre expectations that have acquired a "natural" reality through repetition and memory are challenged. As this novel was a huge international success, such a challenge may actually be what skilled crime readers expect today.

Works Cited

Alewyn, Richard. "The Origin of the Detective Novel." *The Poetics of Murder: Detective Fiction and Literary Theory*. Ed. Glenn W. Most and William W. Stowe. New York: Harcourt, 1983, pp. 62–78.

Choderlos de Laclos, Pierre. *Les liaisons dangereuses*. Paris, 1782.

Day, William Patrick. *In the Circles of Fear and Desire: A Study of Gothic Fantasy*. Chicago: University of Chicago Press, 1985.

Delamotte, Eugenia. *Perils of the Night: A Feminist Study of Nineteenth-Century Gothic*. New York: Oxford University Press, 1990.

Ellis, Kate Ferguson. *The Contested Castle: Gothic Novels and the Subversion of Domestic Ideology*. Urbana: University of Illinois Press, 1989.

Fletcher, Don and Rosemary Whip. "Exploring Sexual Violence in *The Dark Room*." *Social Alternatives* 17.4 (1998): 27–31.

_____. "Minette Walters's Feminist Detective Fiction." *Clues: A Journal of Detection* 18.1 (Spring/Summer 1997): 101–2.

Hutton, Patrick. "Mentalities, Matrix of Memory." *Historical Perspectives on Memory*. Ed. Anne Ollila. Helsinki: Hakapaino Oy, 1999, pp. 69–90.

Klein, Kathleen Gregory. *The Woman Detective: Gender and Genre*. 1988. Urbana: University of Illinois Press, 1995.

LeBihan, Jill. "Tearing the Heart out of secrets: Inside and Outside a Murder Mystery." *Journal of Gender Studies* 10 (2001): 287–95.

Molander Danielsson, Karin. *The Dynamic Detective: Special Interest and Seriality in Contemporary Detective Series*. Uppsala: Acta Universitatis Upsaliensis, 2002.

Pridmore, Saxby. Madness of Psychiatry. Special issue of the *German Journal of Psychiatry*. 2004. 15 Aug. 2005. http://www.gjpsy.uni-goettingen.de/gjp-madness-download.htm.

Punter, David. *The Literature of Terror: A History of Gothic Fictions from 1765 to the Present Day*. London: Longman, 1980.
Rabinowitz, Peter. *Before Reading: Narrative Conventions and the Politics of Interpretation*. Columbus, OH: Ohio State University Press, 1988.
Reddy, Maureen T. "The Feminist Counter-Tradition in Crime: Cross, Grafton, Paretsky, and Wilson." *The Cunning Craft: Original Essays on Detective Fiction and Contemporary Literary Theory*. Eds. Ronald G. Walker and June M. Frazer. Macomb: Western Illinois University Press, 1990, pp. 174–87.
_____. *Sisters in Crime: Feminism and the Crime Novel*. New York: Continuum, 1988.
Riggan, William. *Picaros, Madmen, Naïfs, and Clowns: The Unreliable First-Person Narrator*. Norman: University of Oklahoma Press, 1981.
Rowland, Susan. "Margery Allingham's Gothic: Genre as Cultural Criticism." *Clues: A Journal of Detection* 23.1 (Fall 2004): 27–39.
Walters, Minette. *The Dark Room*. London: Macmillan, 1995.
_____. *Disordered Minds*. London: Macmillan, 2003.
_____. *The Ice House*. London: Macmillan, 1992.
_____. *The Scold's Bridle*. London: Macmillan, 1994.
_____. *The Shape of Snakes*. London: Macmillan, 2000.
Walton, Priscilla L. and Manina Jones. *Detective Agency: Women Rewriting the Hard-Boiled Tradition*. Berkeley: University of California Press, 1999.

Society, Evil, and Other

Nancy Eliot Parker

Every society gets the kind of killers it deserves.
— Robert Kennedy

According to James Waller, in *Becoming Evil: How Ordinary People Commit Genocide and Mass Killing*, in 1969 Kurt Wolff of Brandeis observed, "No social scientist as a social scientist has asked what evil is" (quoted in Waller 11). However, by 1991, an entire issue of *Personality and Social Psychology Review* was devoted to social scientific perspectives on evil and violence (Waller 11). Authors, of course, have been examining evil through the behavior of their characters for centuries. The contemporary world of crime novels offers subtle and probing examinations of human behavior, and the work of Minette Walters is most notable in its emphasis on sociological interactions as it does so. The scholarship of social psychology will clarify how insightful Walters is in her understanding of what creates the behaviors we label as evil and the varieties of ways they can manifest themselves. She uses sociological interactions, characterization, and, at times, physical illness to illustrate the ways in which society creates those diseases that form the bad behavior; and she shows how societies interact to create "others" that can be victims.

In his study of human behavior, *Becoming Evil*, James Waller defines evil as the deliberate harming of humans by other humans. He states evil in terms of an action, not in terms of intentions. This definition does not allow an act to be seen as evil when the motives for an action may be, should the act fail to cause harm (Waller 11). Clearly, the murder of Priscilla Trevelyan in Walter's *Disordered Minds*, according to this definition, is an evil act, though, perhaps, not an intentional one. In defining extraordinary evil, Waller, throughout the entirety of *Becoming Evil*, focuses on the harm inflicted on a helpless group that is targeted by legitimating the behavior through social, political, or religious authority. Minette Walters' helpless groups or "others" include minorities, the disabled, and those in less advantaged classes. She is clearly immersed in the downside of British culture.

There is no doubt that humans have a history of particularly harming those defined as other, from the crusades to the inquisitions, from pogroms to holocausts. How is this behavior still possible in modern societies that define themselves as just? All of Walters' novels examine this issue, using a variety of in and out groups to illuminate behavior. In particular, three novels illustrate Walters' understanding: *Disordered Minds, Acid Row* and *The Tinder Box*.

If we understand evil, must we forgive it? Walters also examines this issue in her novels. Understanding seems to reduce perceived responsibility; however, understanding how social forces *can* lead to a given outcome does not mean they *must* always lead to that outcome. For example, two characters in *Disordered Minds* suffer abuse as children, but only one murders. In fact, understanding may show us ways to prevent that outcome in the future. Fiction can be a positive tool for understanding social forces, and Walters is careful to attend to causes and degrees of guilt and to show ways of healing, through caring and commitment, those who are the focus of hate as well.

Does attempting to understand evil carry a risk of contamination? This question suggests the heart of darkness, a view that humans control behavior only because of being surrounded by a civilization that requires it. Walters, however, shows us a society that bears responsibility for creating the problems and shows us individuals who overcome them, particularly in *Acid Row*. We do risk paralysis and apathy if we do not attempt to understand causes; not to understand only ensures that behaviors will continue. Unfortunately, it is ordinary people who commit crimes as, given the magnitude of harmful activities, there cannot be enough exceptional people to be responsible for all the behaviors. Walters' characters come from a range of backgrounds and sociological groups to suggest universality.

It will be helpful to begin with a model, based on research from social psychology, to examine how Walters creates characters and situations that are true to how social situations lead to certain behaviors such as bullying, ostracizing, attacking and, physically harming others. James Waller's research has led him to propose the following four-pronged model to explain how humans can engage in such behaviors. First, he cites facets of ancestral shadow: ethnocentrism (our group is the right group), xenophobia (fear of outsiders or strangers), and desire for social dominance (leading to aggression and violence). Second, there are forces that mold identities of perpetrators: their cultural belief systems (authority orientation, ideological commitment), moral disengagement, and rational self-interest. Third, there is an immediate social context of a culture of cruelty: socialization built on escalating commitments, ritual conduct, and repression of conscience; binding factors of the group including diffusion of responsibility, de-individuation, and conformity to peer pressure and the merger of role and person that enables evil-doing organizations to change the people within them. Finally, these three influences lead to the social death of the victims: us-them thinking, dehumanization of the victim, and blaming the victim (Waller 18–20). Of course, not all of these are applicable to any one Walters novel, but some elements do appear, some multiple times.

It will be instructive to first explain the model in more detail, and then relate those elements that fit to the novels mentioned. What Waller defines as the ancestral shadow is the human tendency to believe our group is the right group; others are not. As examples of "them," these groups are usually members of an ethnically, religiously and economically different group from the majority population. They may also speak a different language or speak with a particular accent (as do the Irish). As they belong to the powerless other, they are marginalized politically as well as socially and are open to being destroyed. The most obvious characters in this group in Great Britain are the various peoples of different skin color — blacks, Arabs, Asians. As Walters shows in *Disordered Minds*, Muslims currently are particularly feared for their difference and are labeled as dangerous. The social dominance factor is also obvious in regard to these minorities.

Second, cultural belief systems mold the perpetrators. Systems that believe control is external to the individual cede the locus of control to chance, luck, or fate. Belief systems that cede authority seem to be factors in predisposing the individual to obedience to authority, away from any sense of personal responsibility. The individual is not to blame for the behavior. It is just the way things are. At its extreme we have Hitler's comment, "One must not have mercy with people who are determined by fate to perish," (quoted in Waller 179) as an excuse to dehumanize an entire group. Religious belief systems may also influence the individual's proneness to prejudice. In the Walters novels to be discussed, however, there is only a passing reference to an alien belief system with the Irish Catholic lower class in *The Tinder Box*. There is also a side of belief systems that frequently merges with ethnic and national identities. As a group distinguishes between "us," the committed, and "them," the outsiders, it can be perverted to justify horrible deeds. The response of Roy Trent in *Disordered Minds* to being called Welsh immediately comes to mind here. It is an adult indication of how easy it was for him as a youth to objectify young girls. His loyalty was to his two friends; girls were merely objects, outside those who matter. This attitude is also apparent in his initial response to Jonathan Hughes, who is the wrong color, black as opposed to the white man he expected.

The orientation toward authority in a group affects its approach to both power and child rearing. "People high in authority orientation prefer hierarchical relationships with clear delineation of spheres of power. They enjoy obeying authority and exercising power over those below them" (Waller 180). To an extent, this need to exercise power in the treatment of children is seen in the comments of Siobhan Lavenham in *The Tinder Box* as to the differences between English and Irish child rearing. Her husband fears their children will grow up wild because the Irish nanny is not disciplining them enough: "And Siobhan would look at her happy, lively, affectionate sons and wonder why the English were so fond of repression" (*The Tinder Box* 24). The English approach is illustrated in the behavior of Martin Rogerson toward both his wife and daughter in *Acid Row*. When his wife, Laura, is questioned by Deputy Chief Inspector Tyler, she tells him her husband was abusive. Asked to define this abuse, Laura replies that he was a bully, "Exercising power without love.... Inadequate people need to dominate" (*Acid Row* 43).

This orientation is affected by cultural child rearing practices, schools, and social institutions. For example, research confirms that intense violence occurs with significantly greater frequency in cultures in which children are physically and emotionally abused or denied affection. Children may be viewed as servants and obedience is stressed. In *Acid Row*, Jimmy James suggests such a background in his childhood under the care of Aunt Zuzi after the death of his mother. Jimmy was raised in a "regime of constant disparagement ... merciless belittling had led him inevitably to prison." (188–89). However, in contrast, the children and grandchildren of Gaynor Patterson are raised in a completely permissive environment of unconditional love. But to make it clear that her focus is on individual responsibility, Walters shows both Jimmy and Colin, Gaynor's son, to be brave, decent humans when challenged by a threat to their loved ones.

Commitment requires indoctrination into an ideology of antagonism built on differences in values that have been in opposition, or an ideology of hate that is nurtured and shaped to accomplish evil ends. According to Waller, there are three components of hate: negation of intimacy by separating as an individual from the other; passion, the strong emotions of anger and fear in response to a threat; and finally, decision or commitment — cognitions of devaluation of the target group (Waller 185). This devaluation is most clearly exemplified in *Acid Row* by Franek Milosz's hatred and objectification of women. His treatment of Dr. Sophie Morrison is the most horrific element of the novel. Pratto and Sidanius of Stanford show that those with high social dominance orientation show more racism, more patriotism, more political-economic conservatism, less support for social programs and women's rights, and less tolerance for diversity and less altruism, all of which lead to moral disengagement (Waller 185). While the example mentioned focuses on women's lack of rights, most of these elements are addressed in Walters' novels.

The social psychologist, Albert Bandura, maintains that to view a group as "other," an active process of detachment is required that includes the following: First, there is moral justification in that the evil acts serve a socially worthy purpose, a moral imperative, and are self-defense to protect community (194). Ridding Acid Row of a pervert becomes the moral justification for stoning and throwing fire bombs at what is presumed to be his house. This redefining prevents self-censure. Second, euphemistic labeling of evil actions removes their sting. The perpetrators cleanse, purify, or otherwise improve the community. As a next step, exonerating comparisons are made. The contrast effect is used to define the enemy (Bandura 195). For example, the rioters of *Acid Row* see themselves as heroes when their actions are compared to cruelties that have been inflicted on those whom they represent. Killing perverts prevents them from doing harm to the innocent children of the community. In addition, nonviolent actions are judged as ineffective and violent actions are believed to prevent more suffering than they cause. Removing the pedophile has not been done by the authorities; in fact they are responsible for his being there. Thus, there is an element of rational self-interest involved in the extreme behavior. The women who began the demonstration are all parents of small children whom they seek to protect. For Wesley Barber, the most violent of the young males in the attacking mob, there may have been, in his mind, prestige as well. He becomes Wesley Snipes as avenger. Extreme actions may seem to be needed for the individual to be respected. Finally, self-interest, including ego needs relating to power, may come into play. Wesley Barber has been previously controlled by his friend and is criticized by his mother, but, unconsciously, he realizes an opportunity to become admired for his naturally violent nature.

A social contest of cruelty can also be relevant. Stanley Milgram's famous experiments using subjects to shock learners revealed that the shock situation carries its own momentum toward increased cruelty. Equally famous is Philip Zimbardo's experiment using students as prisoners and guards that demonstrated individual behavior is in control of social forces to the extent that the pseudo "guards" soon treated the pseudo "prisoners" as deserving of punishment. Zimbardo then stopped the experiment. (Zimbardo 168). According to Waller, professional socialization begins by suggesting that the organization is legitimate, and then requires escalating commitment. This socialization leads to ritual conduct such as is found when gangs require a murder as a requirement to membership. The conscience is repressed through keeping secrets; individuals are desensitized through the repetition of acts, and criticism of these acts is prohibited.

The group prohibits the mentioning of the act or uses euphemisms. This combination leads to a numbness combated by the thrill of repeating the act (Zimbardo 188–89). While repression of conscience is seen in *Acid Row*, this distorted thinking can also be seen in English-Irish hatred in *The Tinder Box*, in which it is permissible to terrorize a disabled couple because of accusations against their son. Walters makes it clear in this novel that open communication among the different social groups could have prevented the misunderstandings that led to death.

The final phase in Waller's model is the social death of the victims. As other, the victim is outside moral obligation of the group. The in-group is defined and the victim is dehumanized. Killing is made easier as the distance between the perpetrators and their victims increases (Waller 236). When the mob charges the house of the Zelowski's in *Acid Row*, such a final breakdown has taken place.

Whenever groups form, the members sense a boundary between them and other groups, and comparisons follow. As cognitive tools to aid in organizing and simplifying, social categorizations include groups, roles, or occupations. Using these tools creates four effects: assumed similarity, out-group homogeneity, accentuation, and in-group bias. First, we assume others in our group are more like us than they may be. Second, we also assume those in the out-group are to be stereotyped. This combination produces, third, the accentuation effect, over-crediting both of the first two. Finally, in-group bias is seen to have the greatest impact in creating the social death of victims. "Their mere perception of belonging to two distinct groups — that is social categorization per se — is sufficient to provoke ... discriminatory responses on the part of the in-group" (Tajfel quoted in Waller 242). However, social categorization alone is not enough to lead to hatred of out-groups. The final element is to remove the victim from the human species. Those in the out-group are not human. In *The Tinder Box* it is revealed that one of the most evil individuals in the group is the one who has objectified the Irish, Jeremy Jardine; his comment that they are rats is quoted two paragraphs below.

For victims to be dehumanized, they first must be deprived of their identity by defining them entirely by a category, then by excluding that category from the human family. According to the researcher Haig Bosmajian, "The distance between the linguistic dehumanization of people and their actual suppression and extermination is not great" (quoted in Waller 246). Linguistic dehumanization begins with references to victims as something naturally evoking disgust — vermin, bacilli, cockroaches, dogs (bitches) — or with names that become dehumanizing: Asked whether he wants a young woman to burn during the riot, Wesley Barber in *Acid Row*, slow-witted and pumped up on drugs and adrenaline, bellows furiously into the silence: "Who fucking cares? It's only a white bitch" (193). Or people may be dehumanized as things: not corpses but figures, pieces, rags. This dehumanization is complemented by actions that force victims to focus on survival as opposed to being humans themselves: starvation, filthy living conditions, etc.

If victims cannot present a "worthy self" (Waller 248), they cannot demand moral and humane treatment. Dr. Sophie Morrison in *Acid Row* is never addressed by her title befitting an MD by her captor, Franek Zelowski; he says, "You so clever, little girl. You work it out for yourself" (114). Thus she is a stupid girl, not even a woman. The dehumanization is reinforced by visualizing the victims as representing all that is evil, as in *The Tinder Box:* "All you Irish are despicable. You flood over here like a plague of sewer rats looking for handouts" (53). Dehumanization is important to social death because it ensures psychological distance and rationalizes evil actions to avert danger. The victims deserve extreme treatment in order to prevent their actions against the primary group. Such prevention is manifested in the justifications given for burning out the child molester in *Acid Row* when some believe the missing girl is in the house.

Redefining a social category of people and dehumanizing them leads to blaming the victim. We need to believe in a just world, but this makes us blind to the fact that bad things happen to good people. Sadly, a strong belief in a just world is concomitant with rigid social rules and an emphasis on convention as opposed to empathy and concern for others (Waller 252). The belief in a just world is probably a result of socialization, but socialization does not explain why the belief is so pervasive. Possible reasons include that the belief is self-protective, enhances self-esteem, and provides scapegoats. It is self-protective because the plight of others may cause us to realize our own fragility. It enhances self-esteem because it allows the perpetrator to believe an atrocity is appropriate proof of his own superiority. And it provides a scapegoat upon which to displace hostility and diminish our own responsibility for problems. For the inhabitants of Acid Row, the pervert located among them by the authorities is responsible for their living conditions and provides them the perfect scapegoat.

With this background in mind, it is appropriate to note specific applications of Waller's model found in Minette Walters' works. *Disordered Minds* is, according to the *Daily Mail,* "a brilliant piece of psychological deconstruction ... which works on several levels" (paperback jacket) to illustrate perceptions of "other" based on class, race and disability. Misassumptions on the part of the characters immediately come into play. The reader first perceives the plot through Hughes as he arrives at Heathrow airport from New York, post 9/11; he has experienced uncomfortable scrutiny because of his physical appearance, and he feels that tolerance is yet another casualty of the terror attacks (67). Because the reader is not told that Hughes is dark skinned and can be taken for either a black or an Arab, this omission allows the reader to make assumptions from Hughes' perspective without realizing he is automatically "other" in the culture. When Hughes enters the Crown and Feathers Pub to meet the individual he assumes is male, George Gardener, he is treated rudely and called "a jumped-up wog in fancy dress" by the landlord (77). When he gives his card to the landlord, he receives an apology of sorts, along with this admonishment: "You should have said ... who you were, for Christ's sake. I've been expecting a white bloke. Does George know you're a darkie?" (78). There could not be a clearer example of prejudice based on an out-group, but it is presented to the reader from both sides.

Not surprisingly, Hughes decides to leave rather than become more aggressive. As he walks away, the reader learns more of his background. Hughes could be taken to be Moslem, is black, and speaks with an upper-class accent. To the landlord his appearance is "not right." His color is wrong, his accent is wrong, and his dress represents an inappropriate social level. Hughes thinks of his friend, Andrew, accusing him of repressing his emotions to the point of being unfeeling. His response was, "You try being half Iranian, half Libyan ... with a dark skin, Caucasian features and an English name no one believes you're entitled to" (80). He is also hypersensitive to Britain's involvement in Iraq because he believes that war generates hate: "His anger and aggression had increased by leaps and bounds since his passport started being questioned [after 9/11]" (80). The reader now knows that Jonathan Hughes is only partially revealed by his status as an author, an Oxford graduate, and a research fellow at the University of London. He is insecure as to who he is because he is trying to be something that does not seem to fit in this culture. In fact, he has even selected a background other than what he actually is, perhaps because it is more relevant to the current issues in the Middle East. The reader later learns, however, that Hughes' actual parentage is a combination of Jamaican and Chinese. While he is clearly ill treated, he will also soon be revealed to lack tolerance himself, an illustration of Walters' subtlety and evenhandedness in dealing with complex social issues.

When Hughes eventually meets George Gardener, he immediately judges her based on her looks. George is a sixty-year-old plump female who, according to Hughes, "looks like a squat garden gnome" (98). Here, Hughes clearly buys into society's judgments based on appearance, and he re-enters the fray of racism, misunderstanding, social class, and concern over background and heritage. As he returns to the pub for his meeting with George, Hughes recalls his friend's remonstrance, "*You have such an inflated opinion of your intelligence, Jon. You think it puts you above everybody else ... but clever people do not set out to patronize everyone they meet*" (85) as Hughes seems to at this point. He defines himself as intellectually superior because of his education, but is unable to see this degree of education in someone else. He has objectified George.

Hughes rolls out his education like a weapon against Roy Trent, the landlord, by explaining why Roy must be Welsh. George Gardner knows what he is doing: "He's teasing you ... Dr. Hughes was joking about endomorphs [being Welsh] — I'm one, you're one.... For most of us nationality is a choice Roy ... not a birthright" (90). This comment is particularly ironic in that Hughes has chosen his background. At the end of this exchange, the reader learns that Hughes is in a foul humor after being held by immigration because his appearance suggests he could be an Arab. Roy accepts the olive branch and expresses his sympathy to Hughes with this clear sociological truth: "At times like this, when people are frightened, there's always a presumption of guilt if your face doesn't fit" (91). At this point, the present and past and the various conflicts are coalesced — race, social background, possible ethnic heritage — and all sorts of possible hate groups come into play. Revealing his own snobbery in his response to Gardener, Hughes never bothers to establish her credentials.

The conversation between Hughes and Gardener, which does not go well, is an ongoing example of Hughes demanding respect because of his insecurity but not giving it. Wondering why an author would not bother to research the locals about a crime as she has done, Gardner has clear information from an eyewitness exonerating Howard Stamp, but she will not share it with Hughes. He has revealed his insecurities as "other" through snobbery and is set up either to change or be defeated. At this point, Walters has also made it clear that judgments oversimplify reality. As he waits to leave, Hughes overhears Gardener's opinion of him: "He's a fake, a bloody little con man who'd rather exploit other people than do the work himself" (117). She is correct to an extent, but she too has rushed to judgment. Roy Trent explains to Hughes,

> She has two open university degrees, one in psychology and one in criminology — also an external Ph.D. from Sussex in behavioral science.... You shouldn't make assumptions, mate. George is far too modest to call herself doctor — unlike you — but she's *just* as entitled ... she earned her qualifications the hard way: in the evenings while she held down a full-time job ... she doesn't like bullies, she doesn't like people who take advantage and she doesn't like snobs.... And you're all three [119].

As the book progresses, the reader will become increasingly aware of how and why Hughes is a fake, why he is so insecure. However, Walters will soon turn the "other" issue around, using Gardener and Hughes as foils, each with the skill to reevaluate the other, even bringing about change in both. In the novel this juxtaposition makes the clear point that no one should make unfounded assumptions about a group or status. Things may not be what they appear to be.

Hughes' friend Andrew Spicer is also a character who has been the focus of misunderstanding. He is not dark, of mixed race, like Hughes, or a plump, homely woman in her 60s like Gardener; he is a short, balding man who lost his wife to a handsome neighbor. He observes, "We're all in the same boat. When strangers look at me, they see a bald short-arse with zero status. It's just as painful ... particularly when women do it" (173). Accepting what he is, he forces honesty on both Hughes and Gardener and is able to establish a working relationship between them. In their relationships, Walters underscores the need for human empathy and open communication to counter negative human behaviors.

As a result of their improved rapport, Gardener and Hughes pool their resources to solve what have now become two mysteries: who killed Grace Jeffries and what happened to Priscilla Trevelyan, the thirteen-year-old girl who disappeared at the time of the murder, and whose rape opens the novel. Is the Cill who stole Hughes' passport the girl who vanished? Or is Cill the other girl who was present at the time of the rape, Louise Burton? As the two pursue their investigation, George Gardener learns that Jonathan Hughes was an abused child; and ironically, she and Jonathan suspect that the same must be true of either Priscilla Trevelyan or Louise Burton. The questions are which of the two is still alive, who was abused, and who is whom? At this point there are various ways in which groups and individuals have dehumanized "others" by race, or sex, or social status. In the novel, disease takes many forms, including not just the abuse of Hughes, and as is revealed, one of the girls, but also that of Gardener's cancer. Although it is suggested that Hughes' care and affection may be the help George needs, overcoming disease works for some and not for others. There are those who are doomed to repeat their past in an effort to escape it.

By the end of the novel, Hughes and Gardner have completed their investigation, and his friendship with her has brought him a new life, a possible girlfriend, and a mother. He now has an identity and claims it: "She's my mother," he told Wyatt over her head. "She had a one night stand with a Jamaican road sweeper thirty-five years ago and she's been regretting it ever since. I wouldn't mind so much but she keeps trying to pass me off as her toyboy" (533). His joke claims his actual origins, flatters Gardener, and makes his love for his acquired parent obvious — a total change from his former secretive self. He has ceased to allow himself to be "other" and become part of a group.

Various character pairings in the novel are obvious. Both Gardener and Hughes are highly educated, both in some way are ill (he with a bleeding ulcer, she with cancer), and both are overcoming their limitations through commitment to others by the time they have solved the crime.

Both Hughes and Louise Burton have suffered childhood abuse — one mental, one physical — but Hughes is driven to acquiring education and accepts an identity; Burton, however, is driven to anti-social behavior and a constantly shifting identity. The novel exhibits to some degree all four stages of Waller's model. There is ethnocentrism and xenophobia among the four responsible for the rape, and cultural issues have molded several belief systems to define groups as "other." There is a culture of cruelty that leads to an "us versus them" dichotomy, making it acceptable to blame a murder on an innocent mentally retarded individual. Hughes' and Gardner's growth, change, and commitment to others overcome these negatives in the end.

While *Disordered Minds* focuses on two crimes that coalesce, and individual or small gang acts of evil, the novel *Acid Row* focuses on one *type* of crime, pedophilia, and social responses to it. It examines what can go horribly wrong when society's throwaways are crammed together in a situation of *No Exit*, but it also shows the redeeming virtues to be found in individuals who have been labeled as other by society at large. In the novel, Walters makes it clear that doing evil is not a matter of victimhood or social forces; it is a matter of choice. Is the pedophile to be found only in a project for the poor, or is he a wealthy lawyer, or his friend? Evil may be found at all levels of society, but so can good.

The novel opens with Milosz Zelowski, a registered pedophile, being re-housed in Bassindale, subsidized housing that is "a place of deprivation where literacy was poor, drugs endemic and fights commonplace" (*Acid Row* 10). Graffiti has reduced the welcome-to-Bassindale sign to "assid row," or Acid Row, an indication of how its inhabitants view their monument to social engineering: "They were the Jews in the ghetto, the blacks in the townships, the people without a stake in the affluence beyond their boundaries" (99); they are all the consummate "others." Although the relocated Milosz is more of a coward than a pervert, he is accompanied by his father, Franek, a truly atrocious human. The reality of a pedophile in their midst brings the mothers of the community into action; they believe a demonstration can bring about the removal of someone whom they consider a danger to their children. At the same time, Amy Biddulph, a ten-year-old middle-class child, has disappeared. Although Milosz is a natural suspect, he is not attracted to little girls; his crimes have involved consenting teenage boys. The novel plotlines alternate between the building social chaos of Acid Row and the police efforts to find Amy.

The other major characters in Bassindale include Melanie Patterson, a nineteen-year-old, pregnant with her third child by Jimmy James, a black man who has just been released from prison; her mother, Gaynor; her brother, fourteen-year-old Colin; his friend Kevin Charteris; and Wesley Barber, an out-of-control, drug-addicted black youth who represents the opposite of what Jimmy proves to be. What the women intend to have as a peaceful demonstration to remove a danger to their children quickly deteriorates into a riot and Acid Row is cut off from outside help by the gang response that overrides the demonstration.

To complicate matters, Dr. Sophie Morrison is taken prisoner by Franek and Milosz Zelowski when she responds to a call to their house to treat the asthmatic father. She is not only in danger — at the mercy of Franek and trapped in the house the mob is attempting to burn — but she also exemplifies the treatment of women as "other." While the men had called for an ambulance as a way to escape the mob, they instead have a small, tough female doctor who they believe will provide an element of safety until the police arrive. Franek clearly has no respect for females. To him, the doctor is a girl, easily killed: "I snap your neck ... like this" (115). Within a short period of time, Sophie has been badly beaten and is clearly at the mercy of a man who sees women only as objects to be used any way he chooses. Presumably, issues from his childhood experiences in Poland have instilled in him a culture of cruelty that he brings to his son and that leads him to objectify women. Not only has he brutalized prostitutes, but it becomes apparent that he also murdered Milosz's mother. The abuse Milosz has suffered, however, does not lead him to act to protect Sophie; his abuse has turned him into a tool of his father. Franek represents the worst of the end point of Waller's model. To him, not only is Sophie a toy, but Jimmy James — his other would-be rescuer — is merely a stupid "nigger." All are objects to justify his reality. Just as he has rejected any of Sophie's logic when she attempts to reason with him, when the mob threatens his house, he rejects Jimmy's plea to leave with him to be saved.

As the mob's frenzy escalates, Jimmy reveals himself as the opposite of Wesley Barber. Although he is also a large, frightening black male, he is a smart, kind one. He works hard during the growing riot to help those who are hurt or trapped in their homes. Through the establishment of the phone tree called Friendship Calling within the elderly and disabled of Acid Row, Sophie had created a world of caring within a hostile environment, and thus had developed an alternative to being "other" because of age, or disability or race. Jimmy's involvement with the elderly Mrs. Eileen Hinkley, a former nurse who is now wheelchair bound, exemplifies this alternative. She has been told to expect the arrival of a "big nigger with blood all over him who had just come out of prison and couldn't speak without uttering obscenities" (163). In the continued wonderful exchange, the old white woman and the rough young black man come to understand and respect each other when she adds how the ambulance man had said Jimmy was a hero in his opinion and someone who could be trusted. At the end of the conversation she asks for a kiss, which he gives her before leaving, and through other connections created by Friendship Calling, he continues to help people while trying to get to "his woman" Melanie and her children.

One relationship he forms is with an old soldier with a tin helmet and a machete who believes adversity makes people behave at their best; unfortunately, it is also working to bring out the worst in people. The irony is that the old soldier's subsequent inability to believe the best of Jimmy quickly enough endangers him further. Once he has labeled someone as other, it is hard to change his view. When Wesley and the mob break into the Franek house, the old soldier, who had followed Jimmy because he assumed he was entering the house to steal, becomes the object of Wesley's rage as he becomes Wesley Snipes' character in *Blade:* "Killer of vampire perverts. *White Ones*" (313). Clearly, those who are white are things to him.

When enough horror has occurred to end the violence, of all those in the mob only Wesley Barber is brought to justice. At this point in the novel, Walters makes a strong point of what is and is not to blame, what can and cannot be blamed on society:

> Drugs were cited in mitigation.... He was deprived. He was abused. He was black. Blame all those things that were part of his environment and of that day. But the judge is unmoved, noting that people had tried to reason with him and he was no more "socially damaged" than his victims [317].

All the social issues that create evil — all the elements of Waller's model — affect those in the novel, but Wesley, Jimmy, Colin, and Franek each choose different behaviors — some positive, some criminal — during the heat of the riot. Franek, in particular, has never accepted responsibility for any of his behavior, and has opted instead to blame his victims. But issues in the culture are not allowed as excuses in Walters' world. Jimmy sees the error of his ways and not only accepts responsibility for what he has done but also continues to carry the burden of the community.

Walters knows the limitations of those living in Acid Row, but her final vision is one of hope. Two heroes of the riot, the elderly Eileen Hinkley and young Jimmy, clearly believe in human limitations and personal responsibility. Eileen also realizes that Jimmy told Milosz to get lost, in effect holding him responsible for his inability to act against his father and protect the doctor; Jimmy told him, "next time good and evil wage a war outside your door, find some guts and pick the side of angels instead of taking a coward's way out" (353). Jimmy's position is, at this point, not to blame others for one's actions: "Okay, he had a lousy childhood, but then so did a lot of us. You have to make choices in life ... and all he ever chose was to make his father worse" (354). Rather than blaming society, Jimmy believes in personal responsibility, is going straight for the first time in his life, and is proud to be the father of his little daughter. Through the new life of his own child, he focuses on the heroism of all those who have overcome their social limitations to make a better society. He has gone beyond Waller's model, or outside it, to overcome evil.

Walters' much shorter novel, *The Tinder Box,* has much in common with *Acid Row.* Written in 1998, at the request of the Organization of Books in the Netherlands, when Walters was working on ideas for *Acid Row,* "*The Tinder Box* portrays immigrant Irish tinkers as hate figures in a wealthy Hampshire village, but a similar hatred is demonstrated against a convicted pedophile in a sink estate in *Acid Row.* Both stories depict the dangers of ignorance, and how unrelated, misunderstood events combine to trigger violent reactions" (Author's Note, *The Tinder Box*). This brief book deals in a simpler manner with issues found in *Acid Row,* as well as those in *Disordered Minds.* It begins with a newspaper account of Patrick O'Riordan's being charged with the double murder of Lavinia Fanshaw and her nurse, Dorothy Jenkins. According to the press account, a neighbor stated, "Whoever killed them is a monster" (1). But the police insist that "Vigilante behavior will not be tolerated" (1) and O'Riordan denies the charges against him. In short order, both class and ethnic background become grounds for casting a suspect as "other" and therefore outside any need for appropriate concern.

The action of this novella and the issues of class differences are experienced through the perception of Siobhan Lavenham, an upper-class Irish woman married to a wealthy Englishman and living in the small village of Sowerbridge. It is impossible not to consider that the name suggests the moral "You reap what you sow" because the story bridges what the O'Riordans were to what they are now. Siobhan confronts class issues in two ways: her own perceptions as the descendent of an Irish landowner dealing with descendents of roaming Irish tinkers, and the constant anti–Irish attitudes of her upper-class neighbors, which blind her to whatever virtues the English may have. Her circle of neighbors includes the recently murdered Lavinia Fanshaw of the Manor House, Peter and Cynthia Haversley of Malvern House, Jeremy Jardine of the Old Vicarage and grandson of Lavinia, and Dr. Sam and Norma Bentley of Rose Cottage, all of whom live clustered around a crossroad. Across from Jeremy's Vicarage is Kilkenny Cottage, home of the O'Riordans and an eyesore to the neighborhood. Jeremy moved out of the Manor House and bought the vicarage at a bargain rate for its basements, as he is presumably making a living as a wine merchant.

Despite their class differences, Siobhan Lavenham fiercely defends the O'Riordans when their son Patrick is arrested; since they are Irish, they are outside the concern of the community. Her efforts to secure police protection for them uncover a series of sad truths about the family and the parents' disabilities, revealed by the police inspector who knew them in London. Liam abused his wife and son for years until his son retaliated; then Patrick injured his mother when she attempted to intervene in their fight. Patrick's attack on his father ended Liam's life of crime; he retired to Sowerbridge and the son was given a reduced sentence because of his years of abuse from Liam. Bridey's story, however, is that Liam was injured in a car crash and Patrick was scarred by a terrorist's bomb in Ireland. Clearly, the suffering O'Riordans do not feel bound by the truth; and in typical Walters' fashion, the truth is even more complicated than it appears.

When Kilkenny Cottage burns down, and Siobhan's nanny Rosheen is discovered to be missing as well, class conflict is further complicated by the issue of money. Bridey's O'Riordan's niece from Ireland, Rosheen becomes the pivot of Walters' complex examination of who is worthy of what. It seems Lavinia's death should improve the fortunes of the Cynthia and Peter Haversleys and Jeremy Jardin, but the money will not be forthcoming because, according to Peter Haversley, murder really complicates the distribution of assets. Jeremy is not only one of the anti–Irish neighbors, but he also should be among those suspected for the murders as he so clearly expects to benefit from them. An argument between Jeremy and Siobhan over Patrick as a suspect in Lavinia's murder further underscores class differences:

> "You're a fool, Siobhan. Patrick's guilty as sin. You know it. Everybody knows it. Just don't come crying to me later when the jury proves us right and you find yourself tarred with the same brush as the O'Riordans."
> "I already have been.... If you and the Haversleys had your way, I'd have been lynched by now, but, god knows, I'd give my right arm to see Patrick get off, if only to watch the three of you wearing sackcloth and ashes for the rest of your lives" [49].

According to Jeremy, the two relevant "in" and "out" groups are the English and the Irish.

At this point, it would seem that being Irish trumps class, and the local English gentry are obnoxious; but even these contrasting views may derive from the coincidence and misunderstanding that are characteristic of Walters' writing. Cynthia Haversley's criticism of Rosheen's sexual liaisons is accurate in the sense that she is having them, but in error in who the male partner actually is. Rosheen had been leaving Siobhan's sons with the crippled Bridey while having the affair; and Cynthia was disturbed by the boys being in the care of a cripple, or left alone, but never made this concern clear. When she does, Siobhan realizes that Cynthia is kinder than she had given her credit for and must face her own anti–English prejudice. When the truth of Rosheen's disappearance comes out, class conflict erupts in a new way. The community learns that Rosheen had looked down on her relatives and envisioned herself marrying Jeremy to become lady of the manor. Her commitment was not to being Irish, to an ethnic group, or to family, but to some vision of class she was determined to attain.

According to Siobhan, "Moral support is alien to Irish culture, Inspector. We only really enjoy fighting with each other. I thought every Englishman knew *that*...." (85). Her assertion becomes one stereotype that is true: the greatest enmity is among the Irish. But the ensuing story of the night the cottage burned is, in Walters' fashion, ambiguous. Liam and Bridey give one account involving Rosheen and Kevin, but the police inspector — the one who knew the O'Riordans in London — is suspicious; he knows "there is something. I've known them too long not to know when they are lying" (112).

In yet another version, off the record, Siobhan gives her scenario of what the O'Riordans have actually done. She believes that they have been obtaining government benefits under false pretenses and have concocted their version of events to cover the fraud. The inspector's response to Siobhan's version is that Bridey must believe he is a complete idiot; she tells him, "Not you personally. Just your ... er ... kind.... The Irish have been getting the better of the English for centuries, Inspector.... And if the English weren't so blinded by their own self-importance ... they might have noticed" (115). Once again, ethnocentrism and xenophobia have molded beliefs, and cultural issues have created their expression. To an extent, this part of Waller's model has created a culture of, at least, mental cruelty, as well as murder. It takes overcoming the "us versus them" mentality for Siobhan to see the truth. A lack of openness and understanding led to misjudgments that led to disaster. Minette Walters' vision has revealed this truth about human nature: Humans must work to overcome their own prejudices or be trapped, even destroyed, by them.

For at least the last one hundred years, the field of psychology has touched upon and illuminated the field of literature; however, literature has understood human psychology much longer. This author's undergraduate introductory psychology text caught her attention because of its epigram: "The proper study of mankind is man." This is a quote, not from a psychologist, but from the writings of Alexander Pope; its truth is that literature is the study of humanity that can be validated by psychology. James Waller ends his study with the following:

> We are left with the humbling and painful recognition that the persistence of inhumanity in human affairs is incontrovertible. It is hard to argue that we can do something beyond merely make the world a little less horrible. This is a humbling recognition, but — in this case — humility will serve us well. It is only in accepting the limits of who we are that we have a legitimate chance to structure a society in which the exercise of human evil is lessened [278].

Minette Walters not only examines these human limits effectively in her novels but also illustrates that the way out of evil is led, one person at a time, by those who take full responsibility for their actions.

Works Cited

Bandura, Albert. "Moral Disengagement in the Perpetration of Inhumanities." *Personality and Social Psychology Review* 3 (1999): 193–209.
Waller, James. *Becoming Evil: How Ordinary People Commit Genocide and Mass Killing.* Oxford: Oxford University Press, 2002.
Walters, Minette. *Acid Row.* New York: Jove Books, 2003.
_____. *Disordered Minds.* New York: Berkley Books, 2004.
_____. *The Tinder Box.* London: Pan Books, 2005.
Zimbardo, Philip. *The Lucifer Effect: Understanding How Good People Turn Evil.* New York: Random House, 2007.

The Tangled Web of Justice and Revenge: Narrative Devices and Subtexts in *The Devil's Feather*

Gerri Reaves

Fans of Minette Walters' detective novels have come to expect a broad range of narrative devices and inserts. Open any one of her eleven novels, and you're likely to confront photos, maps, newspaper stories, legal documents, quotations, definitions, letters, medical reports, police documents, excerpts from academic texts, journal entries, telephone messages, fables, and more. Handwritten text, as appears in the faxes in *The Dark Room*, adds documentary flavor and visual variety. Walters instituted this practice with her very first detective novel, *The Ice House*, which opens with two newspaper stories written ten years apart, about a man's disappearance and presumed murder, and a map of the village where the body is found. The novel also weaves in tantalizing narrative devices such as a long-hidden letter we never get to read and a hypothetical map — presumed to have existed although it never appears in the story. Taking this practice to new proportions, Walters' 2006 novel *The Devil's Feather* is layered with narrative devices, mostly in the form of electronic documents — even digital movies and cell-phone text messages — as befits the new millennium. The most intriguing of these "illustrations," as Walters calls this grab-bag of what I title subtexts, are the nods to literary convention: lost, found, hypothetical, or faked texts.

Walters argues that the illustrations serve a two-fold purpose in her fiction, realism and variety:

> The books of the 30s by Agatha Christie and Dorothy Sawyers [sic] didn't have detail in them, like police memos or letters. They were more concerned with the puzzle of the crime. That's not to knock what they were doing, but it's very important to me to make it realistic. I see the articles and memos etc. as a way of breaking up the narrative, changing the style from narrative to documentary, and giving readers information in a different way [Baird].

These illustrations also recall the era of Victorian fiction and revive a writing tradition whose demise she regrets: "Up until the First World War, all adult fiction was illustrated, but shortages during that time meant that the industry decided to save paper by not printing the pictures any more. I always think it's sad that adult fiction isn't illustrated" (Baird).

To discuss any Walters novel is, inevitably, to explore narrative structure — layering, juxtapositions, conflicting narrative authorities, and the various devices by which she ensures that readers receive "information in a different way." In *The Devil's Feather*, the structurally complicated narrative is particularly daunting. The sheer number and types of narrative devices and the resulting chronological fluidity heighten our participation in protagonist Connie Burns' struggle to recover her sense of self, shattered by her horrifying abduction in Iraq. In essence, the novel chronicles her fight to control her own narrative — in this case, the narrative being her life. She orchestrates this recovered control not through brute force or a passion for deliberate revenge, but by using her only weapons: her intellect and her talent for collaboration.

Walters' heavy reliance on a network of subtexts complicates and intensifies the pleasure of reading her work: "My job is to keep them guessing for as long as I can," she has said ("FAQ"). Readers searching for tidy, well-made, unambiguous plots will not find satisfaction in Walters' novels; she is more Raymond Chandler than Christie. She figuratively throws the disordered evidence onto a large desk and invites her main character — along with her readers — to engage in the delicious process of sorting through it. Her avowed writing habits attest to this attitude. In answer to a reader's question, "Is it true that you often don't know 'whodunit' until halfway through writing a book?" she answers, "It's not sometimes ... it's always! It's a much more exciting way to write. The challenge is to create a puzzle for the readers." Walters' risk-taking cultivates the sensation that readers are writing with her. She goes on to describe it as "embark[ing] with nothing, just a tightrope across a chasm" ("FAQ"). Because, for at least the first half of the novel, she is as clueless as her character is about the murderer's identity, the engagement of our detective instincts strengthens our identification with the main character(s). However, *The Devil's Feather* departs from this pattern in one respect; the question is not "whodonit?" but if, when, and how he will do it again.

The first twenty-five pages of *The Devil's Feather* compactly cover Reuters correspondent Connie's experiences in war-torn Sierra Leone and then Iraq, spanning May 2002 to 2004. In Sierra Leone she begins to suspect that a British mercenary, most recently calling himself Keith MacKenzie, is responsible for a series of brutal murders of women there. She begins to investigate, but gets nowhere. Two years later in Iraq, she resumes her investigation; as a result, she is stalked and terrorized. Forced to leave Iraq, she is abducted on the way to the airport and held hostage for three days. Sadistically brutalized, she is kept blindfolded and naked in a crate in a basement, terrorized by vicious dogs, and repeated orally raped. Her instinct and logic tell her that her tormentor is MacKenzie, who is avenging her attempts to expose his crimes. The abductor calls Connie his "devil's feather," a term that signifies his extreme misogyny that drives the plot. The term of Turkish derivation refers to "a woman who stirs a man's interest without realizing it; the unwitting cause of sexual arousal," a definition that opens and frames the book. For MacKenzie, any innocent woman he addresses as a devil's feather asks for and deserves whatever violence he inflicts.

After her release, Connie remains silent about what really occurred. She assumes her mother's maiden name and seeks refuge in the English countryside at eighteenth-century Barton House. The bulk of the novel takes place in the Dorset village where she continues her research to track down MacKenzie, becomes interested in the mysterious history of her absentee landlady, Lily Wright, and begins to make friends. But

MacKenzie comes after her only two months later. He brutalizes her parents to force them to tell him her whereabouts, and then invades her country refuge.

The enigmatic ending of *The Devil's Feather*, when all the strands of narrative and subtext converge, powerfully dramatizes Walters' moral questions: How does one simultaneously procure justice and resist the seduction of revenge? Is justice tainted by rage necessarily a corrupt justice? Those questions constitute "the abyss" on whose edge Connie stands at the novel's end.

The Subversive Web of Subtexts

The Devil's Feather's panoply of narrative devices range from authoritative sources of information to alternative narratives that contradict or confuse. On the one hand, the Reuters newspaper articles that open the novel provide straightforward trustworthy information. As with the news stories that open *The Ice House*, the online Reuters articles in *The Devil's Feather* conveniently and objectively summarize years of events and set the stage for the action of the novel. Other authoritative texts, such as the academic excerpts on stalkers, sadistic rapists, and torturers, allow readers to vicariously experience Connie's Internet research and the thrill of investigation. These devices lend a documentary feel and give readers a respite from Connie's focus on her victimization in Baghdad in spring 2004. Ultimately, the mix of multiple sources of information reinforces her credibility — an important function in this intense, psychological first-person narration.

On the other hand, some narrative devices mislead, suppress, confuse, fictionalize, and even lie. Even as they ostensibly inform and establish narrative authority, subtexts such as Connie's journal notes and Peter's verbal account to the police of MacKenzie's invasion of Barton House can in fact undermine the logic of the story. We are put in a position similar to Connie's: grappling with a morally ambiguous world, where the desire for revenge competes with an ongoing terror, rage, and the need to find the truth. We too attempt to accurately "read" her situation, out-think her stalker and tormentor MacKenzie, and make sense of the gothic history that envelopes her rented house and its owner, Lily. As we reconsider characters' motives and intentions, we repeatedly reconstruct the logic of the case, as we question what we know and what we can believe.

Often, the narrative devices in *The Devil's Feather* operate as do subtexts in both literature and drama, running below the surface of the main narrative. Literary theorist Terry Eagleton defines a subtext in fiction as

> a text which runs within it [the novel], visible at certain "symptomatic" points of ambiguity, evasion or overemphasis, and which we as readers are able to "write" even if the novel itself does not. All literary works contain one or more such sub-texts, and there is a sense in which they may be spoken of as the "unconscious" of the work itself. The work's insights, as with all writing, are deeply related to its blindnesses: what it does not say, and how it does not say it, may be as important as what it articulates; what seems absent, marginal or ambivalent about it may provide a central clue to its meanings [178–79].

In drama, a subtext is the combination of unspoken or even unconscious thoughts and motivations of characters — what is between the lines of dialogue. Subtexts have the capacity to reaffirm, subvert, silence, or suppress the more obvious interpretations of a narrative. In *The Devil's Feather*, these tensions foreground the puzzling relationships among journalistic truth, moral authority, and personal responsibility. In addition, a number of hypothetical or fabricated texts alternately unravel or elucidate the facts.

A Question of Courage: Morality as Subtext

Detective Inspector Alan Collins, Connie's friend, confidant, and collaborator in her ordeal, is the one character who reads Connie correctly every step of the way in a novel riddled with misreadings of characters and situations. As a somewhat external subtext, their e-mail correspondence provides the most accurate, objective reading of the entire MacKenzie case, from the first murders in Sierra Leone to the last details of Connie's ordeal in Dorset. His e-mails synthesize information from several sources and as a body are a stabilizing subtext, a reference point outside the maelstrom of Connie's trauma. Collins provides the organizing principle of the novel, a Thucydides quotation that Collins passes on to Connie: "The secret of happiness is freedom; the secret of freedom, courage" (187). This subtext, which insinuates itself into every aspect of the novel, is a lesson Collins' father told his son when he was being bullied by his schoolmates. Taking on the softening voice of his father, Collins warns Connie that the mind can easily distort facts and remember incorrectly, an observation that proves to be true in her case.

Connie and Alan Collins' relationship as colleagues and friends begins in 2004 when he investigates the very first of the Sierra Leone murders. Collins had provided Connie with information and connections to aid her investigation of MacKenzie; he shares her beliefs that the wrong young men had been charged with the crime and that the confessions were forced. Collins can easily and correctly read the subtext she does not share in their correspondence. With psychological insight and superior detection skills, he also infers the unspoken horrors of what MacKenzie did during Connie's abduction — just as he is able later to correctly infer what she and Jess actually did on the night MacKenzie disappeared after invading Barton House.

Collins' insights about Connie's state of mind, chronicled in the subtext of their e-mails, reaffirm her confidence and courage. This e-mail comment to Connie typifies his forthrightness in evaluating the threat she is taking on alone: "Any man prepared to imprison and brutalize a woman is certainly capable of murder, and there was nothing to stop him following his well-tested MO of disfiguring (even beheading) you, leaving Iraq, changing his identity, and letting terrorists take the blame" (187). He accurately discerns that she is distorting her memory of the abduction to exaggerate her cooperation with MacKenzie, and he attributes that distortion to her shame.

It is largely Collins' stabilizing honesty that helps Connie avoid being engulfed by the fear and doubt that would ensure MacKenzie's murder of her in Dorset, and his investigative expertise and friendship are crucial in enabling her to even imagine she can stand up to her torturer. So conditioned is Connie by her abduction that she will not break her silence; MacKenzie still controls her will if not her body. This fear leads her to tell D.I. Collins that only under two ironclad conditions will she reveal to him all her evidence and research: MacKenzie must be in custody and her evidence must be necessary for his conviction. The professional and personal bond established in the running subtext of Connie and Collins' e-mail correspondence intensifies after MacKenzie disappears following his invasion of Barton House. When she meets with Collins at his office after that disappearance, he shares an anecdote from his childhood that indirectly reveals two things. One, he suspects that she killed MacKenzie and has possibly hidden his body in the unused covered well at Barton House. Two, he feels she is morally justified in doing so — even though he is professionally bound to uphold the law in every particular. After telling her that he thinks MacKenzie died the night of the invasion, Collins tells Connie about a holiday he and his family once took in Dorset, where they stayed in an old cottage. The subtext of this narrative is clear: On that visit, they learned from a neighbor that redundant wells were common in rural Dorset.

Most important is the intent of these random comments: Collins willingly collaborates with Connie in helping her evade the punishment she and Jess are due for pursuing a private justice. His comments also serve as a friendly warning to Connie — after all, Inspector Bagley of the Dorset police continues to doggedly investigate, hoping to charge her with murder. Seeming discrepancies between Connie's and Peter's accounts of that horrific night make the police suspect Connie and Jess of murdering MacKenzie during the time that Peter left to summon the police. He will not accept her story that MacKenzie must have wandered off into the night, become disoriented in unfamiliar terrain, and fallen off a cliff.

In the more than five years they have fought to bring MacKenzie to justice, the legal system has failed Collins and Connie. They tacitly collaborate on a hypothetical narrative that offers a solution to the dilemma. When Collins pointedly ends their meeting by asking if anyone will ever ask to see the suspect's file, Connie answers, "Maybe a body will wash up on the Dorset coast one day, and put us all out of our misery." He expresses a hope that there will be salt water in its lungs. Collins and Connie meet again after part of an arm washes up on the coast and DNA evidence confirms that it is MacKenzie's. This evidence allows for the closing of the criminal case and the end of Connie's ordeal. Their hypothetical subtext about MacKenzie falling off a cliff — the figurative "abyss," as they call it — becomes the official record, closes the case, and ends Connie's terror.

A Dorset Morality Tale

No narrative device better explains Connie's moral dilemma than "the old morality tale of the death-ray and the elderly Chinaman" (179). Along with quotations by Thucydides and Nietzsche, this tale constitutes a moral framework that illustrates the extreme choices she is faced with, as the horrors of that Iraq basement threaten to infect the Dorset countryside. Connie is already alarmed over her parents' safety because they have been receiving anonymous nuisance phone calls that focus on her whereabouts. Although her instinct tells her MacKenzie is making the calls, she does not share her fears with her parents, and her failure to warn them about him adds to her guilt. The tale of the elderly Chinaman deals with taking responsibility for a choice and being able to live with the consequences: to press or not to press a button that will kill an elderly, unloved Chinaman on the other side of the world. Choose to press the button, and you will receive a million pounds for doing so. Connie summarizes the three choices as one, press the button and enjoy the million pounds, and assume the set-up is a scam; two, press the button and enjoy the million pounds knowing you have committed murder; and three, refuse to press the button and therefore refuse the million pounds.

MacKenzie's actions toward her parents make the tale's abstract moral ultimatum real for Connie. She is forced immediately to come to terms with her guilt, fear, and shame. The responsibility she feels for that threat to her parents catalyzes the recovery of her former confident and independent self. With brutal self-analysis, she directly compares her own situation with the choices in the morality tale and finds herself lacking. Her moral dilemma pits safety against danger, and silence against formal accusations and the pursuit of justice for MacKenzie. But she misreads herself, failing to see that only someone of moral courage and conscience would hold herself to such an unbending abstract concept of morality. She logically dismisses the "impossible" first choice because free lunches do not exist. One's soul would forever be owned by the rich man who offered the money, because doubts that it was a scam would always linger. But she accuses herself of having tried to exercise exactly that impossible choice since her abduction: reap the benefits — her life in exchange for silence about the abduction — and bear no responsibility for anyone else's death. For her, this self-centered view is morally reprehensible. It contradicts her eye-for-an-eye strict morality and the principles of social justice that undergird her work as a war correspondent. She simplifies the tale's last two honest choices: accept the million pounds for committing, along with the consequences, or refuse. The ambiguous phrase "payment for murder" refers to theoretical deaths: the women MacKenzie has already killed and the ones he will kill, if he remains free. Connie is all too aware that the euphemistic language of war makes it easy to distance oneself from responsibility for killing. Killing from afar in war is the same as pushing the button to kill the elderly Chinaman. She knows that no one will know, it will not change your life for the worse, and you will never be held responsible.

The moral crisis precipitated by the threat to her parents — a crisis configured in the tale of the elderly Chinaman — compels her to fully disclose to Collins everything she has pieced together. Knowing, however, that her own parents' lives are threatened makes the act of killing all too real. And she knows she cannot live with those consequences; thus, refusal is the only alternative. She realizes that silence is also a form of collaboration, an empowering of MacKenzie. Her silence provides him sanctuary and the opportunity of committing more crimes without ever being held accountable. Despite her recurring dream of bludgeoning MacKenzie to death, the horrors of her abduction had trained her to submit rather than rebel, to bargain for her safety with silence and compliance.

Assuming responsibility for her parents' safety marks a dramatic change in her. She can no longer lie to herself, as she did a mere two years before when she abandoned her investigation of MacKenzie because there was insufficient evidence to present to the police. She had rationalized that because she was due to leave Sierra Leone and didn't want to create a delay, she could excuse herself of responsibility for pursuing justice. Once her parents are threatened, she no longer has the option of refusing moral responsibility, nor can she shunt the responsibility onto unmotivated, disinterested law enforcement. She is forced to act or live with the unbearable consequences.

On the night Barton House is invaded, Connie undergoes an immediate transformation that she attributes to that very morality tale, her memory of what she said in her e-mail to Collins about the Chinaman, death-rays, and living with guilt. The panic attacks she has experienced since the abduction have rendered her helpless. In her memories of her days in the crate, she sees herself cowering and MacKenzie ramming himself into her mouth and telling her to smile for the camera. She reasons that, as long as she is not killed, what did it matter that others died? But when she actually sees MacKenzie sitting in her kitchen at the computer, she is not disabled by fear but transcends it. Later, however, she does not credit herself with courage or heroism. She attributes her courage to her inability to live with the overwhelming guilt that would engulf her if Peter and Jess were killed before her eyes in Barton House.

Another subtext that frames Connie's moral choice and infiltrates her memory is the story of the woman in Freetown, a story that parallels her abduction and thus haunts her. Connie had seen the woman roaming the streets of Freetown and loudly condemning herself for being alive. When rebels had attacked her village, she hid under her house while everyone else, including her husband and children, were massacred. Connie identifies with the mad Freetown woman, likening her ordeal and guilt to her own abduction and guilt. She imagines the hours the woman remained terrified and silent under the house. How did *she* handle the guilt? And was that the beginning of her madness, Connie wonders?

In the Freetown woman, Connie witnesses the anguish that results when one collaborates with murder through silence — the moral burden of reaping the benefit of staying alive oneself without suffering consequences. Like the survivor of the Freetown massacre, Connie feels guilty for being alive. No logic can convince her to see Peter's logic: that during her abduction, her choice of obedience and survival is blameless. She holds herself to a stricter standard: Blood will be on her hands if she remains silent and others die.

This unwarranted guilt derives from what she calls her journalist's exploitation of people's anguish for years. Questioning whether silence and inaction are moral, she goes so far as to say that if she suffers the same fate, it will be the punishment she deserves. Coincidentally, that very narrative comes to be, for that statement foreshadows the predicament MacKenzie forces on her when he first takes her parents hostage, tries to force them to reveal Connie's whereabouts, and subsequently threatens her friends as well.

With Collins, Connie debates the moral dimensions of the justice she eventually endorses. Because he is familiar with the serial murders in Africa and with Connie's research, only he perceives the broader context the local police cannot. When an arm washes up on a beach miles away, he sees the suggestive "interesting symmetry" to the arm having been detached in the same place where MacKenzie's deliberately broke the arm of one of his African victims (348). Only Collins and Connie are concerned with a fuller justice — seeing that MacKenzie is punished for the murders in Africa as well as his crimes in Dorset, whether the law allows for it or not. Connie insists to Collins that she would never exercise such vigilante justice because she does not believe in an eye-for-an-eye retribution. She furthers her case by pointing out, among other things, the asymmetry: to achieve perfect revenge, she would have imprisoned MacKenzie in a crate for three days. In answer to her question whether he could really believe her capable of murdering MacKenzie and disposing of his body in order to escape justice, he responds with not only iron-clad logic, but with an implied understanding of the act he assumes she has committed, an understanding that borders on approval: "Why not? He was a killer. A sadist. He liked hurting people. He boasted about what he'd done to your father ... humiliated your friend and killed her dog. You're good at hiding your feelings, Connie. You have a brain ... and you have courage. Why wouldn't you kill him if you had the chance?" (348). Collins also implies that there is no conflict between morality and a willingness to kill. But Connie's subsequent responses to him have a rehearsed quality; it's the subtext that matters. Relying on the Thucydides quotation passed down to him by his father as a moral legacy, Collins defines a brand of courage that, if it results in personal freedom leading to happiness, sanctions even what appears to be eye-for-an-eye revenge that is criminal under the law.

Implicit in this courage defined by Thucydides is taking responsibility for whatever actions or deceptions it entails. Connie and Collins' last conversation ends the book — perhaps with some readers not entirely sure about what Connie and Jess did to MacKenzie before the arrival of the police at Barton House. And what is the alternative to not acting and taking responsibility? Their conversation and the novel conclude with the answer that the alternative is "the abyss," as defined by Friedrich Nietzsche. Collins can count on Connie to correctly read his paraphrasing of Friedrich Nietzsche's famous saying: "When you fight with monsters take care not to become one yourself" (349). He mentions it as an admonition to all policemen, but she discerns the subtext that is especially applicable to her.

Connie and Collins' electric exchange that ends the novel occurs over tea and biscuits, a prosaic situation reminiscent of cozy mysteries, in which the final scene ties up all the loose ends and restores order and tranquility to the community ruptured by violence. But in this closing scene of *The Devil's Feather*, Connie trumps Collins as she tells him, "It goes on: 'If you stare too long into the abyss, the abyss stares back at you'" (349). She well knows the danger and temptation of succumbing to the moral void into which MacKenzie has plunged. Pursuing revenge threatens to take her there, too. She matter-of-factly observes that it was MacKenzie, not herself, who was unable to step back from the brink of the abyss and save himself. She was able to save herself, she assures Collins — and then offers him a biscuit. They tacitly agree to excuse their circumvention of an unresponsive, inadequate legal system to ensure that MacKenzie meets justice.

Left to her own devices to make sense of her private hell and survive, Connie has learned precisely where to draw the moral lines for herself. And unlike the Freetown woman, she survives mentally and emotionally intact, believing she has accomplished what seems logically impossible. She has perpetrated revenge but escaped without its taint, without being pulled into its hellish domain, the abyss. She has found the key to courage: knowing when to act and when to exercise restraint.

Mastery of Space and Escape

Despite its "cozy" English-countryside setting and romance plot worthy of Agatha Christie, *The Devil's Feather* explores territory where the personal and political collide. The world of the cozy — a subtext itself — whets readers' expectations: a desire for justice, the English countryside village restored to moral order, and lovers who finally get together. However, the cozy setting of *The Devil's Feather* is ironically unsettling, as it both uses and subverts conventions. Connie initially seeks refuge in Dorset not only because of its remoteness from Iraq — and presumably MacKenzie — but also because of its implied cozy factor. She rents the house sight-unseen based on a website description, the deciding factor being that it is the only property available for a six-month lease. The details about the condition of the house are deceptive, she realizes immediately upon taking possession of the house; but looking back she knows that so strong was her instinct to remove herself from the world she would have rented it even knowing about its run-down condition.

Opposite the novel's title page, a photograph of Barton House promises the literary trappings of a cozy mystery; further, Connie recalls that the photograph on the agent's website featured the homey element of climbing plants on the stone building. However, the text of the novel begins with a Reuters article titled "Spate of brutal killings" (5) about the Freetown murders of five women. Notwithstanding the authority it carries, the photo misleads. Connie's hopes of evading MacKenzie are undermined, too, within moments of her arrival at Barton House. No sooner has she stopped her car and taken a look at Barton House than she realizes that the online texts and photos of the eighteenth-century house are misleading. She bravely resists the urge to get back into her car and flee. As she attempts to unlock the front door, MacKenzie symbolically arrives at the front door in the form of Jess's five threatening mastiffs. Connie suffers a panic attack — a residue of MacKenzie's terrorizing dogs — and barricades herself in her car. These are her first moments at Barton House in cozy-land.

Although Connie seeks isolation and control over her living environment at gothic Barton House, at first it offers not refuge but more anxiety. The high hedges and vine-covered walls that greet Connie paradoxically offer not only protection but also a space in which she can be caught and victimized. Being hidden, she realizes, works to the advantage of an attacker, who could lurk in a wild garden shielded by tall hedges. Although confronted with a menacing setting, she is forced to settle in because she has "nowhere else to go" (34). So intimate does the reader become with the house that it becomes a character, partly because it seems to stand in for the absent but central character of Lily. Readers share Connie's experience of adapting to the house as if it is a protective second skin, whose every detail she must master in order to feel safe. Interestingly, her safety derives from the escape potential, not from confidence that she can fend off an intruder. She is comforted by the knowledge that each upstairs room has two entrances — or in the case of an intruder, two escape routes.

Her new friend Jess coaches Connie — albeit untactfully — on rebuilding one's life after trauma. After all, Jess had lost her entire family in a car accident twelve years ago. She criticizes Connie for being so vulnerable — how visible she is in lit-up rooms without the curtains drawn, for example. She brings her a baseball bat to keep at hand and lends her a watchdog, Bertie, the mastiff that used to belong to Lily. But Connie's unorthodox idea of caution and defense differs greatly from that of Jess, whose puzzlement is understandable, since Connie's peculiar safety plan is influenced by her abduction. Caged in the crate, she had come to feel safest there in the dark. In fact, when she's frightened at Barton House, her abduction conditioning compels her to turn on all the lights except in the one room where she hides in the dark. For Connie, control over space means the ability to vacate it without being caught, not defending it from intruders, as it does for Jess. Connie also realistically assesses her body strength and nerve; she knows she would be at a disadvantage in a physical encounter.

She ironically finds comfort and a sense of safety in ignoring or contradicting standard safety rules. The detailed descriptions of the layout of the house, the view or lack of one from various windows, the rickety doors that, despite being locked, are easily breached — all point to her mastery of the situation through mental mapping. She reasons, "Why bother to locate every light switch, oil the door locks, arm myself with torches and devise exit strategies if my conditioned response to terror was to curl into a ball in the corner with my eyes closed? Just as the mutilated victim had done in Freetown" (139).

Nevertheless, inexplicably, illogically, Connie gradually cultivates peace at Barton House. Even she realizes that she should have been ultra-vigilant over every shadow and sound, but she is lulled into a confidence that she can defend against an intruder because she knows the floor plan and oddities of the house so well. The very things that logic tells her are reasons for caution, she is able to overlook: vines tapping on the window at night, sinister silhouettes on the curtain panes, and numerous insecure French windows. From the first days, it is clear that her defense against terror and threat is critical thinking, knowing the lay of the land — a triumph of wits against brawn. Within days of her arrival, she perceives the isolating hedges and darkness of Barton House quite differently. They now make her feel secure; the same hedges that can hide an intruder can also hide her. She begins to revel in the quiet of the Dorset countryside, far from the chaos of Baghdad, and in the sheer beauty of the land where corn and rapeseed grow. She simultaneously cultivates an everyday life and friendships, while never abandoning her intensive research to track down and prosecute her abductor.

Like many readers, Connie draws her idea of England's countryside from fiction and poetry, and she is aware of it. She and the reader share those clichéd images of the quiet, safe English country village. Forced to flee Iraq because of MacKenzie's stalking and terrorizing of her, she returns to a country she admits to barely knowing, having spent no more than two months there since leaving Oxford fourteen years before, but the imagined safety of the pastoral setting lures her. She dreams of summer rain, country lanes, and soothing corn fields. In fact, it is the house's very decrepitude that seduces her into staying rather than fleeing, after the terrorizing welcome she receives from Jess's mastiffs. At first glance, the shabbiness of the eighteenth-century house had been off-putting, but within minutes, the lived-in, worn-down appeal of the house begins to attract her.

After her panic attack subsides, she stands in the hall, soothed by the contrast to her minimalist flat in Singapore. Wallpaper tacked up with Blu-Tack is peeling away from the wall, and unlike the cream-colored modern flat in Singapore, Barton House is "spacious, lofty and red-wine-friendly" (54). The faded exotic-patterned wallpaper, the worn Victorian furniture, and the threadbare rug remind her of her lost family home in Zimbabwe. The touching neglect and hominess of Barton House comfort her, contrasting as they do with the sterile or war-torn places she has lived in as a journalist. Within a short time, she e-mails her lover and boss Dan Fry in Iraq, and reassures him that she has tucked herself away in a peaceful chocolate-box village. Although the assertion is ostensibly true, Connie intentionally misleads Dan with another kind of silence — a withholding of the full truth — to lessen the pressure on herself to reassure him that she is safe and well.

Even though the novel is set in the seemingly benign English countryside, involves amateur sleuths, and has a romantic subplot involving Jess and Peter, the novel's level of violence and number of loose ends contradict the genre. Unlike the classic cozies of Christie, in *The Devil's Feather*, the offenders aren't caught and punished, at least not by the law. The person who tortures Lily suffers no legal repercussions. Connie and Jess's investigation alone gives Lily's solicitor the evidence to fairly execute her estate and attain what justice is possible. Eventually, MacKenzie is punished, no thanks to the law.

Connie's and Lily's Parallel Terrors

The parallel terror narratives of Connie and Lily Wright inextricably intertwine upon Connie's arrival at Barton House. Once sufficiently recovered from the panic attack brought on by Jess's dogs, Connie is frantic to wash her hands, and finds herself by the fishpond in the same spot where Jess had discovered Lily, collapsed and nearly dead of exposure, on a cold January night. Lily remains in a nursing home — fragile and suffering from Alzheimer's. Connie is strangely and unknowingly drawn to that spot where Jess Derbyshire found Lily, when, in frantic need to wash her hands, she recalls from the website description of the house that there is supposed to be a fishpond in the back garden.

Gradually it is revealed that Lily was the victim of terror, too — right at Barton House. Little does Connie know that her experiences there will not only exorcise MacKenzie from her life, but will expose Lily's tormentor as well. Connie finds justice not only for herself, but for Lily, too. Woven into the close bond that develops between Connie and Jess are two secrets they want buried. Connie conceals exactly what happened to her in the cellar in Iraq, and Jess wants to keep her true parentage concealed. Coincidentally, the two friends end up almost literally burying a mutual secret at Barton House.

The conclusion of the first chapter, titled "England," highlights the suspense and, more importantly, establishes the hidden well as the intuitive nexus of Connie's and Lily's narratives: "I knew nothing of [Barton House's] recent history as I stooped to wash my hands, and if I had I wouldn't have stayed. It was a place of anguish" (50). Connie ponders Lily's last night at Barton House before Jess found her freezing by the fishpond and she ended up in a hospital. Connie wonders, was the elderly Lily, deprived of water and heat in January weather and in a confused state, prompted by a memory to search for water at a well long built over with planks and a woodshed? Connie's examination of Lily's connection to the well through memory—trying to understand why and how she came to be there on a cold January night—eventually leads her to feel close to solving Lily's riddle.

Although strangers to each other, Connie and the owner of Barton House are linked in at least two ways. Both women have been terrorized, and both are invaded by memories and unable to remain in the present. Lily's Alzheimer's-induced dementia causes her to move fluidly through the years, confusing or overlapping the present with events of fifty years ago. Only the loosening of her logic betrays that she has intentionally perpetrated a misreading for decades, one that benefited her both socially and financially. One moment Lily knows she's speaking to Jess in the present, and the next she imagines she is speaking to Jess's grandmother, her family servant of decades before. Jess gradually realizes that a thank-you from Lily meant she was remembering the nineteen-nineties and an order from her meant she was reliving the nineteen-fifties. When she experiences a panic attack, Connie's sense of time also becomes fluid. She is involuntarily transported back to her abduction and even re-experiences the near-suffocation MacKenzie induced by almost drowning her.

Connie's acute intuition and journalistic instinct lead her soon after her arrival at Barton House to ask the right questions and discover the discrepancies in Lily's confusing narrative, as conveyed by Jess. In contrast, the community of Winterbourne Valley and even Jess have misread Lily for decades. To some extent, the community is culpable for the sadistic terrorizing that Lily experienced over a period of weeks. Jess alone knows the two versions of how her family came to own the substantial land she farms, and those are as drastically different, she tells Connie. Jess's own grandmother perpetrated a half-true narrative rather than reveal who Jess's parents are. Ironically, it is Lily, her memory and self-control loosed by Alzheimer's, who provides the counter-narrative that effects justice in her own case.

Jess's grandmother was not merely a maid at Barton House, nor are the family relationships what they seem. The community misreads the Wright family's treating Jess's family like unpaid servants as a holdover obligation from the grandmother's days as a maid, maligning Jess's character (e.g., a "predatory lesbian" [70], radical animal rights activist, and stalker), and even going so far as to suspect Jess's kind attentions to Lily as a ploy to influence her will. The community fails to effect justice when it also misreads Lily's Alzheimer's-induced bizarre behavior when she begins wandering into neighbors' houses, tiptoeing upstairs, bathing herself, and falling asleep in their beds. Her neighbors fail to discern — or even question — the motivation behind her odd, unprecedented behavior, attributing it to rudeness and the presumption of class. The community's failure to see the cruelty going on under their noses results in yet another injustice: the unfounded assumption that Jess was responsible for not looking after Lily, in keeping with the "servant-mistress" role she had inherited from her grandmother and father. Not privy to the complications in the Wright and Derbyshire families, the community has embraced a narrative of lies.

Both Jess and Connie unwittingly become catalysts for justice on Lily's behalf. Connie follows up by piecing together the truth and, through Lily's lawyer, insuring that Lily's estate is executed fairly. The income from the rental of Barton House will support Lily comfortably in the nursing home until her death. In matters unrelated to her own trauma, Connie can easily apply more objectivity and restraint. For example, she sensibly hands over to Lily's solicitor all the evidence she and Jess have about the elderly woman's tormentor. They relegate to him the responsibility of deciding whether to proceed with legal charges and to what extent he will follow his client's wishes regarding the dispensation of her estate. The result is the greatest degree of justice Connie and Jess can reasonably expect.

Connie's "Notes": The Master Narrative

The dated "extracts from notes" interspersed throughout the novel constitute a subtext that documents Connie's private day-to-day struggle with the terror that still grips her. In these ruptures in the main narrative, she shows a vulnerable, self-reflective, and still-frightened side of herself. The notes also reveal Connie's paralyzing guilt and shame over her abduction. The sexual violence, her terrorized submissiveness, and her obedient silence since McKenzie released her — all increase her shame and feelings of cowardice. And she is also shamed by hiding behind the journalistic hype perpetrated by her Reuters boss, the myth of her "courage and professionalism" (150). We accept the extracts from notes as authoritative, private, and honest; but they are incomplete. This specialized set of narratives chronicles Connie's struggle to recover and preserve her lost life and self. She writes in her journal-like notes that her life will never be the same again and she will never again be the person she was.

In fact, the notes give readers a privileged view of her preoccupation with revenge she at first adamantly denies having: "The artist Paul Gauguin once said, 'Life being what it is, one dreams of revenge.' *I* dream of revenge. All the time" (65). The seeds of revenge are sown during her abduction, when she used the promise of it to survive, even as she obeyed MacKenzie's every order. Although outwardly compliant, she rebelled inwardly to maintain her sanity, vowing that should he let her live, *he* would die. In the privacy of the notes, she hypothetically faces the truth about the impotence of the law in procuring justice, and in those entries readers learn the details about what parts of the truth she acknowledged and to whom. She reveals that although the police suspected her of evasiveness, she was nevertheless honest when she told them she had no more to tell them. Nor could she be more forthcoming with Dan. Besides, she concedes that the one unknown bit of evidence she does not reveal would be dismissed by the authorities: the evidence of MacKenzie's smell. This honesty forces self-reliance, and in these pages, she bravely faces the fact that she is on her own.

Her dreams of revenge are not general, not merely about inflicting physical and psychological damage on her abductor; her ideal revenge is a specialized one focusing on personal relationships the abduction caused her to lose. The revenge she fantasizes about involves recovering the fragile trust she once enjoyed among the people she cares about. Her revenge is about not living with a permanent suspicion of others or enduring their suspicions of her— particularly the suspicion that she faked her abduction for publicity. MacKenzie's care to not leave the marks of his torture further complicates the aftermath of Connie's ordeal, for she has no evidence to prove the torture occurred. Her unverifiable abduction evokes doubt instead of the unquestioned sympathy that her fellow journalist Adelina receives after her abduction. Oddly enough, however, the absence of marks works to her advantage immediately after the abduction. Able to deceive the press into believing that essentially nothing happened to her, Connie creates a false narrative that thus aids her silence and reclusiveness.

The notes further testify to Connie's insight in analyzing the tangle of subtexts by perceiving discrepancies, lies, and connections. Within the privacy of those notes, we see her detective instincts at work. For example, even after first hearing Jess's accounts of Lily and Madeleine, Connie correctly divines that the tension between Jess and Madeleine derives from something other than a past romantic rivalry. These notes also document how Connie constructs and manipulates her own narrative of recovery. As a narrative strategy, the extracts from notes reveal yet more facets to her prodigious talents for dissembling — not for malicious ends but for self-protection. For example, even though she has settled into Barton House, early on she e-mails DI Alan Collins that as yet she has no permanent address and phone number and that she is still unsettled. Her analytical and research savvy enables her to master the situation and rescue herself and others. Even in her instinctive leaps of imagination, her ingenious fabricated narratives become tools that help her and others to survive.

Collaborative Subtexts: Instruments of Justice

In the course of their investigation, Connie and Jess share or co-create a group of specialized subtexts, and their collaboration on texts and images emphasizes the trust between them as they correct misleading versions of the truth. The video of the family of weasels that Jess shares with Connie reveals a creative side of her that, up until then, no one but Peter has seen. Other creative and healing projects such as Jess's family photomontage also testify to Jess's emotional health and strength. She is not the psychotic, depressed, anti-social person most of the community believes her to be.

Upon seeing the interior of Jess's house, Connie is instantly struck by the discrepancies between the community's view of Jess and the reality. The popular view is that after the death of her parents and siblings in a car accident twelve years ago, Jess converted the house into a monument to them, a home frozen in time, a morbid shrine. Instead, Connie finds a tasteful, well-kept house crammed with high-tech equipment and a modern home office. The shrine to the family consists of a touching and artistic corridor filled with family photos — in natural and happy moments — that impress Connie as a tribute to life and love, not a morbid fixation on death. In addition, Jess runs a successful farm with the help of several employees. All evidence undermines the narratives Connie has heard about a supposedly psychologically disturbed Jess.

Their first collaborative project is the enhancement of a photo of MacKenzie, with Connie contributing her research on MacKenzie and Jess applying her impressive photography and computer skills. Her skill and success show a woman at home in the digital age, not stuck in a morbid past. This project undercuts the false narrative that the village has spun about Jess and produces an authoritative text that contributes greatly to the investigation. The most significant of the collaborative subtexts, however, is a videotaped confession by Lily's tormentor. Connie plays the provocateur who angers the subject into confession, and Jess plays the hidden technical person capturing it all on digital video. Connie's use of taunts, baiting, and fabrications — the same tactics she uses in conquering MacKenzie — strengthens the parallels between these narrative strands. The strategies entrap both a murderer and a would-be murderer. In tricking Lily's tormentor, the women gain evidence that verifies their version of Lily's recent history. Later, they hand over the video to Lily's solicitor, who is able to correct his own misreadings of Lily's history. That confession, secretly caught on video by Jess, becomes yet another subtext, a subset of truth-telling that is subsequently viewed, analyzed, and discussed by four characters. Like other invented or nonexistent subtexts, it also substantially affects the direction of the main narrative.

The malicious narratives perpetrated about Jess's family history and standing initially infect Connie's mind and lead her to many misconceptions about the Derbyshires and the Wrights. Without knowing the full intricacies of Jess's family history, Lily's daughter Madeleine pointedly discredits and maligns Jess. She says that Jess is a lesbian — something she knows the rural village certainly condemns — and accuses her of mental instability. She slanders Jess by saying she stalks people she wants to befriend and, after she alienates them, makes threatening phone calls to them. Connie's ability — and willingness — to read Jess correctly helps to catalyze the eventual unraveling of Lily's narrative. Connie's rejection of the community's long-held misconceptions about Jess also makes possible their friendship and teamwork that bring justice to both MacKenzie and Lily's would-be murderer.

Faked and Hypothetical Subtexts of Truth

The most interesting, quirky, and consequential narrative devices are ones that are faked or hypothetical, each of which operates as investigative tools or weapons. Connie's fear that MacKenzie will come after her if she does not remain silent motivates her to create a misleading public narrative for the press. Her boss and lover Dan aids her in evading heavy press coverage and she escapes to London incognito. She misleads him, saying that in the end she was lucky, compared to her colleague Adelina. She emphasizes that she survived and that little of consequence happened during those three days. Rather than face the unpredictable consequences of the story of her abduction coming out, Connie preferred to risk being thought a fraud.

Connie strongly resists Peter's suggestion that she speak out about her abduction. To counteract his logic, she shares with him her imaginary impromptu news story that invalidates and rewrites the published Reuters news stories that open the novel. In effect, those terse "factual" news stories nevertheless lie to protect Connie's fragile sense of self:

> Yesterday, at London's Old Bailey, a 36-year-old newswire journalist sensationally revealed details of her Baghdad kidnap. Far from the lucky-to-be-alive version she gave at the time of her release, it was a three-day ordeal of torture and sadism that persuaded her to change her name and go into hiding. Claiming to be deeply scarred and still in fear of her life, the blonde Zimbabwean named the defendant, Keith MacKenzie, as her attacker [170].

This hypothetical text is her way of sharing the truth with Peter. Like the photograph and video she co-creates with Jess, these imaginary news stories are a means of building intimacy and justifying her silence.

On the night he invades Barton House, MacKenzie brings with him a DVD recording of his oral rape of Connie during her abduction and plays it on Connie's computer for Peter and Jess. But contrary to what he expects, Connie is not intimidated and shamed into submission as she sees the horrifying film and hears her own voice repeatedly pleading with MacKenzie to stop. Before this showdown with him, the shame and humiliation associated with that video had haunted and controlled Connie, even given her nightmares; she had assiduously monitored the Internet, fearful that the film would be posted. Connie's and Peter's interpretations of that film differ significantly. The version of the video that she carries in her memory is self-deceiving; but Peter, who has an uncanny ability to read Connie accurately from the first moment he meets her, tries to help her realize how she is misreading her own memories, to her detriment: Whatever she did, he reassures her, she did because she was forced to. Her shame merely affirms MacKenzie's continuing control over her life. A key dynamic of Peter and Connie's relationship is her fighting for control over her own narrative and Peter persistently offering alternative readings.

Peter wants to correct her misreading — that video in her head — her feeling that she eagerly complied with the rape and she is now forever degraded and repulsive. Although she purports to fear its being shown in court because it is the only evidence of his crime — and she has no doubt that it will be shown — Peter rightly perceives that Connie misreads the video as condemning *her* rather than MacKenzie. Peter points out that she similarly grossly misread the news video of fellow journalist Adelina after her abductors released her, which included close-up shots of her badly beaten face. Despite Adelina's small stature and black eyes, Connie sees Adelina as "indomitable," although Peter insists that in the news video he saw "a frightened woman" (175). Connie repeatedly berates herself with the thought that she was not as brave as Adelina, a false assumption that Peter is determined to disabuse Connie of. Peter does not see a brave Adelina at a press conference, as Connie does; he sees a terrified woman. Realizing that she has misread her own actions and memories is a blow to Connie's self-confidence. Because Peter is familiar with international guidelines for the investigation and documentation of torture, he clearly sees that much of her behavior corresponds to indicators for catastrophic ill-treatment and abuse.

On the night of the invasion, Connie fights back by simply out-thinking MacKenzie. They are frozen in a standoff, she with axe in hand and he at the computer playing the humiliating DVD of her abduction. Both Peter and Jess are unwilling and incapacitated witnesses. Connie's flair for the impromptu subtext does not fail her in the crisis. Just as a series of creative, logical leaps had led her to the truth about the crimes against Lily, her imaginative leaps now confuse and stall MacKenzie. Connie's intellectual arsenal includes the invention of an imaginary police statement made by MacKenzie's mother. She bases the document on psychological profiles of his type, on Internet information about sadists and rapists, and on one stunning detail with a personal touch. In Africa, MacKenzie had once given Connie a letter and asked her to post it while she was in England. She remembers the addressee, Mary McKenzie in Glasgow, and uses this random information to fabricate a narrative to distract and disorient her adversary.

Connie's use of this invented statement marks a turn in the battle with MacKenzie, when she tells him that the police know about him, and that, moreover, his own mother has given a statement about him. She begins to detect doubt in his demeanor, and the entrapment works when MacKenzie's curiosity compels him to ask what the statement says. She ingeniously invents yet another narrative, complete with a devastating detail — that his mother told the police that she thinks her son is responsible for several unsolved murders of prostitutes. So convincing is her spiel that even readers cannot be sure at first if it is true. Connie discerns that the confrontation begins to turn in her favor when she sees that a confused MacKenzie did not know whether to believe her fabrications or not. So ingenious is she at fabricating texts, improvising, and manipulating MacKenzie that even Bagley later questions her role of mastermind of imagined texts. He is amazed that she is able to invent a plausible narrative from both Mrs. MacKenzie's statement and MacKenzie's psychological profile.

The missing invoice for filling Lily's fuel tank, whose existence Connie and Jess easily infer, is key in helping them to piece together the details of the systematic torture of the elderly woman through deprivation. The absence of an invoice from the full set of records in Lily's shed is but one piece in the complex puzzle. Lily's "fantasy will" (205) too is also a crucial document in solving Lily's riddle, although the will does not physically exist. The will's contents and Lily's intent are known, but only from Lily's demented ramblings to Jess. Connie theorizes that the will is something Lily wanted, even intended, to have drawn up but never did; Jess, however, surmises that it does indeed exist. Therefore, the two women brilliantly use the hypothetical document as ammunition to provoke the person guilty of torturing Lily into a confession.

The Convergence of Narratives: Justice and Revenge

Connie's sense of Old-Testament justice is needlessly unforgiving, as Peter points out. Believing that everyone gets what is coming to him is a comforting but cynical thought, since she tends to hold herself overly responsible for MacKenzie's actions post–Iraq. Convinced that the English public has a right to know about MacKenzie, she is torn between her need for privacy — and the safety she feels her silence about her abduction will earn her — and the obligation to inform that public. She is haunted by the thought that it will be her fault if MacKenzie continues his killing spree in England. Despite her assuming responsibility for his potential further violence, she doubts the effectiveness of her testimony, and imagines a worst-case scenario if she were to testify — MacKenzie's getting away scot-free and her being accused of faking the abduction for publicity. Connie sees the futility of relying on the criminal justice system; her cynical view combines realism, self-loathing, and doubt. Two years ago, she had abandoned her investigation of MacKenzie, knowing that the evidence she could present to the police in Sierra Leone and Iraq would not result in a conviction. At that time, she had the luxury of convincing herself that ensuring justice was not her responsibility; but now in Dorset, Peter is a healthy counter-force to her blindnesses about herself. Intuitive enough to have divined the facts of Connie's abduction and informed about the psychological effects of torture, he bolsters her resilience and her courage. When she counters with the assertion that she was MacKenzie's devil's feather and was to blame, Peter retorts that she was a prisoner. On the night of the invasion, Connie adamantly rejects MacKenzie's repeated use of the pejorative term in addressing her — a name she was forced to accept during her abduction. This repudiation of even MacKenzie's control over the language of their interactions epitomizes her courageous fight to own herself once again, to live without fear.

On the night of the invasion, the extremity of the situation instantly corrects Connie's misreadings of MacKenzie himself. Her first impression of more than two years ago in Sierra Leone had been a threatening one. Ironically, she had likened him to a dog: "the build of a terrier — middling height, lean muscular frame, strong neck and limbs — and a terrier's ferocity once he had his teeth into someone" (8). But the MacKenzie she sees sitting at her computer desk in her kitchen in Barton House is significantly diminished, despite his initial advantage. Realizing she is not as afraid as she had expected to be, she intuits that her self-control gives her an advantage over the now-isolated MacKenzie. No longer the ferocious terrier who literally had played God with her body and life, he now appears "smaller" and "seedier" (246) and his repulsive odor betrays his unwashed state. Her terrorizer is reduced to "a dirty little runt" (283). Observing his body language and nervous facial expressions, his former victim sees his debilitating doubt and relentlessly presses her luck, improvising as she goes.

Connie's sharp intellect is essentially her only weapon when MacKenzie invades Barton House and threatens her and her friends. As she uses her intelligence to lie, mislead, and confuse her adversary, MacKenzie attempts to use threats to her friends' safety to manipulate her into a fate that is unknown, unspoken, but lethal. What are the possibilities? Leaving with him to end up dead? Being raped, humiliated, and killed in front of them? Initiating a violent physical confrontation that she has no hope of surviving? It is in this moment that all the narratives, readings, and misreadings coalesce for Connie into an accuracy that makes her courage easy and inevitable. All of Peter's and Collins' warnings about how the memory distorts, all the research, all the excerpts, all the narratives she interpreted as evidence of her cowardice and stupidity — all give way to the realization that she had never really seen MacKenzie or herself accurately. With this empowering coalescence, Connie counters each of MacKenzie's demands with an implacable refusal. She quickly escalates from irrefutable noncompliance to taunts and provocation, and even resorts to vulgar jokes about his genitals. In only moments, she turns the tide of terror, and it is MacKenzie who is under siege.

Peter's comments to Inspector Bagley about that night's event provide an arguably objective measure of Connie's self-control and courage in her encounter with MacKenzie — an assessment that surprises her. Peter characterizes her actions as calculated from the first moment she enters the kitchen to find MacKenzie there and her friends in danger. And not only does he state that she knew exactly what she was doing, but that MacKenzie had that impression as well — perhaps an insight into why he eventually crumbled under Connie's challenges and aggressive taunts. Connie disputes Peter's memories of the events. Does she argue because she is motivated to dissemble? We must wonder if his impressions reflect her on-the-spot courage or his misreading of Connie's state of mind when she finds MacKenzie in her house. Is Peter offering the most accurate version of the narrative when he tells Bagley that MacKenzie certainly thought Connie was out for revenge — so much so, that he was frightened of his former abductee? In fact, she answers that she improvised the events; she relied on instinct, knowing she was incapable of using a weapon. Peter fails to take into account one crucial fact, that bearing the responsibility for her friends' lives bolsters Connie's courage during the siege. The mere presence of her friends, she argues, gave her the courage to face her adversary. When Jess also credits her friend with courage, Connie falls back on her habitual self-deprecation and guilt by saying that she was responsible for putting everyone in danger in the first place by coming to live in Barton House.

When pondering the horrendous chaos of the dog attack and MacKenzie's mortal wounding of Bertie the dog, Connie herself cannot even be sure if revenge motivated her. She has no idea what she really intended when she seized the axe, and remembers thinking only that the violence against Bertie was unfair. Even though she meant to hit MacKenzie's head with the axe, she only manages to break three of his fingers. Only the intensity of the moment pushes her to pick up and use an axe she had concluded she had neither the physical strength nor the guts to use on MacKenzie. Instead, she relied on her intellect, her ability to out-think and confuse him. Her motives, however, are ambiguous, even to herself. Should we believe her when she tells Bagley that she thought about hitting MacKenzie on the head to knock him out once he was tied up, but did not want to kill him accidentally? It is clear that Bagley suspects her of murderous intent. She concedes that she regrets not using the axe earlier in the fight; doing so would have saved Bertie the mastiff, who was killed when MacKenzie slashed his carotid artery: "There was no contest between which of them deserved to live and which deserved to die" (272).

Does the reader feel complicit in Connie's illegal, if not vengeful, acts? She is aware that in the eyes of the law, revenge is a criminal offense, and she feels it hanging over head during one of the many sessions of intense police questioning. The photograph of Barton House, the Reuters articles reporting the murders in Sierra Leone, and the Thucydides quotation encapsulate the salvation and the damnation of Connie's psychological journey before the narration even begins. The quotation also establishes the moral framework of *The Devil's Feather* and echoes a perennial Walters theme — a woman's hard-won personal salvation. Connie learns that courage is the ability to respond, not to refrain or freeze. The restraint and inaction commonly thought to ensure a civilized society are, in her situation, actually dangerous. Acting, however, involves the overriding of involuntary responses, a daunting task. She is shocked at how the Pavlovian responses instilled by three days in a cellar could override a lifetime of behavior patterns and contradict the very self she unquestionably believed she was and always would be. Awash in a sea of misinformation and false narratives in the Dorset countryside, Connie Burns masters them, composes her own, and picks up the dropped narrative thread of her former life. The result, finally, is justice that coincidentally exacts a satisfying measure of revenge.

Works Cited

Baird, Emma. "Minette Walters — In It Together." *Minette Walters*. 25 Oct. 2006. .
Eagleton, Terry. *Literary Theory: An Introduction*. Minneapolis: University of Minnesota Press, 1983.
Walters, Minette. *The Devil's Feather*. New York: Knopf, 2006.
_____. "FAQ." 25 Oct. 2006. http://minettewalters.co.uk/babout_minette/faqs.htm.

Everyday Heroes: Women of Valor

RACHEL SCHAFFER

Minette Walters has written an impressive collection of socially conscious crime novels that address a wide variety of issues, from race and class prejudice to rape and domestic violence, focusing, as she says on her official website, "on the trauma that exists within families and communities when a murder is committed, and explor[ing] the tensions that necessarily arise from it" ("FAQ" 3). In most of her novels, it is a female protagonist who, through her attempts to uncover what really happened in connection with a crime, serves as readers' surrogate righter of wrongs, avenger of victims, or most essentially, revealer of the truth. Walters' women are neither professional crime fighters nor even amateur detectives with experience gained over years of solving cases; rather, they are ordinary women doing the best they can day to day when they are caught up in a criminal investigation that changes both them and their lives. While some focus on seeing justice done, most are primarily interested in simply finding out the truth, regardless of how their revelations may (or may not) be used afterward. They pursue their various goals with integrity and determination, often facing down their own fears and considerable opposition to do what they believe is right. They exhibit qualities that while not stereotypically bold and daring still qualify as quietly heroic in nature. In general, Walters' protagonists are ordinary women who prove themselves to be *everyday* heroes: women who do what they feel they must — and more than most of us would or could do — in the face of serious obstacles.

Walters has often been asked why she chose to write stand-alone novels rather than a series; she explains on her website, "I was never interested in creating a series character because I wanted to be free to tackle whatever I wanted, when I wanted, without being shackled to a particular person or place" (2). Her decision has left her free to explore her characters unrestricted by the need for consistency in developing a series protagonist's personality and behavior. The result is a variety of protagonists, mostly female, from different backgrounds — different social classes, family situations, professions, and educations — and with different motivations and personalities, some more heroic and selfless than others, but all well rounded and at the very least, like the children of Garrison Keillor's Lake Wobegon, all well above average. Few of the women are ostentatiously feminist, but their personal qualities make them the best exemplars of feminism: they lead by example and serve as worthy role models for readers of both sexes. All of them have attributes that enable them to carry out a crime investigation and deal with the repercussions of their actions, which sometimes include direct attacks on them. And all of them share certain basic traits that readers can admire and identify with and that keep readers' sympathies firmly with them in their quest to achieve their goals.

Everyday Heroes

The familiar heroes in history, mythology, and literature — the epic, tragic, and romantic heroes — are men whose noble qualities far exceed those of the average person, who pursue dangerous quests, win great battles, and find true love, and whose deeds are admired by all. Northrop Frye, in his discussion of the archetypes of literature, describes the hero in myth as "conceived in human likeness and yet hav[ing] more power over nature" and belonging to "an omnipotent personal community" (1455).

More modern views, however, broaden the list of traits that qualify as heroic. Dixon Wecter and Andrew Bernstein, for example, emphasize traits of intellect and character as well as courage and physical strength in their discussions of heroes. Bernstein defines a hero very specifically as "an individual of elevated moral stature and superior ability who pursues his goals indefatigably in the face of powerful antagonist(s)" (4). He distinguishes the hero from mere moral men, achievers, or role models, all of whom may be great men, certainly, but who do not qualify as heroes unless, in addition, they "[hold] rational values and [fight] for them, if necessary against every conceivable form of opposition" (4).

Another view is offered by John Cawelti, who recognizes two kinds of heroes: superheroes, like Frye's heroes of myth, with "exceptional strength or ability," and "'one of us,' a figure marked ... by flawed abilities and attitudes presumably shared by the audience" (40). Roger R. Rollin uses Frye's label for this second type of hero: Everyman-Heroes, people who are "ordinary mortals thrust by chance or circumstances into extraordinary situations. Unlike most mortals, however, they do not back off: they accept the challenge, rise to the occasion, and thereby raise themselves above the legions of the average" (29). Frye's description fits Walters' protagonists perfectly: when they are forced to deal with the aftermath of crime and violence, they display not completely uncommon but still highly admirable forms of heroism. Will Wright's label, "popular heroes," also describes them well: "Popular heroes are popular because they represent accessible and effective kinds of actions. In an important sense, we are all the heroes of our own stories" (147). This explains why female readers can identify closely with Walters' protagonist-heroes: they can well believe that if they found themselves in similar circumstances, they could indeed emulate these women and take whatever action would be required to achieve a positive outcome.

Walters' protagonists are not powerful, either physically or socially; with one exception (military officer Nancy Smith in *Fox Evil*), they do not work in dangerous occupations or charge themselves with saving humankind. They are simply good women who display the kinds of qualities that make them ideal role models: intelligence, courage, and heart. Perhaps what makes them most truly heroic in their own quiet way is that they care about others, about fighting injustice, and about protecting the innocent. They are heroic in their desire to bring a little more order into their own small corner of a highly disordered world, to do what they can to make things just a little bit better, even at their own peril.

Walters' protagonists are by no means superwomen, but they are all educated, professional women, with careers ranging from teaching, medicine, and the military to journalism, photography, and social work. Most of them are also attractive: Walters' male characters often comment, both to themselves and others, about the effect their beauty has on people. Jinx Kingsley, in *The Dark Room*, for example, is described as "a bit of a stunner" (103); Mrs. Ranelagh in *The Shape of Snakes* is addressed as "Pretty Lady" by a neighbor (351); and Anne Cattrell, in *The Ice House*, is beautiful "in her own way" (133). They also tend to be perceptive, determined, and physically brave when they need to be even though, for the most part, they have no special training in fighting and have little or no prior experience with dangerous situations. More than anything else, however, what makes them heroic is their willingness to risk something of vital importance to them, whether reputation or physical safety, in order to see a wrong righted.

Fighting for Truth and Justice

If, as Bernstein maintains, "the hero is the man who lets no obstacle prevent him from pursuing the values he has chosen" (3), then the values that Walters' heroic women have chosen to pursue are most often truth and justice. Indeed, the majority of Walters' protagonists are engaged in some kind of search for truth, whether an impersonal truth about a crime that gradually becomes personal or an intimately personal crime-related truth that directly affects their lives. Jinx Kingsley, in *The Dark Room*, exemplifies the latter. She is struggling to learn a truth that is as personal as a truth can be: because of an automobile crash, Jinx has retrograde amnesia. She has lost the last few days, during which she supposedly tried to commit suicide. Not only is Jinx trying to recover her memory of what happened to her during that time, but she is also a prime suspect in the recent murders of her fiance Leo and best friend Meg, just as she was in her husband's murder several years previously.

The stress of her situation might paralyze a less formidable woman, but as a result of her husband's murder and the subsequent criminal investigation, Jinx has learned to be tough and stoic. When her doctor, Alan Protheroe, says, "'I've never met anyone, man or woman, who is as self-reliant as you are,'" she replies, "'It's something you learn very quickly when you find yourself on the wrong end of a murder inquiry.... You never stop watching your back'" (295). She exerts an iron control over her emotions and gives nothing away about her true feelings, preferring to put on a brave face. After Alan has been attacked on the grounds of the clinic that he runs and where she has been recuperating, she decides to go for a walk in the grounds despite the fact that there is danger for her, as well. When Alan tells her that she is brave for going out alone with his assailant still at large, she explains that she does not want to be like the fox in a trap another patient told her about. The fox tried to escape by biting off its own leg, but died of fright. Jinx wants to prove to herself that, unlike the fox, she will not die of fright if she exercises her desire for freedom (313).

Underneath her brave public face, however, Jinx experiences real fear about what she might remember. She tells Alan at one point, "I like it the way it is. I don't want to *remember* anything. I don't want to *know* anything. I don't want to *feel* anything" (192–93). Nevertheless, as flashes of what happened begin to come back to her, she deals with them, eventually regaining full memory of the ordeal she went through. The night of the murders, despite her fear of Meg and Leo's killer — who tried to kill her as well — she exhibited true courage and love in risking her own life to try to save them. She too would have died if not for some good luck. After hearing the full story from Jinx, one of the investigating officers acknowledges her heroism: "You obviously have a very strong will to live, Miss Kingsley. I envy you your courage, and whichever guardian angel is watching over you" (332).

In *Disordered Minds*, in her pursuit of the truth about a decades-old murder case she has become interested in, George (short for Georgina) Gardener displays the same kind of fortitude and determination as Jinx, though without her more personal motivation. As a social worker living on the same street where Grace Jefferies was murdered more than thirty years ago, George feels a natural interest in the case of the accused killer, Grace's grandson Howard Stamp. George's highly developed sense of justice tells her that he was wrongly convicted, and after hearing about a book by anthropologist Jonathan Hughes in which the case is discussed, she contacts him and offers her help in trying to establish Howard's innocence.

At sixty, George is older than the other female protagonists, has never been married, and is far different physically from the typical Walters woman. She is described by Jonathan as fat (81) and "astonishingly ugly" (96). However, she is extremely well educated, and as Jonathan comes to know her better, he realizes that she is also "unassuming and kind" (93). The owner of the local pub tells him that "she's been trying for years to get someone interested" (118) in Howard's case, not for money or credit — "That's not George's way. Never has been" (118) he adds — but to see justice done. Clearly, through her motivation and actions, George demonstrates all the qualities of a quietly heroic woman, determined to pursue her mission even though she is seriously ill, and to persevere in the face of Jonathan's initial reluctance to work with her, as well as ongoing deception, manipulation, and discouragement from those with something to hide. She contacts Jonathan's agent, enclosing information that intrigues Jonathan enough to persuade him to reply, and they form a tentative partnership that deepens as they get to know each other better.

By the end of the novel, thanks in large part to George's efforts and insights, the truth has come out, the guilty look likely to be punished, and Jonathan and George have become good friends. Jonathan, who was initially hostile toward George and suspicious of her motives, has grown so fond of her that he teases her by referring to her as his mother, claiming that she once had a brief fling with a Jamaican and now tries to act as though he is her much younger boyfriend. George's determination to see justice done, even in the face of serious illness, makes her a role model that even a distinguished anthropologist decades younger can admire.

Fighting to Do the Right Thing

Not all of Walters' novels feature a woman as a crime investigator, but even those protagonists not actively engaged in investigation are still affected by crime and must often make difficult decisions guided by their inherent sense of the right thing to do in a given situation. They demonstrate Bernstein's heroic "unbreached and unbreachable allegiance to the good in the face of any possible form of opposition" (3). Walters' first novel, *The Ice House*, illustrates this theme by presenting an ethically complex attempt to do the right thing that involves covering up a crime. The three women living together on Phoebe Maybury's country estate are suspects in the death of a man whose body was found on their property. Phoebe Maybury was also the prime suspect in the disappearance of her brutally abusive husband David ten years ago, but the police could find no trace of his body on the grounds of her estate. Her best friends, Anne Cattrell and Diana Goode, supported her throughout both her turbulent marriage and the hostile police investigation that followed David's disappearance, keeping what they knew about what happened to him to themselves. In the end, unlike those Walters protagonists who try to uncover the truth, these three women do their best to keep the truth hidden because they believe that the right thing to do in this case is to protect Phoebe and her children from yet more pain and suffering caused by David even long after his death.

Phoebe shows true courage in dealing with David's death and its aftermath in two additional ways. Ten years ago, CI Walsh was eager to prove Phoebe guilty of killing her husband, not just because he believed she was guilty but also because she refused his sexual advances. When Phoebe "turned him down and told him where to stick his protection" (256), Walsh started a "malicious smear campaign" (257) to make sure the whole town thought not just that she was guilty of murder but also that she was part of a lesbian menage à trois. Phoebe bravely decides to end the resulting gossip and ongoing social ostracism by appearing in public for the first time in years and reaching out to the local community; she tells Diana, "I will brave that wretched pub tomorrow. Someone's got to make the first move and it might as well be me" (294).

Acid Row also presents a woman caught up in a difficult situation demanding difficult decisions about what to do. Like many of Walters' novels, it uses shifting points of view, with the key female protagonist, Dr. Sophie Morrison, facing extreme danger because she does the right thing. At the end of a long day, given a choice between leaving a public housing estate where she keeps pepper spray in her pocket to ward off thugs or making one more house call, she decides in favor of the patient, an elderly man suffering from asthma. As a result, she is swept up in a mob attack on the man's home and is threatened and hurt by the man himself. When Sophie does escape the siege of the house in which she is trapped, she has yet another choice; she can abandon the man and his son, who has fallen unconscious during their escape, or do what she can to keep them safe.

Once again, she chooses to help, telling the woman in whose home they have taken refuge, "I can't leave my patient" (300).

In *The Scold's Bridle*, it is the teenager Ruth Lascelles who shows enormous courage in striving to do the right thing by helping the police convict a manipulative thug who has developed a horrifyingly effective method for coercing girls to steal for him. In Ruth's case, the thug wants her to steal from her grandmother. When Ruth objects, he breaks her will and enforces obedience by locking her in a van with a group of his friends, who repeatedly rape her, and then promises more of the same unless she agrees to do what he wants (191). Ruth is thoroughly traumatized by the experience and terrified that if she helps the police in any way, the mastermind will find her and punish her again. Nevertheless, she gives the thug's address to a friend, thus prevents another young girl from being raped, and, together with three other victims, agrees to testify against him. Another friend points out that all four young women should be admired for the courage they show in being willing to face the gang leader at his trial (357).

Fighting Back

Some of Walters' protagonists do display the more familiar heroic qualities of physical bravery and a disregard for their own safety in the interest of defending their values and protecting others. When they are pushed to it by necessity and circumstance, their innate motivation to achieve good causes their actions to be raised to a more heroic level: like Bernstein's heroes, they will "expend all their energy, engage in any struggle, take on every foe" (4) to attain their goals. Rosalind Leigh, in *The Sculptress*, for example, may be depressed to the point of considering suicide as the novel opens, and she can be naive in her trust of Olive, the woman she is trying to free from prison and who may in fact be manipulating her. But Roz's heroic traits far outweigh the negative ones; she is fiercely independent, has a well-developed sense of responsibility and justice that prevents her from abandoning Olive, and has reserves of courage in the face of danger that allow her to fight back when physically attacked and to proceed with her quest for truth even when threatened with retaliation if she notifies the police about the assault. Clever and resourceful, she uses the weapons at hand to protect herself—in one fight, sticking a hatpin into "the buttock" of one of her attackers (219)—and concealing a small tape recorder in a box of Tampax to gather incriminating evidence against a thug, knowing that he would search her and her purse but not that particular item.

Dr. Sophie Morrison in *Acid Row* is also a fighter and does her best to protect herself against an assailant. When she is threatened with assault by a sadistic patient, Franek Zelowski, she barricades herself in a corner of the room to keep him at bay and gradually realizes it is her own fear that arouses him more than anything about her physical appearance. He knows just how to frighten her, and "[s]he couldn't bear the way he knew what she was thinking.... It was an invasion. A brutal assault on resolve, setting her at war with herself about whether to keep standing up to him or appease through silence " (116). In the face of doubts about whether she is correct, she decides that "[s]he had to stand up to him" (117), and although she pays physically for her decision, she continues to fight back, injuring Franek in return and holding him off. Not a trained fighter, Sophie eventually loses; her rescuer finds her with her "face battered beyond belief" (260). Even so, her rescuer also observes that "[s]he must have fought like a tigress. The old man's face was scratched and clawed as if two-inch talons had hooked into his skin and ripped it wide open" (260). Unlike the other women in Franek's life, Sophie does not let fear win and fights back as long as she can even though she is afraid; and she makes sure the police know that, telling an officer that "this bastard punched me at least twenty times but *still* couldn't get me to submit. There is *nothing* ... in this *whole* world ... that would have allowed me to give in to a worthless piece of *shit*" (303).

In all of Walters' fiction, Nancy Smith in *Fox Evil* comes closest to the classic hero figure: she is tall, fit, tough, smart, and determined not to be bullied. She needs all those attributes as a Captain in the Royal Engineers, where she faces harassment from her sergeant and has to prove that she can do as good a job as any man. Like Rosalind and Sophie, when faced with a threat to innocent people, Nancy decides to involve herself in others' problems to try to protect them, in this case, her newly discovered biological grandfather. Her concern for her grandfather's welfare leads her into a violent nighttime confrontation with the dangerous Fox Evil.

Nancy, who has served in Kosovo, is dismayed to find herself paralyzed with fear in the darkness when she realizes a possible attacker is nearby, although Fox notes that her hand, holding a flashlight, is steady: "And that worried him. It suggested a stronger adversary than he was used to" (297). The decisive moment, however, comes when Fox attempts to take his son Wolfie hostage; faced with the need to protect an innocent child, Nancy's training and instincts take over, and she reacts with courage and resolve. She fights for her life, telling Fox, "I'm your worst nightmare. A woman who fights back.... Let's see how you do against a soldier" (300). In spite of her valiant efforts to fight back, Nancy is no superwoman; when Fox charges her, she "fling[s] [her weapon] away, and curl[s] into a tight ball to present the smallest possible target" (301), suffering a volley of kicks rather than dishing them out. She might very well have been killed. Later, when Fox once more threatens Wolfie's safety, Nancy again refuses to let him succeed. In both cases, someone else comes to her aid; but she puts up a valiant defense, and it is not certain in the later confrontation that she would have lost on her own. Wolfie certainly sees her as a heroic role model; when Nancy returns for a visit months later, another character tells her, "He's always asking about you, wants to be in the army when he grows up" (376).

In *The Devil's Feather*, Walters develops yet another strong woman who is forced to find her inner hero after the terrible experience of being held captive in a Baghdad cellar, where she was sexually abused, physically tortured, and emotionally broken. While on assignment in Iraq, journalist Connie Burns recognizes mercenary Keith MacKenzie from past assignments in other war-torn countries and realizes that he may have been responsible for a string of rapes and murders in each of them. When she alerts the police and MacKenzie's current employer, he finds out, abducts her, and traumatizes her so badly that all she wants to do when he releases her is return to England and find a quiet place to hide. Because of her experience, Connie has become anorexic, is now prone to panic attacks, and has developed phobias about dogs and being touched by men; when frightened, she crouches in the nearest dark corner. Her perception of her behavior while a captive is that she was a craven coward because she obeyed every command and begged for mercy; although she survived, her self-confidence and self-esteem have been shattered.

And yet, once safe in England, Connie eventually resumes her efforts to help authorities catch her tormentor, realizing that if she does not, other women will undoubtedly suffer as she has, and she will not be able to live with the resulting guilt. When he tracks her down in her Dorset refuge and, more importantly, when he takes two of her friends hostage in her own house, Connie finds the strength and courage to fight back. She confronts him, refusing to be intimidated by him any longer and using her wits to keep him off balance and focused on her rather than on her friends. She ignores his commands to enter the room, where she would lose her advantage, and at some point she realizes that she is far from paralyzed by fear. She continues to taunt him mercilessly about all the shortcomings of serial killers that she has been reading about in her research, until he charges her. Then, successfully fighting another fear instilled by him, she takes decisive action that effectively neutralizes him and saves her friends.

Denying that her actions were heroic, Connie admits that it is not bravery that forced her to leave the safety of her kitchen and face her nemesis. Rather, it is guilt that drove her: she could not face the thought of being the cause of her friends' deaths (236). She also admits to being "terrified" (237), but she faces down her fear and acts. She had certainly impressed one friend with her resourcefulness; a policeman later tells Connie that her friend felt she was in control of the situation from the beginning and claimed that her tormentor felt the same way (247). Shortly afterward, she summarizes her reaction to the whole incident to a friend, confiding that the act of confronting him was liberating. It allowed her to see him as he was, not as what her fear had turned him into in her imagination, and that realization diminished her fear to the point where, she believes, he actually feared her more during their confrontation than she feared him (323).

Regardless of her denial of heroism, by overcoming her deepest fears and phobias and by fighting back in spite of them, Connie embodies perhaps the truest definition of courage. And because she had the furthest to go before she was once again capable of fighting back, after being thoroughly conditioned by her victimizer to be a victim, to submit, she is arguably the most heroic of all of Walters' protagonists.

Fighting for Personal Growth

Lee R. Edwards maintains that "heroism involves both doing and knowing, that the pattern of action that characterizes heroism exists to support an underlying development and growth of consciousness" and that "the struggle to achieve [individuation] is perhaps the final goal of personal heroism" (39). These observations certainly apply to Walters' protagonists, who change and grow emotionally, for the most part as a result of their involvement in the cases under investigation, which require various forms of personal courage.

One of the two central women characters in *The Sculptress*, Rosalind Leigh provides a good illustration of the personal growth described by Edwards. When her agent gives her the assignment of writing a book about convicted murderer Olive Martin, Roz is at first reluctant to accept the job. Having recently lost her daughter in a car crash and divorced her husband because he was driving at the time, she is depressed, in no mood to submerse herself in Olive's story. She does meet with Olive, however, and sufficiently overcomes her initial repugnance at Olive's obesity to hear what she has to say. She soon feels enough sympathy for Olive and enough doubt about her guilt to conduct her own investigation, and puts herself in danger in order to learn the truth and free Olive. When she seeks information from Olive's arresting officer, DS Hal Hawksley, now retired and being threatened by someone related to Olive's case, she is gradually drawn into helping him as well. The result is that as she helps her new friends deal with their problems, she becomes better able to deal with her own; by allowing herself to become emotionally involved with Olive and, because of her, with Hal, Roz also recovers emotionally from the devastating loss of her child. She confides her emotional instability to one of Olive's former teachers and further explains how her relationship with Olive has improved her life: Olive helped her realize how repressed she has been during the past year and that she has feelings for Hal (226). By the end of the novel, Roz is able to consider a new romantic relationship with Hal — a purely internal kind of courage that is nonetheless heroic.

Similarly, Jinx Kingsley, in *The Dark Room*, also embarks on an emotional journey. After years of enduring disappointing relationships with a domineering father, a drunken stepmother, jealous stepbrothers, a controlling husband, an unfaithful fiancé and a best friend who was the cause of both her late husband's and her fiancé's unfaithfulness, she has reason to distrust intimacy. Add to that the trauma she suffered when her husband was murdered and she was treated as a prime suspect, and Jinx has understandably resolved to remain detached from other people. After a car accident resulting in partial amnesia, she is sent to a clinic to recuperate, where she confides in her doctor, Alan Protheroe: "I prefer the peacefulness of feeling nothing. For every up there's a down and I hate the sadness of disappointment" (106). As the novel progresses, however, and Alan demonstrates that he cares only about her well-being, she learns to trust him and starts to talk about her feelings, eventually recovering both her memory and her willingness to make herself vulnerable emotionally by entering into a new relationship with him.

In *Fox Evil*, Nancy Smith undergoes a similar widening of the heart. Although she knows that she is adopted, she has had no interest in finding her biological parents. When contacted by her birth grandfather's lawyer about meeting him, she at first refuses; but after learning about the family problems that led to her being given up for adoption and the harassment her grandfather has been suffering since his wife's recent death, she becomes intrigued in spite of herself and goes to visit him. During her stay, she begins to admire him — he is, after all, a retired army colonel, and she is a captain in the Royal Engineers — and she is drawn into the mysterious circumstances surrounding her grandmother's recent death to the extent that her own safety is threatened as she tries to help him. By the end of the novel, the two have resolved their difficulties and have bonded, and she writes to him over the next year and returns to visit him before leaving the country on her new posting. Having successfully overcome her prejudices and preconceptions about her biological family, she now has not just one family but two.

In *The Shape of Snakes,* the growth that Mrs. Ranelagh undergoes, while still emotional, is quite different in nature from that of the first three women: she regains the self-confidence and independence that others had tried to scare out of her when she was a young woman. Twenty years after the supposedly accidental death of her neighbor, "Mad Annie" Butts, Mrs. Ranelagh (addressed as M by others) has painstakingly gathered enough evidence to renew her determination to discover the truth of what happened, not only for Annie but, perhaps even more importantly, for herself. At the time, when she asked too many questions about the accident and tried to make the police aware of racism in their own ranks, she was threatened, harassed, terrorized, and assaulted by those eager to see the case closed quickly with no arrests made.

Because of the way she was treated at the time by her neighbors, by the police, and by her husband and mother, most of whom thought she was delusional, M feels a tremendous need for vindication and revenge. One of the investigating officers at the time, PS Drury, actually told M's family that she needed to be persuaded to stop taking up any more valuable police resources, and their combined skepticism very effectively shut her up. Twenty years later, she arranges the opportunity to confront Drury with the evidence of his racism and abuse that she has painstakingly gathered, and she has the chance to vindicate herself in front of her husband, telling both men for the first time about the intimidation that Drury had set in motion against her. And while that intimidation kept her quiet for twenty years, it did not stop her from gathering the evidence that will eventually lead to the truth. She expresses her long-standing frustration with Drury's sexism and condescension, pointing out that what angers her most is the fact that he underestimated her then and continues to do so — a powerful speech that brings as much satisfaction to readers as it does to her (267). She is no longer intimidated by doubters and has regained her self-confidence after years of conducting research and collecting evidence.

Fighting for the Community

Where most traditional discussions present a lone male figure as the archetype of the hero, recent crime fiction presents heroic female protagonists who live and work not in isolation but within a variety of communities. Glenwood Irons develops this point in his discussion of several mystery authors, concluding that for these authors and their protagonists, "community rather than individualism is the driving force" (140). This motivation is certainly also true of Walters' protagonists. The communities that Walters writes about, however, are far from Frye's omnipotent communities surrounding the heroes of myth; rather, they are the communities of average, everyday mortals: family, friends, neighbors, and colleagues, living in neighborhoods, villages, towns, and cities. Nevertheless, regardless of how ordinary they are, they are still of utmost importance to Walters' protagonists. When these communities are threatened by various social and political ills — whether rape, domestic abuse, racism, blackmail, or murder — it does not take a superhero to make a difference in the fight against injustice; it simply takes an ordinary person who is willing to try to do something to make things better. When Rosalind Leigh (*The Sculptress*), Mrs. Ranelagh/M (*The Shape of Snakes*), and George Gardener (*Disordered Minds*) try to uncover the truth about old crimes; when Phoebe Maybury and her friends (*The Ice House*), Jinx Kingsley (*The Dark Room*), and Nancy Smith (*Fox Evil*) try to protect friends, family, or loved ones from harm; when Sophie Morrison (*Acid Row*) tries to take the best possible care of her patients; and when Ruth Lascelles and Connie Burns conquer their deepest fears to take action against those who have harmed them in order to prevent them from harming anyone else, they all demonstrate the most basic kind of good citizenship and make a vitally important contribution to the well-being of their communities.

A common thread of discussion in mystery/detective/crime fiction criticism concerns the perceived lack of real influence on social change from the work of a variety of women writers. While individual novels present solutions to individual problems, the authors do not offer general solutions to the problems being illustrated. Donna M. Bickford addresses this type of criticism in her examination of Sara Paretsky's *Tunnel Vision*, which focuses on the problem of homelessness as it affects one particular family. Bickford emphasizes that even if Paretsky's novel does not offer a systemic solution to this general social ill, it still performs a very real service by "provid[ing] more accurate understandings of the situations and experiences of homeless people, especially women" (50). She maintains that this kind of global criticism of mystery fiction

> seems too categorically dismissive and final and indicates a refusal to acknowledge the potential impact of this novel.... Paretsky's attention to shattering stereotypes about "the homeless" is vitally important cultural work. Perhaps the greatest contribution that she makes is to humanize otherwise faceless masses [50].

Bickford also maintains that "[a]lthough the solutions presented in her novel are individualistic and do not mend the social fabric, the reader can no longer be complacent about and complicit with the rips and tears in that fabric" (51).

This discussion applies to Walters' novels as well. M. D. Fletcher and R. J. Whip have pointed out that "[Walters'] novels are conservative insofar as the solutions offered are specific rather than systemic, and radical feminist stances are eschewed, but systemic issues are raised" (110). By raising those systemic issues, and with many of her female protagonists as her proxies, Walters too performs "vitally important cultural work"; she calls attention to serious social problems in need of repair, and as her characters battle those problems and do whatever they can to heal them, they inspire readers to care enough themselves to help where and how they can. They may not effect system-wide improvements, but by caring enough to take what action they can, they contribute to the well-being of their communities on some level. As opposed to the majority of people, who are either oblivious to the injustice all around them or else unwilling to risk their own reputations or safety, these women are heroic indeed. Timothy E. Scheurer comments on "the hero's ability to reconcile his individual achievement with the hopes of the community and, in the process, renew the community..." (161). This process of renewal can be seen in several of Walters' novels, as her protagonists address a variety of social problems in ways that Wright says address "basic issues of social explanation, not just transient issues of cultural fashion" (146) and that provide "the explanatory context for effective actions in familiar social situations" (147).

In response to current events, some of Walters' more recent novels have also broadened their social scope to address the effects of war on the community of noncombatants: *Disordered Minds* and *The Devil's Feather* both explore the negative effects of the Iraq War on their protagonists and allow Walters in her strongest language yet to voice opinions on the war, racism, and sexism through those protagonists. In *Disordered Minds*, anthropologist Jonathan Hughes is no fan of the Iraq War — or any war. In Jonathan's opinion, "The war was ... phoney" (70), and he has strong opinions (Walters' own, readers might assume) about how the war has revealed the racist and sexist attitudes underlying the various communities he lives among.

As a child, Jonathan's dark skin attracted attention from bullies; as an adult, thanks to the War on Terrorism, it attracts attention from every security guard at every airport he passes through. Based on his own painful experience of being stopped time and again at security checkpoints for extra screening, he reaches the conclusion that "[i]t might have been Hiram Johnson who said the first casualty of war was truth, but to Jonathan's jaundiced eyes the first casualty was tolerance. As far as he was concerned, the world had gone mad since the attacks on the World Trade Center and the Pentagon" (67).

Jonathan is a man, of course, but nonetheless he is perhaps Walters' most feminist protagonist. His musings on the hypocrisy of the Muslim dress code for women — women agreeing to cover themselves from head to toe rather than expecting men to take responsibility for their own actions — is arguably the strongest feminist statement in all of Walters' novels, while also pointing out the inescapable connection to racism directed at Muslim women as well as Muslim men. Muslim women who wear the veil, in fact, literally wear their faith on their sleeves and thus make themselves highly visible targets, while Muslim men are not required to wear an equivalent garment, an inequity that Jonathan sees as a sign of cowardice (66). The Iraq War also receives comment from Connie Burns in *The Devil's Feather*. A journalist on assignment in Baghdad in spring 2004, Connie has a firsthand view of the increasingly troubled living conditions in Iraq in the aftermath of the Abu Ghraib prisoner-abuse scandal. A self-professed cynic, she presents a far from optimistic view of the human rights efforts being made by the coalition forces, calling the public relations buzz phrases ("in accordance with the law," "absolute commitment to humanitarian principles," etc.) "fine-sounding sentiments" but pointing out that such lip service to high principles is no more likely to put an end to atrocities in the future than were the Nuremberg trials or the investigation into the My Lai massacre in their day. Sadism and war, she observes, are too closely bound for public demonstrations of justice to put an end to them (15).

It may not be Walters' intention — or within her ability — to suggest broad solutions to social issues, but her novels do provide thought-provoking illustrations of the ills that result from these problems and may motivate readers to take action themselves in combating them, starting in their own homes and families. Walters is not a sociologist or a politician, after all, but a writer doing what she can to make people aware of problems, to make them care that the innocent are being harmed, and to think about what they themselves can do to bring about change for the better in their own communities. Eve Tan Gee's online interview with Walters for *Crime Time* clearly reveals Walters' awareness of the need to reconcile her social conscience with her readers' needs. She admires writing that incorporates "gritty realism" or at least "reflect[s] social change," and in response to the question, "you're saying crime novels can sometimes be snapshots of their era?" she replies, "There's no doubt. And I like to utilize social elements ... while never forgetting the demands of the narrative."

Conclusion

In his 1941 examination of what Americans look for in a hero, Wecter maintains that "[w]omen have had a curiously small share in the major hero-worship of America," adding that "the cynical may suggest that no woman is ever a heroine to any other woman" (476). American women who have been considered heroes, Wecter suggests, such as Molly Pitcher, "became heroic by imitation of the stronger sex" (477). Times have changed since Wecter wrote, of course. Wright comments specifically on this point: "The popular stories of an era tell the people of that era what changes are taking place and what those changes mean about the possibility of effective action. In other words, these stories reflect what the new social context is and who gets to be a hero in this new context" (147). Authors like Walters reflect these changes by showing women as heroes — "only" everyday or popular ones, perhaps, but still very much heroes — whom both men and women, of any nation, can admire and strive to emulate. They may not shake the world, but they do shake things up within their communities; and by doing the best they can in difficult circumstances, they act as positive role models for readers of both sexes. Furthermore, because they are not perfect — "they have enough problems to avoid being 'too good to be true,'" according to Fletcher and Whip (110) — they are far easier for readers to relate to and are far more realistic than they would be otherwise.

Walters' protagonists truly exemplify Edwards' definition of "the heroic character": "a patterned fictionalizing and heightening of the mundane, the result of a collaboration, entered into for the sake of human progress, between the hero's self and some surrounding social group" (33). The mean streets her protagonists walk down are those of the neighborhood, not the whole world, and it is their immediately surrounding social groups — their families and neighbors — that they try to heal. If readers recognize them as heroes, it is because, as Edwards says, "[t]he social recognition of the hero depends precisely on society's recognition of its own unhappiness" (34). Walters and her readers are keenly aware of society's many forms of unhappiness; therefore, they are more than willing to recognize — and welcome — whatever aid her quietly unassuming heroes can provide.

Edwards also observes, "The heroic age seems always to be past, and yet, whatever time we live in, we seem always to need heroes" (33). Walters is familiar with this need and fulfills it for her readers by creating characters who, through their everyday lives and personalities, rise to the occasion when they are needed with heartfelt attempts to make things better. Walters' heroes are often paragons, not necessarily of virtue (though many of them are far above average in the decency and kindness department), but of those outstanding qualities of character that ensure they will achieve their goals and survive intact. They perform far better under duress than most of us and do not let opposition stop them. In their own persistent, quietly heroic way, the Walters women, like the women protagonists of other mystery writers, show the rips in the social fabric of their places and times and do what they can to help repair them. They reflect the everyday best instincts — the everyday heroism — in all of us.

Works Cited

Bernstein, Andrew. "The Philosophical Foundations of Heroism." 11 Aug. 2006. http://www.andrewbernstein.net/heroes/2_heroism.htm.

Bickford, Donna M. "Homeless Women and Social Justice in Sara Paretsky's *Tunnel Vision*." *Clues: A Journal of Detection* 25.2 (Winter 2007): 45–52.

Cawelti, John G. *Adventure, Mystery, and Romance*. Chicago: University of Chicago Press, 1976.

Edwards, Lee R. "The Labors of Psyche: Toward a Theory of Female Heroism." *Critical Inquiry* 6.1 (Autumn 1979): 33–49.

Fletcher, M. D. and R. J. Whip. "Minette Walters' Feminist Detective Fiction." *Clues: A Journal of Detection* 18.1 (Spring/Summer 1997): 101–12.

Frye, Northrop. "The Archetypes of Literature." *The Norton Anthology of Theory and Criticism*. Ed. Vincent B. Leitch. New York: Norton & Co., 2001, pp. 1445–57.

Gee, Eve Tan. "Minette Walters: My Glittering Career." *Crime Time*. 20 April 2007. http://www.crimetime.co.uk/mag/index.php/showarticle/756.

Online Interview with Minette Walters

(QUESTIONS SENT FEBRUARY 13, 2007;
REPLIES RETURNED JUNE 4, 2007)

Q: How would you define justice and can it be found inside (or outside) the British legal system?

A: I think for most of us justice means "fairness." If we or someone we love is wronged, we look to the rest of society to step into our corner and fight our cause with us. Justice in the UK, as in most other countries, is delivered by the state on behalf of the victim, and for an individual to have his or her "wrong" ignored is devastating. Justice can certainly be found inside the UK legal system but in too many instances it has to be fought for. This is particularly true when public opinion is not on the side of the victim. Rightly or wrongly, a murdered paedophile, terrorist or drug dealer will never generate the same level of police, judicial and public interest as a murdered child. Yet the rights of the victims are the same. These are difficult moral issues at the best of time but, when the cost of policing affects decisions, fairness is not always evident or automatic.

Q: Why did you choose to make Olive Martin in *The Sculptress* so dramatically overweight?

A: I wanted to create an intimidating character whose appearance and crime evoked fear rather than sympathy. Olive is tall as well as overweight, and I discovered how threatening sheer size can be when I visited a male offender on remand for rape in Winchester Prison. He was 6'6" tall and almost as wide. I spoke to him for 45 minutes alone in a small room and, despite prison officers being able to watch us through a large glass window, I knew I had no easy exit if the man chose to attack me. He didn't, but I was interested in my response to him — not just to his bulk but also to the fact that he'd been accused of rape. The two together alarmed me and made me less inclined to believe what subsequently proved to be true, that the accusation was malicious and the charges would be dropped. I've always been grateful to him for giving me Olive, both in terms of her appearance and also her difficulty in persuading anyone to take her side.

Q: You have said in the past that the reason *The Sculptress* has such an ambiguous ending is that the British judicial system is "only interested in pitting one story against another" and not particularly concerned with truth. What sorts of more general claims are you making about our ability to determine truth from falsehood by letting it appear (perhaps) that Olive has gotten away with murder?

A: I wanted to put the reader into the shoes of a juror. If a defendant pleads "not guilty" — which most do in murder trials — the jury must examine the weight of evidence and decide which way the balance tilts. Often, this means that the truth of what happened — principally, why the victim was killed or why the murderer thought the death of another person would be a solution to a problem — remains obscure. In Olive's case, the jury found her guilty beyond reasonable doubt at her trial; on a re-examination of the evidence, the Appeal Court exonerated her. Who do my readers think was right? I know what I believe, but that doesn't mean another person, having met Olive in the pages of the novel, will agree with me. We all respond to different stimuli in our search for the truth.

Q: When you develop your female protagonists, do you consciously try to make (most of) them heroic? Is heroism even a trait that you consider when writing your novels?

A: I tend to think all protagonists are "heroic," simply by virtue of standing in the spotlight for 100,000 words — an extraordinary achievement for any ordinary person — but I'm just as interested in portraying my characters' weaknesses as I am in portraying their strengths. I believe Graham Greene's approach was right: real heroism is to face adversity with a sinking heart and trembling knees. It's the strength that damaged and vulnerable people find within themselves that I choose to develop and explore ... and, in my experience, women often have deeper emotional reserves than men.

Q: What are your views on victims and victimization, and how does this determine your characterizations? For example, to what extent do you create victims who cause their own fates?

A: As patron of Victim Support in my home county of Dorset, I have enormous respect and sympathy for victims, who are usually devastated by what happens to them. Rape and murder are cataclysmic events in anyone's life, but a burglarized and vandalized house can impact dramatically on a person's confidence. On the other side, I've been a prison visitor for twenty years, and it's difficult to argue that many inmates aren't victims, too — of dysfunctional backgrounds, emotionally deprived upbringings, illiteracy, drug and alcohol dependency and mental health problems.

Nevertheless, I have always been interested in how or whether victims contribute to their fates. Certainly, Mathilda Gillespie in *The Scold's Bridle*— through her cruelty and insensitivity — might be seen to have provoked her killer ... but how far was she responsible for, or able to control, her cruel streak? It could be argued that Kate Sumner in *The Breaker* courts disaster through her own behavior. I paint her in deliberately unflattering terms to demonstrate how easy it is to destroy a rape victim's character, but nothing Kate ever did, however unpleasant, excuses her rapist and murderer.

Q: How did you first learn about the scold's bridle as an early modern form of punishment?

A: My family moved to Reading, Berkshire, when I was six. I was a great reader and my mother took me and my brothers to Reading library every week. My brothers were always rather slow about choosing new books so I used to wander across the hallway to the museum on the other side of the building. In one of the display cases was a scold's bridle — still there, I believe — and I was constantly fascinated by its horrible appearance and the written explanation beside it. Why had men ever been allowed to stop women talking? I have since seen other exhibits, notably the ones in the Tower of London.

Q: *The Shape of Snakes*, as well as some other of your novels, seems to start the narrative in the formula of feminist crime fiction, but then bends the conventions and mystifies the readers' expectations. On the level of how the story is narrated, the unexpected features do in many ways refresh the form and the experience of reading. On the thematic level, however, I have in *The Shape of Snakes* — as well in other novels by other scholars — noticed a tendency to value conservatism that seems to infuse the story more and more as it develops, and finally the story seems quite non–feminist. I would like to know how designed this is. Do you plan the ideological turn in the narratives, or is it merely spontaneous?

A: I tend to be on the liberal side of the feminist debate, arguing for equality rather than an end to domination and oppression. This view may be influenced by the fact that I've been married to the same man for nearly thirty years and have sons but no daughters. An author's personal views invariably flavor their writing, and it pleases me to take characters on a journey that ends in mutual respect. I've been described as offering seeds of "redemption through love" at the ends of my books, and I certainly attempt to achieve small closures through the new, or renewed, understanding that some of the characters find for each other. At heart, I'm an eternal optimist about human decency and kindness, irrespective of gender, but I remain convinced that our failure to communicate with each other is the cause of individual and world problems.

Q: In *The Shape of Snakes*, you use many qualities from the epistolary and gothic traditions of the eighteenth and nineteenth centuries. Are there any particular forerunners from these periods that are important to you, such as authors you admire and novels you reread?

A: *Les Liaisons dangereuses* by Pierre Choderlos de Laclos, 1782, *Dracula* by Bram Stoker, 1897.

Online Interview with Minette Walters

Q: Although you write about children who suffer within their own families or at the hands of society, you also depict them as healing forces in *other* dysfunctional families — i.e., Ruth Lascelles in *The Scold's Bridle,* Terry Dalton in *The Echo,* and Wolfie in *Fox Evil*. Why are they able to fulfill this role after being so badly mistreated or damaged?

A: Even damaged children are more innocent and less judgemental than adults, which allows them to see more freely, I believe. The older we become the more likely we are to categorize people into types and avoid those we don't like.

In addition, although I'm convinced that damage done in childhood has long-lasting effects, I also recognize that a poor start in life does not inevitably lead to a troubled adulthood. There are enough people who rise above deprivation, abuse and neglect for me to believe that dysfunctional family cycles can be broken. In real life, I have enormous admiration for children who make a conscious decision to take a different direction from abusive or neglectful parents and careers. It's very hard to do, and requires a level of self-understanding that few of us possess, but the children who succeed are heroic.

Q: Why is your view of marriage and family — and the plight of children within these social institutions — so consistently bleak in your novels?

A: Simplistically, because I write about murder. Violent death doesn't usually visit stable, loving families unless a predator comes in from outside. I firmly believe that the family unit is the most important and supportive corner stone in anyone's life, but it can also collapse disastrously if the unit becomes dysfunctional. I've seen too many men in prison who have no relationship with their mothers, know only their fathers' names, and who have had no contact with their own children for years. I often think there's no reason for such men to conform since there's no one "outside" who has any expectations of them. It's other people's belief and respect that give us self-esteem and allow us to move forward with confidence. In a vacuum, or as the butt of constant abuse and criticism, most of us become alienated and struggle to make and maintain relationships.

Q: You show great sympathy for and interest in the rejected, the "other," those found guilty of crimes because they are different, or are the object of crimes because they are different. Did something trigger this focus? Do you feel that your sympathy is naturally associated with being a female writer? Is your use of a voice within a voice, for example Jonathan Hughes, a way to move into a male voice?

A: I do have sympathy for the marginalized in society, and I suspect the trigger was my father dying when I was ten. My mother was left alone to bring up three children on benefit, and life was a constant struggle with every penny having to be counted. It was no one's fault, but I've always been incredibly grateful that society didn't leave us to starve.

In truth, I don't think women are naturally more sympathetic than men but I do believe we're better communicators, and better readers of character, which make us quicker to notice when someone's in trouble. The downside is, we can also be highly critical from our long heritage of having to rely on a husband to bring home the money — or not if he drank it first — and fault-finding is the first step to prejudice. Nevertheless, these are all useful qualities for a crime writer, which may explain why women are so successful in the genre.

Q: Connie Burns in *The Devil's Feather* mentions that her idea of England was based as much on fiction and poetry as on real life, and she mentions some of details of the landscape she associates with England (e.g., "soft summer rain, green grass, narrow hedge-lined lanes, and fields and fields of ripening corn"). What kind of non–physical characteristics would this idea of England include for someone like Connie, Zimbabwean, but with strong cultural ties to England?

A: In Connie's case, she's certainly inherited the reserve of the English, preferring to deal with her problems herself rather than "share" them. In her job, she also has our curiosity and pioneering spirit which led us to Africa in the first place, although "adventuring" seems to be a universal quality in the twenty-first century. Connie's tragedy — as is Africa's tragedy — is that foreigners tend to exploit perceived weakness, and the consequences can be disastrous and long-lasting. In those circumstances, revenge seems reasonable, although I've no idea if that's an English characteristic, or the quietly held ambition of every victim everywhere.

Notes on Contributors

Sarah D. Fogle, professor of communication and humanities at Embry-Riddle University in Daytona Beach, Florida, received her M.A. at the University of Florida. She has published articles on detective and crime fiction in *Crime Fiction and Film in the Sunshine State: Florida Noir* and *Crime Fiction and Film in the Southwest: Bad Boys and Bad Girls in the Badlands,* both edited by Steve Glassman and Maurice O'Sullivan. She teaches courses in the genre and has a special research interest in Florida crime fiction.

Tilda Maria Forselius, Ph.D. student in comparative literature at the University of Gothenburg in Sweden, is currently working on a dissertation about the use of letters in Swedish eighteenth-century papers. Her research interests are epistolary traditions, popular fiction, and narrative analysis. Among her publications in English are articles in *Women's Writing* and *Clues: A Journal of Detection.*

Mary Hadley, associate professor of writing and linguistics, teaches crime fiction, freshman composition and English as a second language at Georgia Southern University in Statesboro, Georgia. She received her Ph.D. from the University of Reading, UK. Her publications include several articles and book chapters on crime fiction and *British Women Mystery Writers* (McFarland, 2002). She has also coauthored four crime novels with her husband under the pseudonym Mary Charles; these were published by Twenty First Century Publishers of England.

Donna Waller Harper, a high school teacher in Nashville, Tennessee, received her Ph.D. from Middle Tennessee State University. She has contributed to *Great Women Mystery Writers* and the *Encyclopedia of Popular Culture,* and she is at work on an article for the *Encyclopedia of Women.* Her research interests are mystery fiction and issues of social justice; a special focus is the work of Robert B. Parker.

Rhonda Knight, associate professor of English at Coker College in Hartsville, South Carolina, teaches courses in medieval and Renaissance literature. She received

Notes on Contributors

her Ph.D. from Binghamton University. Her articles have appeared in *Studies in Iconography, The Journal of Medieval and Early Modern Studies, Exemplaria,* and *Studies in the Age of Chaucer.* Her interest in scolds and scolds' bridles emerged from researching the roles of women relevant to Shakespeare's *The Taming of the Shrew* and *The Winter's Tale.*

Deane Mansfield-Kelley and **Lois A. Marchino**, professors of English at the University of Texas at El Paso, received their Ph.D.s from the University of Texas and the University of New Mexico, respectively. They created and teach courses in detective fiction at both the undergraduate and graduate levels and often include detective fiction in other literature courses. They are the editors of *Death by Pen: The Longman Anthology of Detective Fiction from Poe to Paretsky.*

Nancy Eliot Parker, professor emeritus at Embry-Riddle University in Daytona Beach, Florida, received her Ed.D. from the University of Central Florida. She has taught a dozen different courses in the Humanities and Social Sciences Department at Embry-Riddle; she authored the university's first course in technical report writing to be delivered through distance learning, and she served as director of Diversity Advancement. Her research areas include comparative religions, male-female differences, and serial killers in literature.

Gerri Reaves, independent scholar and freelance writer, received her Ph.D. from the University of Miami. She lives in Fort Myers, Florida, where she writes about the arts, Florida history, the environment, popular culture, and literature. Her publications include *Mapping the Private Geography: Autobiography, Identity, and America* (McFarland, 2001), and critical and nonfiction essays. She is currently at work on a pictorial history of Fort Myers.

Rachel Schaffer, professor of English at Montana State University–Billings, received her Ph.D. in linguistics from Ohio State University. She teaches linguistics, composition and literature, and her research and writing interests focus on mystery and crime fiction. She has published several articles on such authors as Dick Francis, Sue Grafton, Sara Paretsky, and Montana writers Jamie Harrison and Jenny Siler in publications such as *The Armchair Detective, Storytelling,* and *Clues*; the latter she serves as a board member.

Caren J. Town, professor of English at Georgia Southern University, in Statesboro, Georgia, received her Ph.D. from the University of Washington. She teaches courses in world, American, and young adult literature. Her recent publications include essays on contemporary female mystery writers Anne Perry and Margaret Maron and a book on late 20th century female coming-of-age-novels, *The New Southern Girl* (McFarland, 2004).

Index

Abuse 3, 7, 8, 13, 14, 26–28, 30, 31, 33–35, 38, 40, 46, 64, 68, 75, 79, 82, 84, 92, 95, 99, 100, 112, 120, 134, 138, 140, 141, 148–151, 153, 179, 194, 198, 199, 201, 209
Acid Row 14–19, 106–108, 113–116, 138–144, 149–152, 191, 193, 199
Alewyn, Richard 126
Amussen, Susan Dwyer 73

Baird, Emma 158
Bandura, Albert 141, 142
Bardsley, Sandy 72
Berlins, Marcel 5, 6
Bernstein, Andrew 186, 188, 190
Bickford, Donna M. 199
Boose, Lynda E. 74
Bordo, Susan 49, 51, 54
The Breaker 26, 28, 29, 35, 88, 90, 96–101, 207
Brown, Pamela Allen 72, 83
Brownmiller, Susan 93
Butler, Judith 50

Cawelti, John G. 187
Chambers, R. 77, 78
Chandler, Raymond 6, 16, 103, 127, 158
Chaucer, Geoffrey 74
Children 2, 3, 7, 11, 13, 14, 16–19, 23–40, 43–47, 75, 92, 100, 112, 115, 120, 128, 133, 138, 140–142, 149–151, 166, 186, 191, 209, 210
Community 19, 24, 25, 30, 34, 43, 46, 52, 53, 72, 74, 77, 91, 106, 107, 111, 112, 114–116, 142, 149, 152–154, 168, 173, 174, 177, 186, 191, 198, 200
Courage 26, 39, 161, 162, 164, 166–168, 175, 181–184, 186, 187, 189, 192, 194–196,

"The Cucking of a Scould" 76
Cunnington, B. Howard 75
The Dark Room 94–96, 119, 120, 188, 196, 199
Davis, Natalie Zemon 81
Day, William Patrick 128, 129
Deats, Sara Munson 25
Delamotte, Eugenia 128
Detmer, Emily 73, 83, 84
The Devil's Feather 157–184
Dilley, Kimberley J. 22, 63
Disordered Minds 19–22, 107, 108, 138–140, 145–148
Dunant, Sarah 52

Eagleton, Terry 161
Earle, Alice Morse 77
The Echo 26, 28, 37, 40–42, 109–112, 116, 209
Edwards, Lee R. 196, 203
Ellis, Kate Ferguson 133
Evil 3, 5, 13, 21, 28, 72, 101, 128, 133, 137–139, 141–144, 149, 152, 156

Family 2, 10, 24, 28–47, 51, 59, 63, 67, 68, 71, 80, 82, 84, 90, 91, 95, 99, 100, 109–111, 116, 122, 133, 134, 143, 153, 155, 163, 170, 171, 173, 176, 177, 186, 197–199, 207, 209
Feminism/feminist 23, 96, 127, 186
"A Fight for Justice: The Stephen Lawrence Story" 9
Fletcher, Don 57, 120, 121, 126, 200, 202
Foley, Catherine 46
Foucault, Michel 74
Fox Evil 26, 28, 37, 43–46, 111–113, 116, 187, 193, 194, 197, 199, 209

Index

Frye, Northrop 186, 187, 198
Gardiner, Jean 25
Gee, Eva Tan 202
Golden Age 1, 5, 23, 88, 89, 97
Greenblatt, Stephen 66, 67, 68
Guilt 10, 20, 27, 30, 32, 44, 50–53, 57–60, 62, 63, 96, 98, 99, 101, 134, 138, 146, 154, 164–166, 183, 190, 191, 195, 196, 206

Hall, Stuart 47
Hamlet 69, 70, 84
Hero 3, 63, 101, 106, 128, 129, 131–134, 142, 151, 152, 166, 185–190, 192–196, 198–203, 206
"History of the Movement of Peoples" 111
"Homeless" 109
Honig, Elizabeth Alice 81
Hutton, Patrick 129

The Ice House 1, 6–9, 18, 26, 28–30, 119, 120, 157, 160, 188, 190, 191, 199
Impelluso, Lucia 76
Ingram, Martin 73, 75
Innocence 32, 50, 51, 53, 55, 57, 62, 63, 108, 189
"An Interview with Minette Walters" 37
Irons, Glenwood 63, 96, 198

Jacobson, Michael 3, 21
Jacques, Martin 47
James, Dean 91, 93
Jenkins, Henry 28
Jobes, Gertrude 76
Jones, Manina 5, 121, 126, 127, 134
Justice 3, 5–22, 26, 39, 52, 58, 64, 103, 106, 110, 112, 119, 124, 131, 132, 134, 151, 160, 163–168, 172–176, 181, 184, 185, 187–190, 192, 199–201, 205

Karen, Robert 46
King Lear 70, 71, 81, 84, 85
Klein, Kathleen Gregory 60, 61, 120, 127, 133
Knight, Stephen 97
Kuchta, David 68

Laclos, Pierre Choderlos de 130, 208
Lawley, Sue 101
LeBihan, Jill 120, 121, 126
Lenker, Lagretta Tallent 25

Maida, Patricia D. 89
Marriage 7, 10, 14, 26, 29, 33–41, 73, 78, 79, 81, 82, 99, 122, 209
Meier, Robert F. 89
Miethe, Terance D. 89
Molander Danielsson, Karin 121, 126
Morrell, Martin 23, 26
Munt, Sally 23, 27, 32, 35

Narrative 2, 10, 26, 27, 39, 51, 54, 69, 118–123, 125–135, 157, 158, 160, 161, 163, 164, 166, 172, 174–184, 202, 208
Parker, Patricia 74
Patrick, Bethanne Kelly 3, 19, 23
Police 3, 5–10, 12–21, 26, 29, 30, 35, 39, 41, 43, 54, 58, 63, 69–72, 79, 91, 93, 95–99, 101, 104, 109, 113–115, 122, 125, 132, 150, 153, 155, 157, 158, 160, 163, 165, 167, 168, 175, 180, 181, 184, 191–195, 198, 205
Pridmore, Saxby 130
Punter, David 128
Puttock, Kay 27

"Q and A" 105, 106

Rabinowitz, Peter 127
"Race" 106
"Racism" 10
Racism 3, 10, 12, 13, 24, 106, 108, 112, 134, 141, 146, 198–201
Rao, Kavitha 2
Reddy, Maureen 6, 11, 14, 24, 53, 127, 133
Revenge 6, 8, 14, 52, 90, 114, 119, 124, 130, 132–134, 158, 160, 167, 168, 175, 181, 183, 184, 198, 210
Riggan, William 126
Routledge, Christopher 27
Rowland, Susan 127

Schober, Adrian 27
The Scold's Bridle 26, 28, 29, 33, 34, 37–40, 47, 66–87, 88, 90–94, 96, 99, 119, 120, 192, 207, 209
The Sculptress 26, 28, 29, 31, 32, 49–65, 91, 120, 192, 196, 199, 205
Segal, Lynne 25
Seltzer, Mark 89, 90, 92, 96
The Shape of Snakes 9–14, 20, 106–108, 112, 113, 116, 118–136, 188, 197–199, 208
Sharpe, J.A. 82
Shengold, Leonard 28, 29, 43

214

Index

Sibree, Bron 2, 6, 13, 14, 46
Silet, Charles L.P. 19, 53, 54, 63
Sloan, LaRue Love 74
Spargo, John Webster 76, 77
Spelman, Judith 3, 5, 24
Spornick, Nicholas B. 89
Sturrock, June 25
Swanson, Jean 24

The Taming of the Shrew 73, 74, 83, 84
Taylor, Gary 81
Thompson, E.P. 75
Thomson, Liz 14, 16, 17, 47, 114
The Tinder Box 138, 140, 143, 144, 152–156
Trodd, Anthea 25
Truth 3, 5, 6, 8, 9, 11–14, 18–22, 24, 38, 46, 50, 53–55, 57, 59, 62, 63, 108, 119, 126, 129–132, 146, 153–155, 160, 161, 171, 174–178, 180, 185, 188–192, 196–199, 201, 206, 210
Twelve Ingenious Characters 72

Underdown, David 73, 75

Van Dine, S.S. 89
Victims 21, 22, 24, 26, 27, 79, 88–90, 93, 95–97, 101, 128, 137, 139, 143, 144, 151, 152, 167, 185, 192, 205, 207
Violence 7, 8, 18, 19, 21, 24, 57, 60, 62, 63, 73, 89, 90, 93, 94, 114, 120, 137, 139, 141, 151, 159, 168, 171, 174, 181, 183, 185, 187
Vives, Juan Luis 74

Waller, James 137–145, 149, 150, 152, 155
Walton, Priscilla L. 5, 121, 126, 127, 134
Waugh, Dorothy 78
Wayne, Valerie 72
Whately, William 74
Whip, Rosemary 57, 120, 121, 126, 200, 202
Woods, Robin 52, 53

Zimbardo, Philip 142, 143